PAINTING WEATHERED TEXTURES IN WATERCOLOR

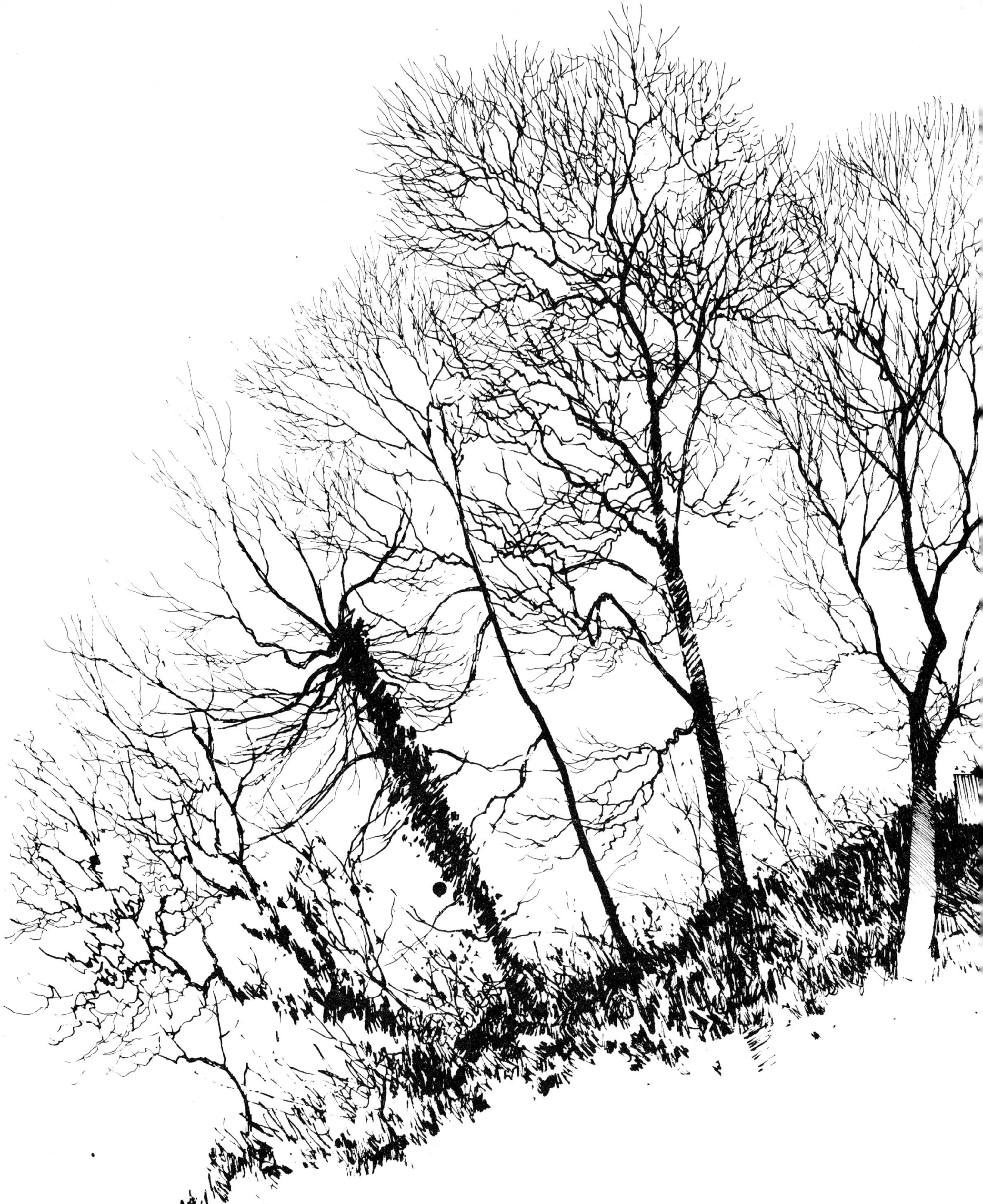

WATSON-GUPTILL PUBLICATIONS, NEW YORK

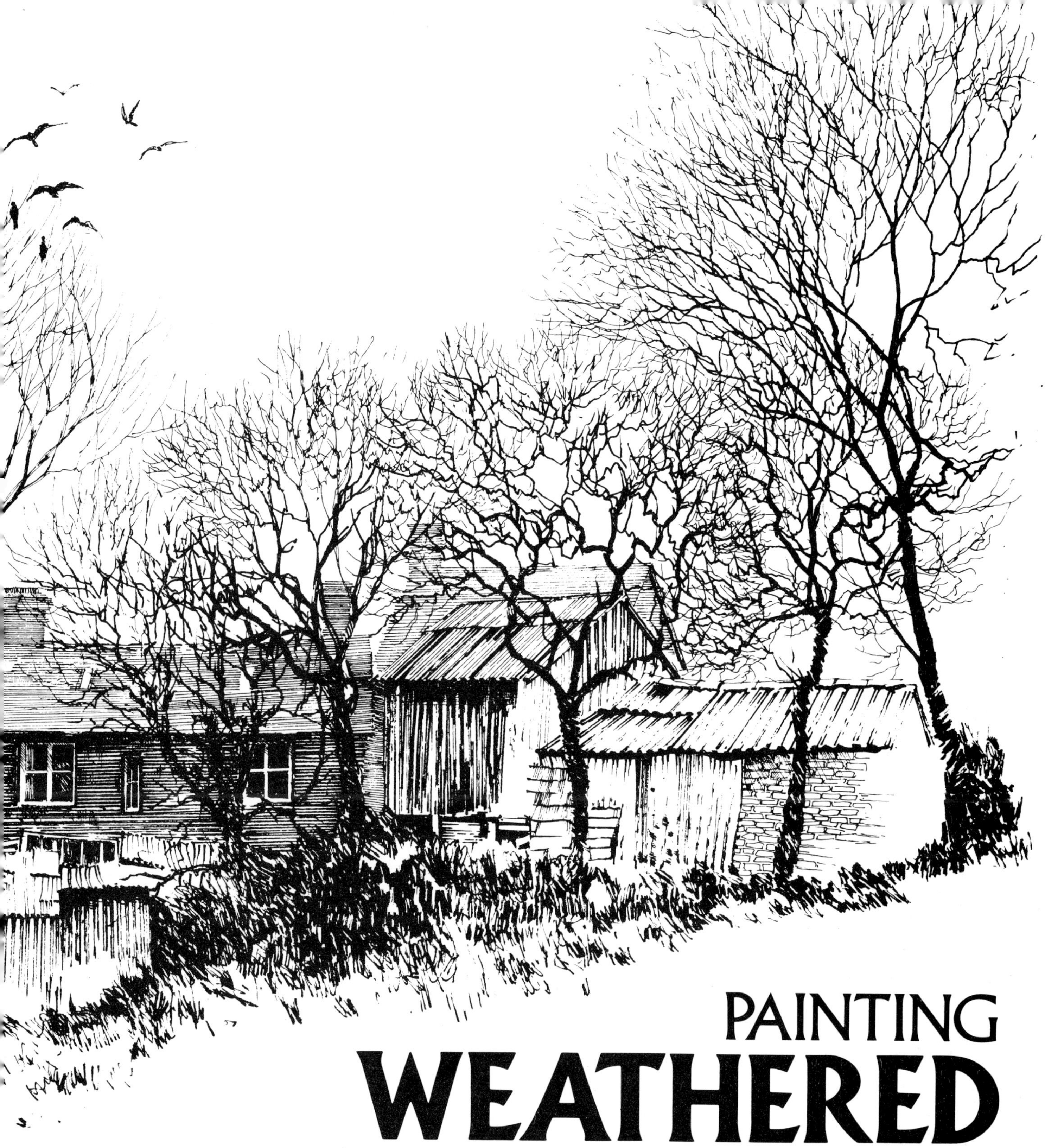

PAINTING WEATHERED TEXTURES IN WATERCOLOR

BY RICHARD BOLTON

First published 1982 in New York by Watson-Guptill Publications,
a division of Billboard Publications, Inc.,
1515 Broadway, New York, N.Y. 10036

Library of Congress Cataloging in Publication Data
Bolton, Richard, 1950-
Painting weathered textures in watercolor.

Includes index.
1. Water-color painting—Technique. 2. Texture (Art)
—Technique. I. Title.
ND2422.B643 1982 751.42'2 82-10999
ISBN 0-8230-3876-9

Manufactured in Japan.

First Printing, 1982

4 5 6 7 8 9 10/87 86

Edited by Candace Raney
Designed by Bob Fillie
Graphic Production by Ellen Greene
Text set in 11-point Palatino

For Margaret and the boys

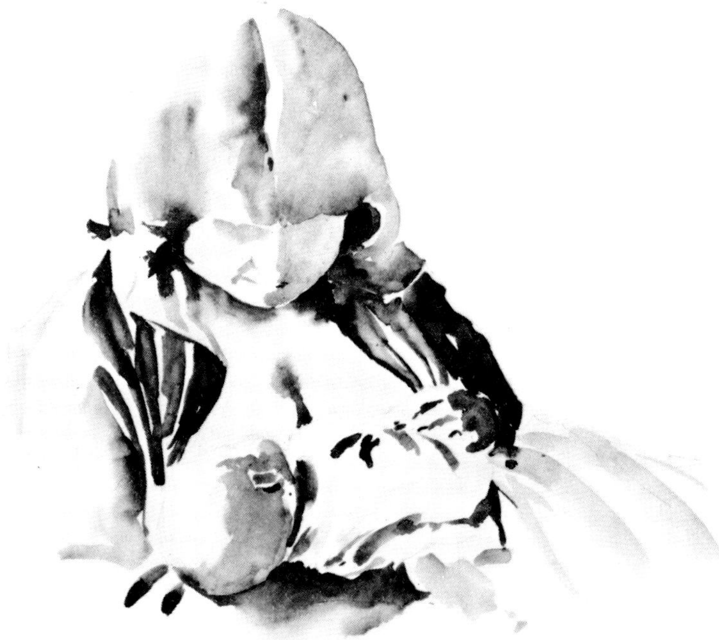

I would like to thank all the people who have made this book possible: my family; Keith Kirk-Spriggs and Edwin Pollard for their encouragement; Michael Petts for the high quality of the photography; Candace Raney who edited the text; and especially David Lewis, who put such a lot of his energy and considerable talent into planning this book.

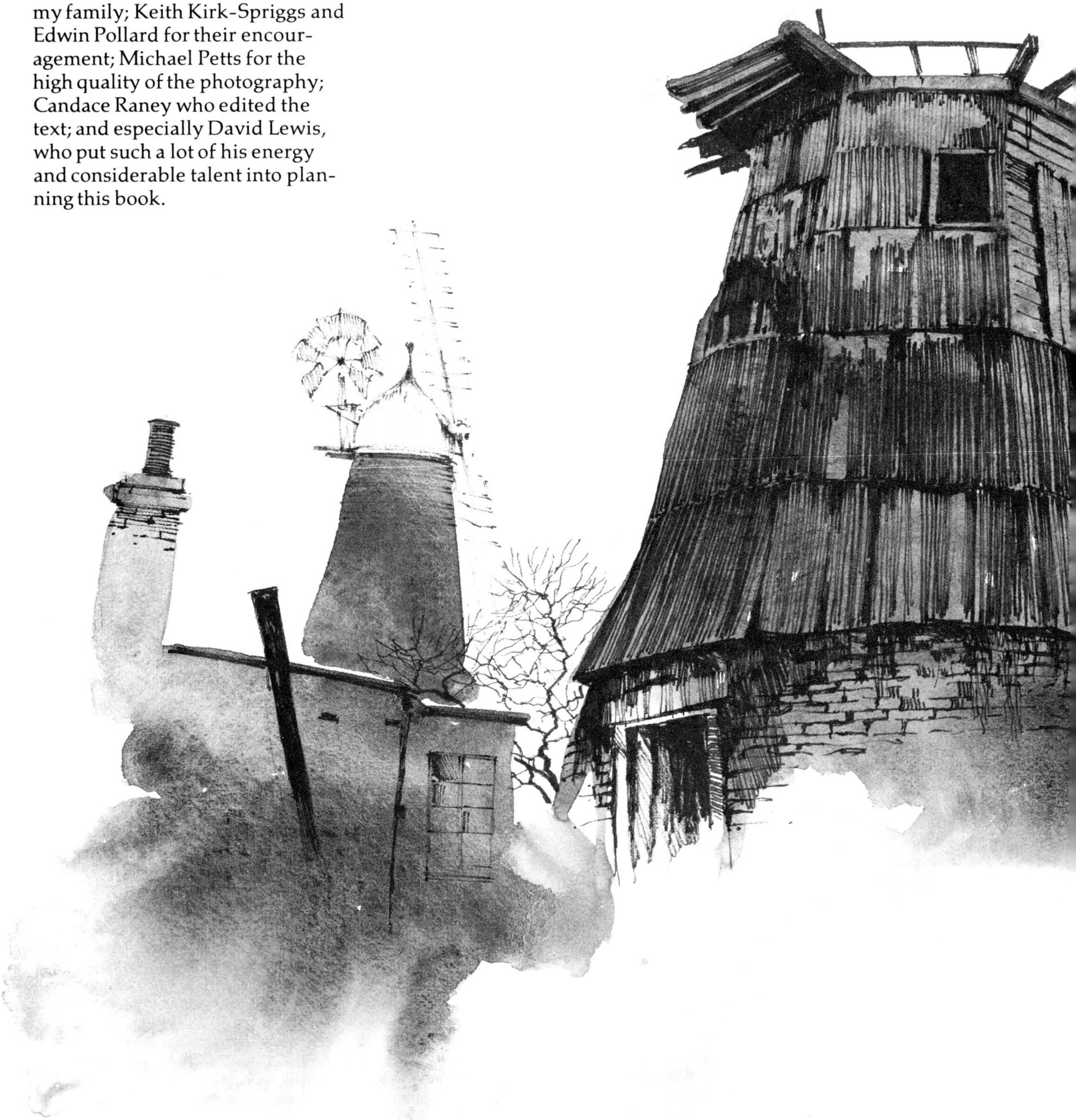

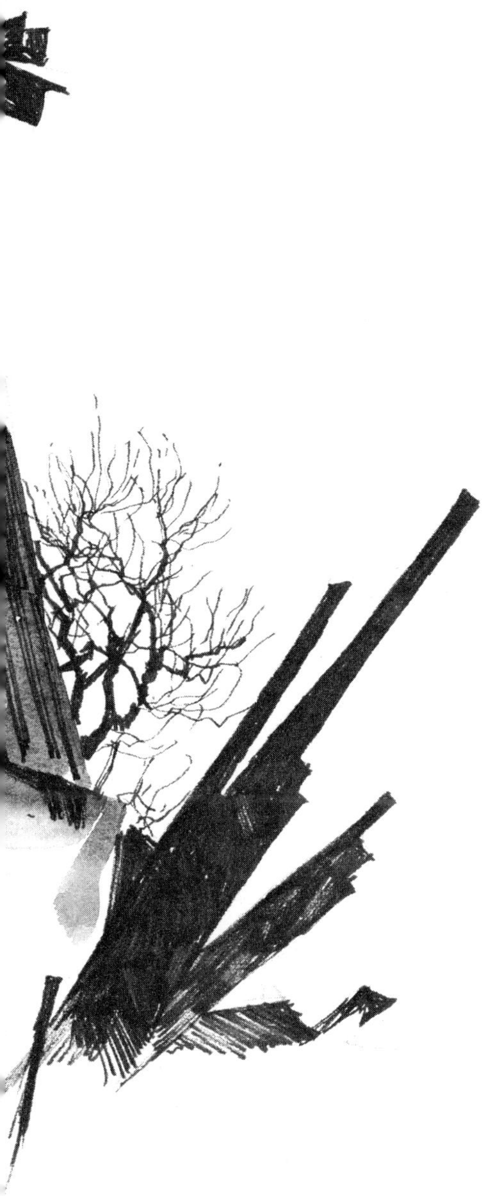

CONTENTS

INTRODUCTION

Why does natural weathering in the landscape make such good subject material for watercolor painting? At first sight, old or crumbling objects are by no means pretty, clean, or neat; and as often as not they lack any sign of life or usefulness. Yet I find that it is for exactly these reasons that I spend hours roaming the hills and the shore looking for spectacularly attractive examples of natural weathering. Perhaps like me, you are excited by painting these things in watercolor, for with skillful brushwork and drawing, there is room for exaggeration, plenty of opportunity to study and render detail, and a whole new range of colors and textures in decaying wood, metal, and stone.

There was a time when I used to paint landscapes for relaxation, but somehow after struggling all day to evoke a sense of atmosphere in a painting, I could never quite find enough satisfaction. At that time I worked as a technical illustrator and spent my working hours making drawings of carefully measured man-made objects. Almost by accident, the idea of a landscape painting containing a precision man-made object seemed to provide exactly the right balance I was looking for. By centering the attention on an old car in a field, the land, trees, and horizon could remain as a quiet area in the painting and play a secondary role. With this new-found painting theme, I became fascinated by the painting possibilities in the natural harmony created by the earth's reabsorption of man-made objects. Once-new, upright, and cleanly painted farm buildings tottered with the onset of years in the wind: paint peeled, doors hung crooked, hinges rusted, and the rust ran in an orange smear down the splitting wood panels; windows grew dusty and blind or were broken by the stones of urchins; roofs sagged under the weight of tiles, and as the ridgepoles weakened the lines of tiles or slates became crooked until the whole roof crashed in, leaving the walls to do the same a few years later. Suddenly I became aware of the myriad painting subjects that existed in the countryside where I lived.

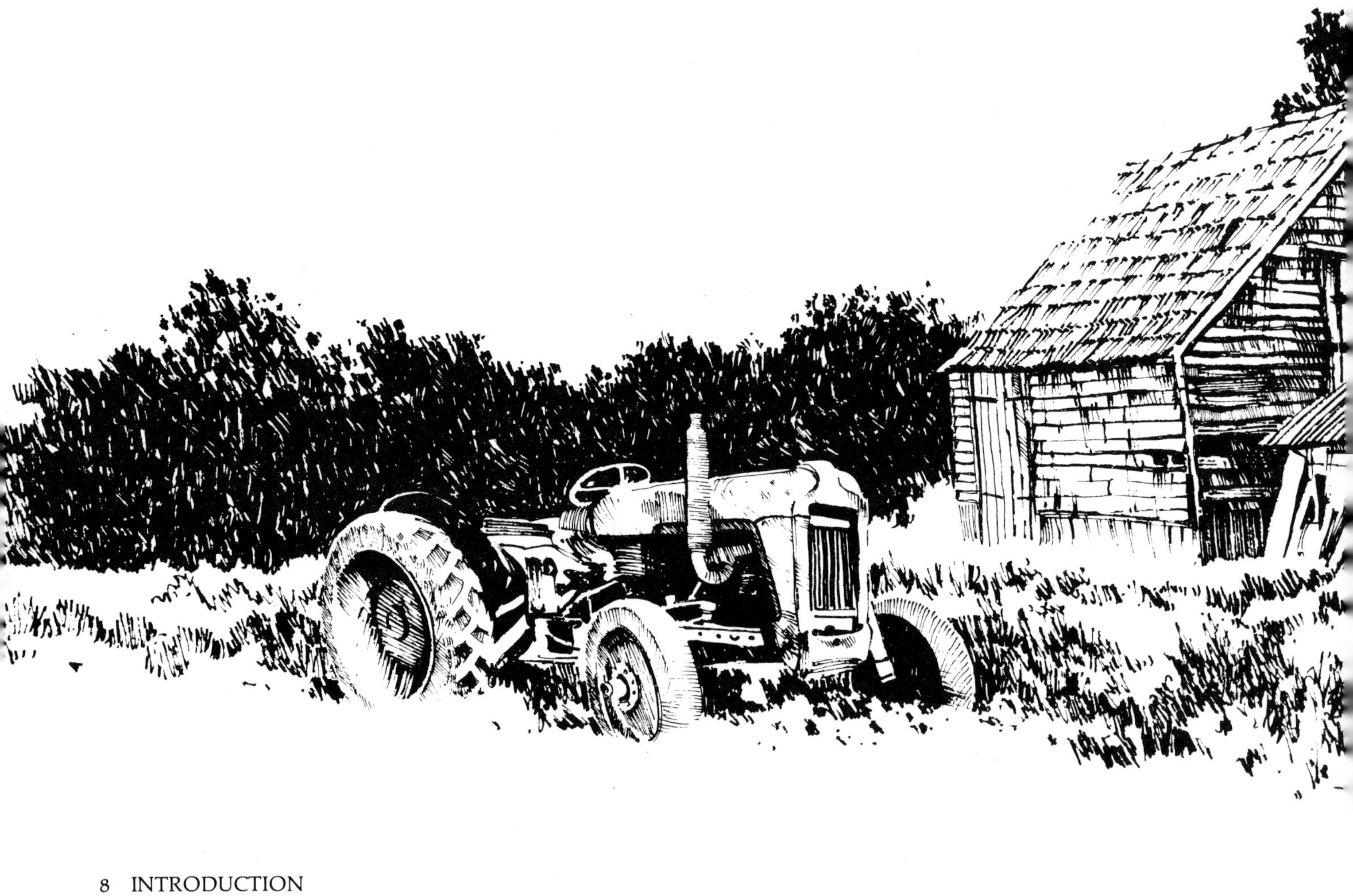

With only a little imagination, it was possible to create most dramatic and intriguing landscape paintings.

You may have already discovered these decaying natural subjects for yourself. If so, then examine the techniques in the workshop section and discover how you can develop a strong graphic style in your work. If you have never before considered painting an old wooden post or a door handle and padlock, turn to pages 66-71 and see what you have been missing. None of these subjects is difficult to paint, and I have only shown one way of rendering the character of each in the two paintings. The relative strength of any of the paintings in this book is due to three things: imagination and foresight, reasonably good drawing (but you need *not* be an ex-technical illustrator!), and confident brushwork. From my experience, I think that positive brushwork is the most important of these assets. You do not need to be wildly imaginative and can get by without highly developed drawing skills if you avoid awkward subjects. But your range of textures and surfaces will be greatly reduced if you cannot handle a watercolor brush with some dexterity. Because brushwork is so important, I have included on the next few pages some of the brushes that I use and the wide range of strokes that they make. These brushes work for me and I recommend that you try them too, especially the Oriental bamboo brush. The most valuable exercise with brushes is simply to practice making as many different sized, shaped, and textured strokes as you can. Mix washes and apply them quickly or slowly, rich or very pale. The more you understand and control the capabilities of your brush, the greater will be the strength and style of your watercolor painting. Let's get to work.

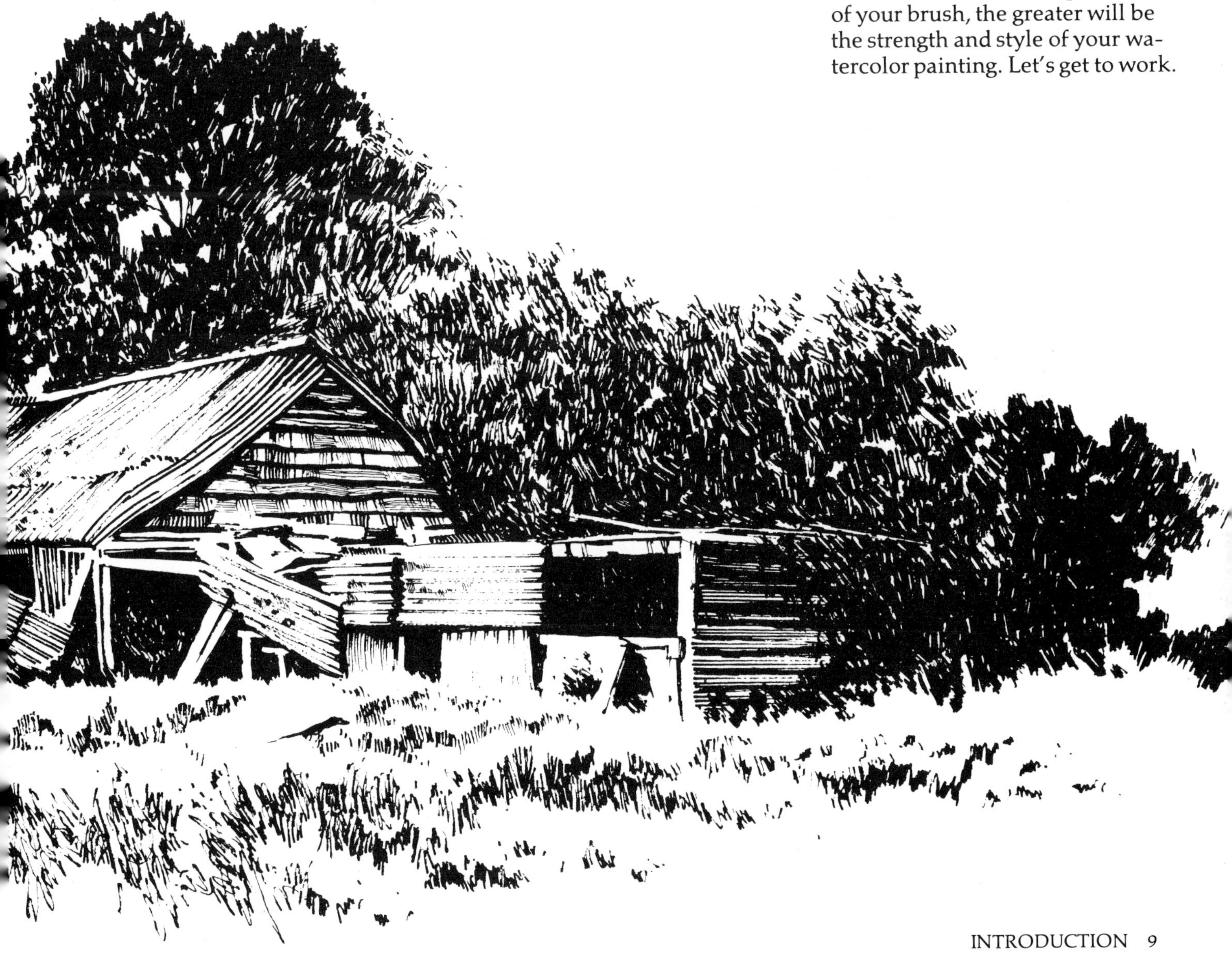

BRUSHSTROKES

1-inch flat sable brush

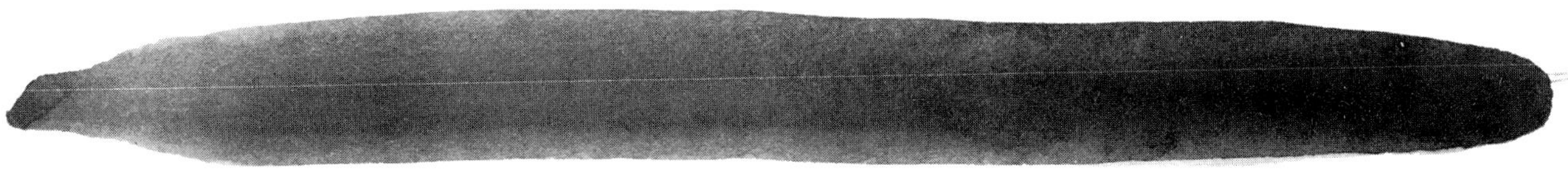

Size 12 round brush

Bamboo brush

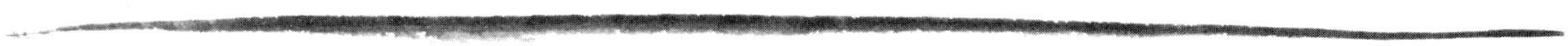

Size 2 sable brush

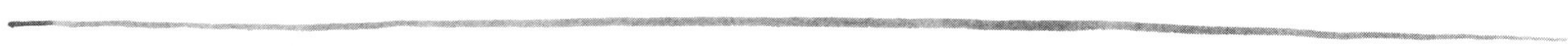

Rebuilt brush

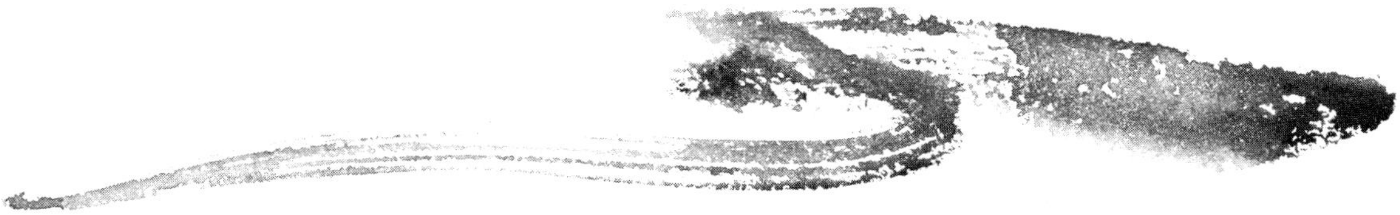

The curved, shapely brushstroke, using the brush's natural flexibility.

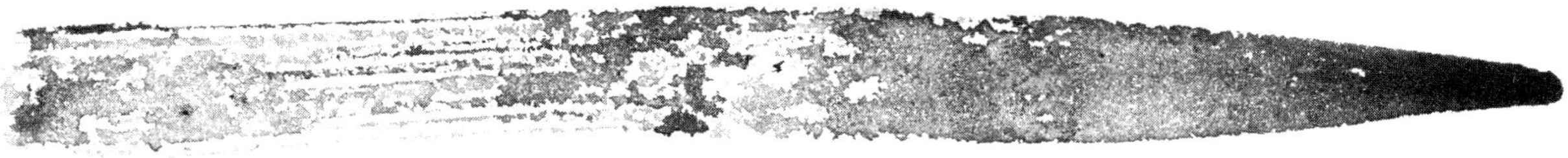

The dragged brushstroke, using a brush starved of water.
This brush technique is very important in my painting.

The brush scrubbed on its side creates a brushstroke of broken line and texture.

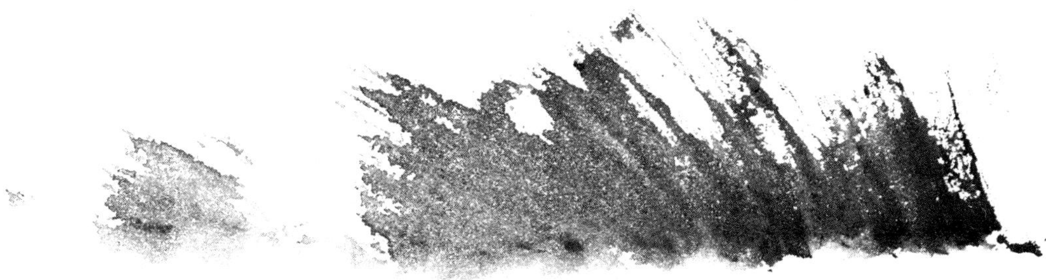

The brush scraped upward on its side. I use this technique extensively for rendering clumps of grass.

The fine-line brushstroke created by the natural fine-tip shape of the brush.

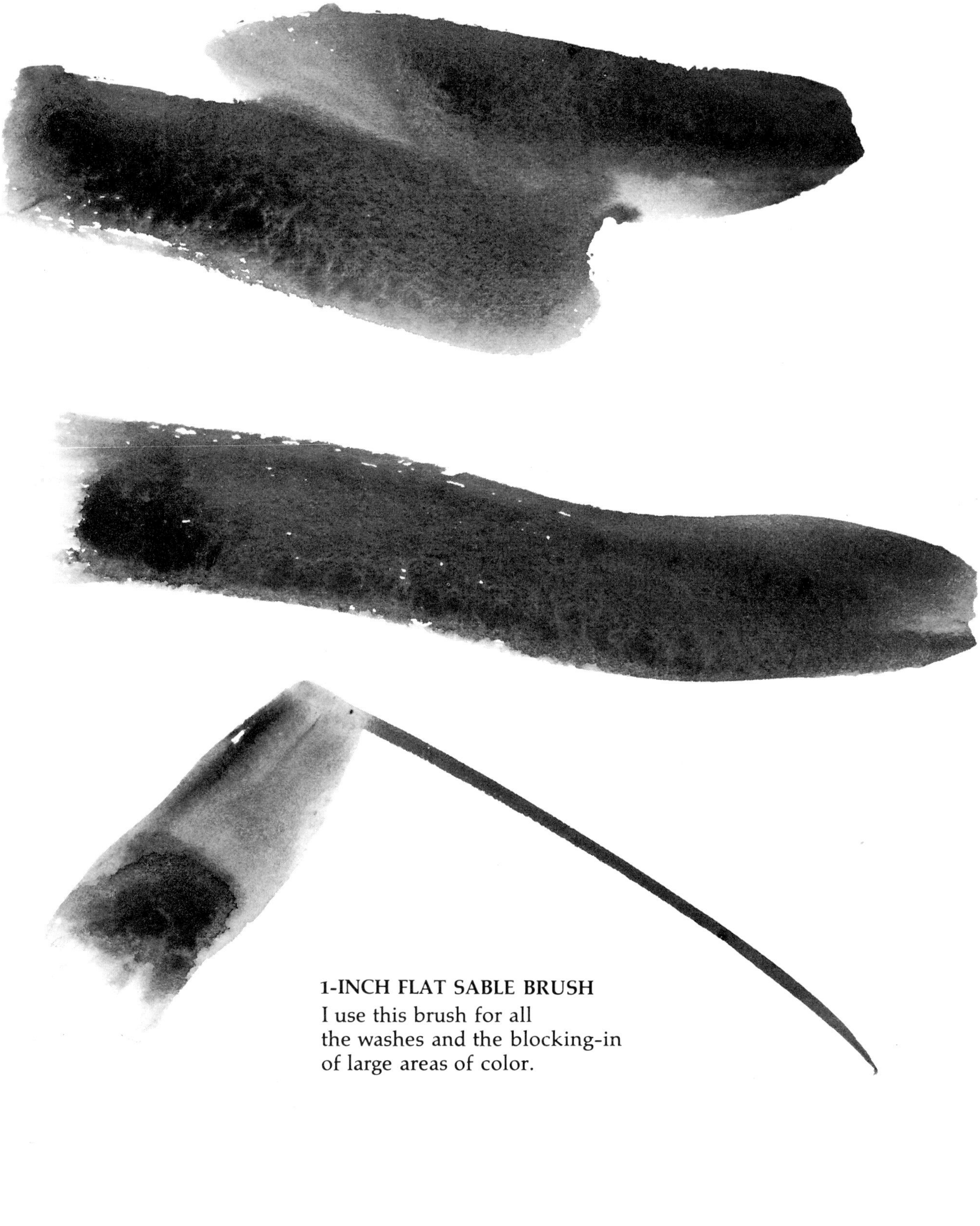

1-INCH FLAT SABLE BRUSH
I use this brush for all the washes and the blocking-in of large areas of color.

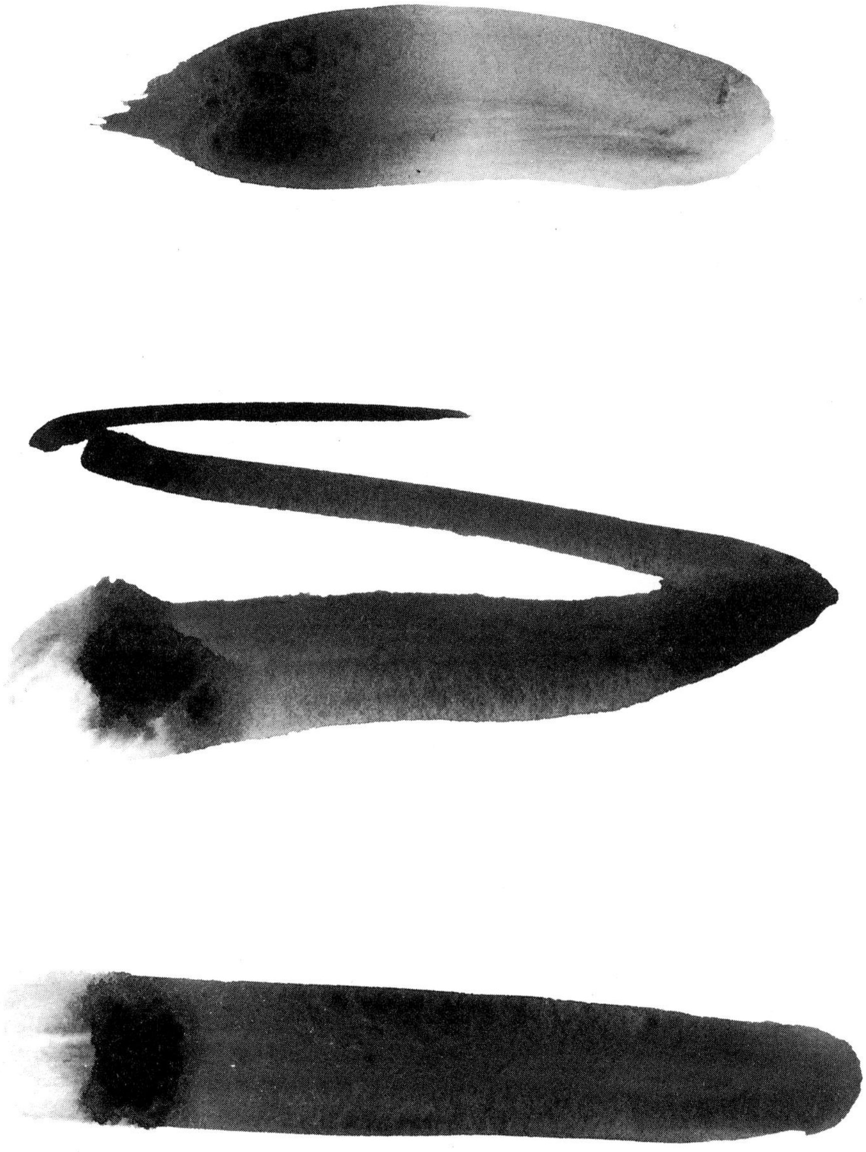

SIZE 12 ROUND BRUSH

This brush holds a great deal of paint, but it is not a brush I use often. I prefer the 1-inch flat sable, although this is probably more from habit than from any fault of the brush. The round brush can be used for the same jobs as the flat sable.

THE BAMBOO BRUSH

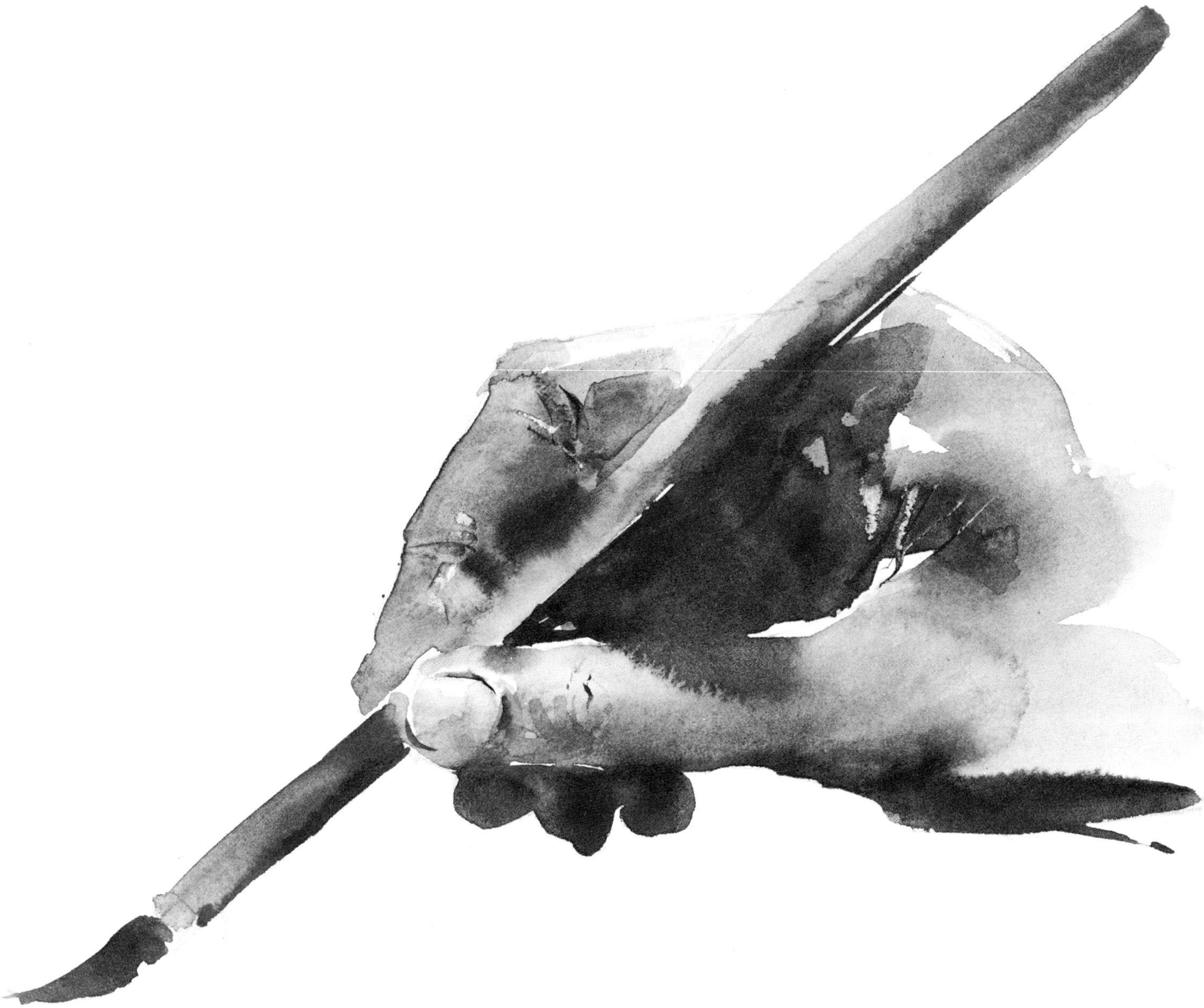

BAMBOO BRUSHSTROKES

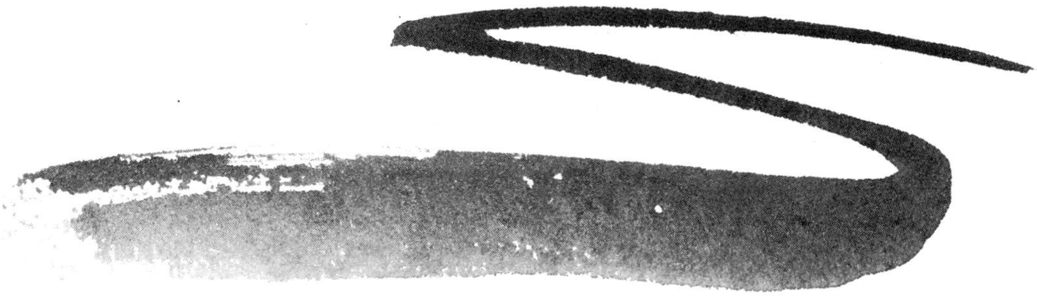

A wide variety of shapes can be produced from this brush, from delicate lines to heavy, broad statements.

A characteristic brushstroke in my work is the quick brushstroke, with the brush running out of paint. This brushstroke could be the start of a piece of wood.

Textural effects such as grass can be made by scrubbing the brush over the paper.

The starved brush dragged swiftly across the paper is another very characteristic brushstroke in my work. This could be the grain effect in a piece of wood.

The drybrush effect, dragging the brush longways, pressing hard into the paper.

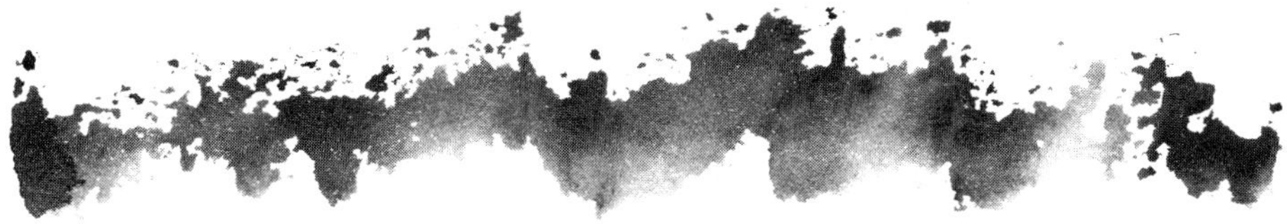

Rolling the brush on its side produces this irregular pattern brushstroke.

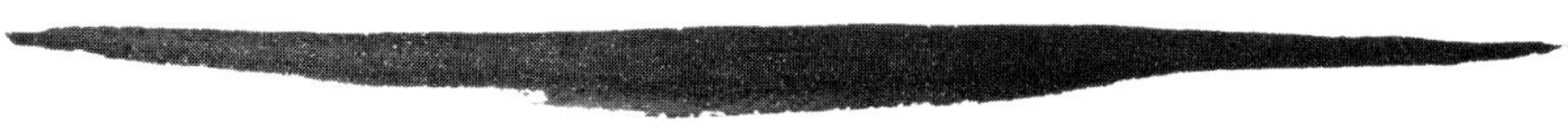

The smooth line brushstroke, going from light pressure
to heavy pressure in the center and back to light pressure.

The drybrush effect, using the brush on its side.

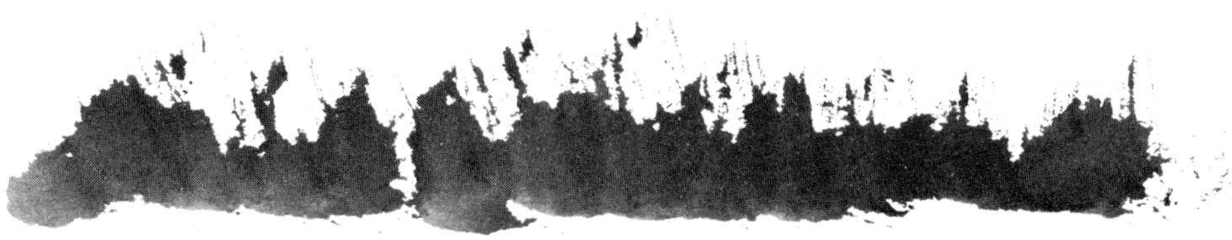

The drybrush effect, scrubbing upward with the side of a brush.

A heavily loaded brushstroke with ox gall added. This stroke is frequently used for washes. The ox gall helps to increase the paint's ability to spread.

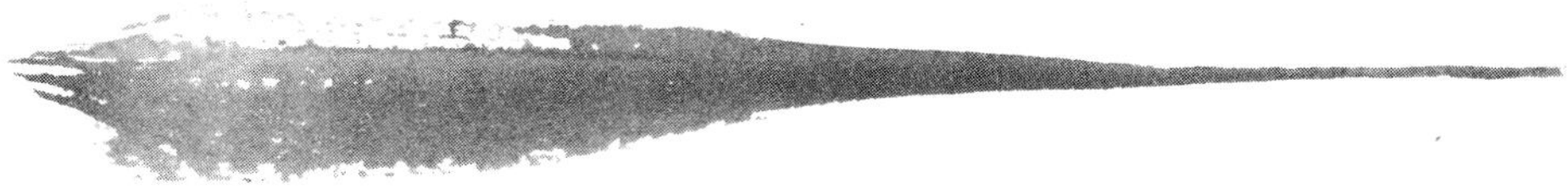

Using the brush's natural pointed shape, and working from right to left, this brushstroke moves from light to heavy pressure.

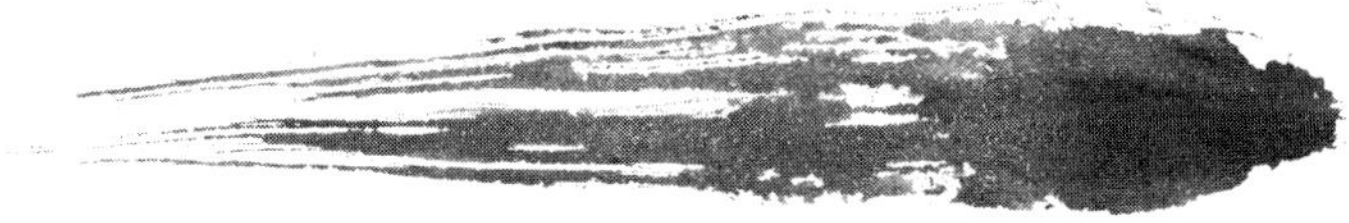

Working again from right to left, this brushstroke moves from heavy to light pressure.

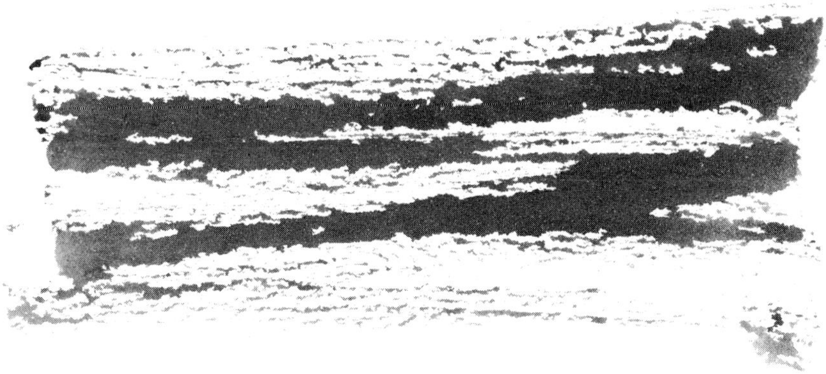

The textural effect, produced by scrubbing backward and forward, using the natural roughness of the paper.

REBUILDING AN OLD BRUSH

My style of painting is very hard on brushes, in particular the smaller sable brushes that I use for many of the textural effects. Unfortunately, the sable brushes are now very expensive and there is not as yet a good substitute, so I have devised a technique for rebuilding sables and turning them into useful brushes again. The process is quite simple, although somewhat time consuming.

Take an old sable brush that has worn out. Cut it down the center of the ferrule with a hacksaw and remove the hairs. These hairs will be tied together and glued at the butt end. The glue is very brittle and will chip off easily. Using a sharp knife, sever the cord holding the hairs together.

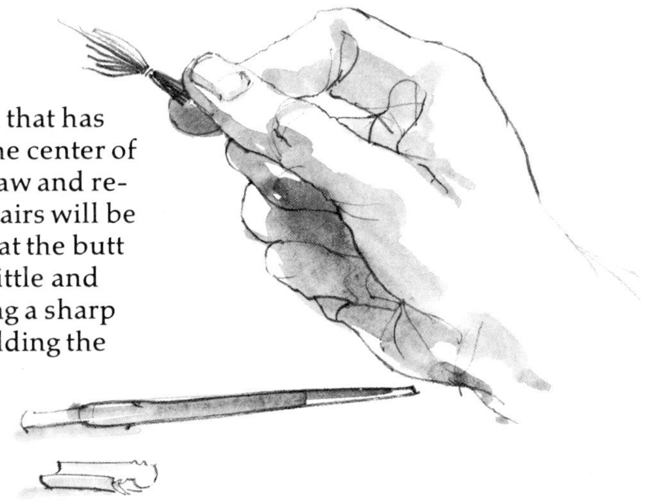

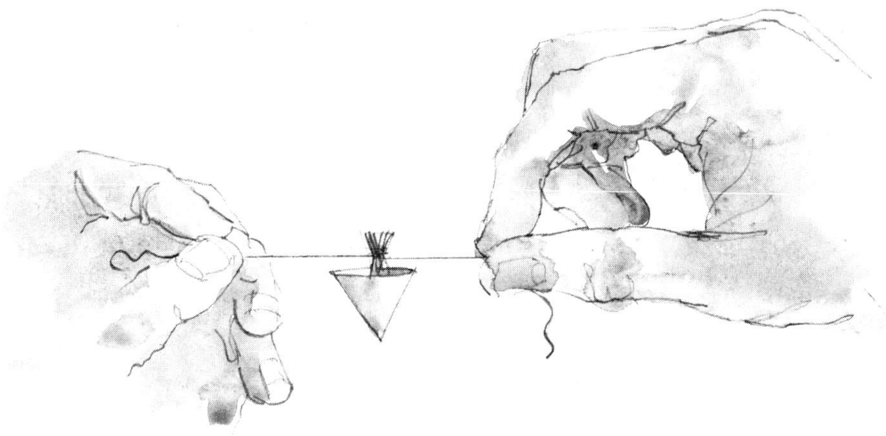

If the brush is large the hairs can be separated to make three or four smaller brushes. Improvise a cone from paper and dip the hairs into it. Make sure that the hairs reach the tip of the cone, then draw the ends together with your fingers. Do this without lifting the hairs up from the tip of the cone and losing the point of the new brush. This will give the brush the sharp point needed for detailed painting. Retie with a piece of fine fishing line to hold the hairs together.

Rummage around and find a suitable old pen—usually an old ballpoint or felt-tip pen will do. I use the kind that has a separate, removable tip, which makes changing brush hairs very easy. Sometimes the tip is difficult to remove, and I use pliers or a penknife to pull or cut the tip away. To insert the brush hairs, wet them first and then push through the small hole of the tip, pulling the hairs through from the other side to the length you require.

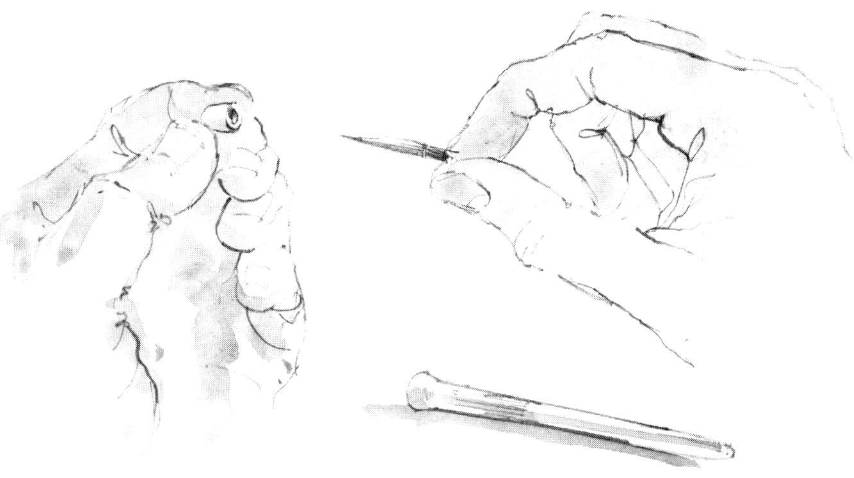

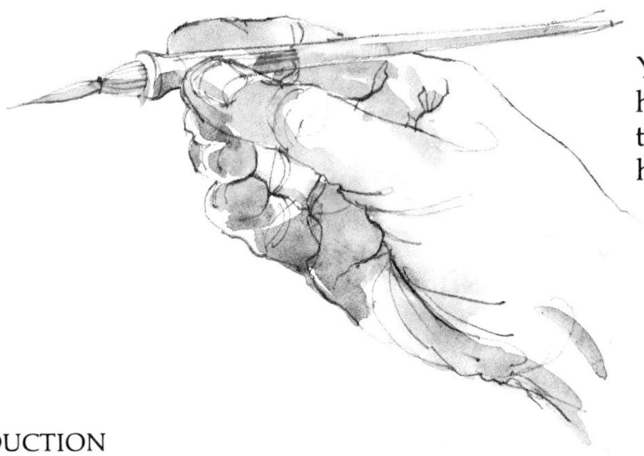

You now have a new brush and have saved some money. When this brush wears out, remove the hairs and reshape them again.

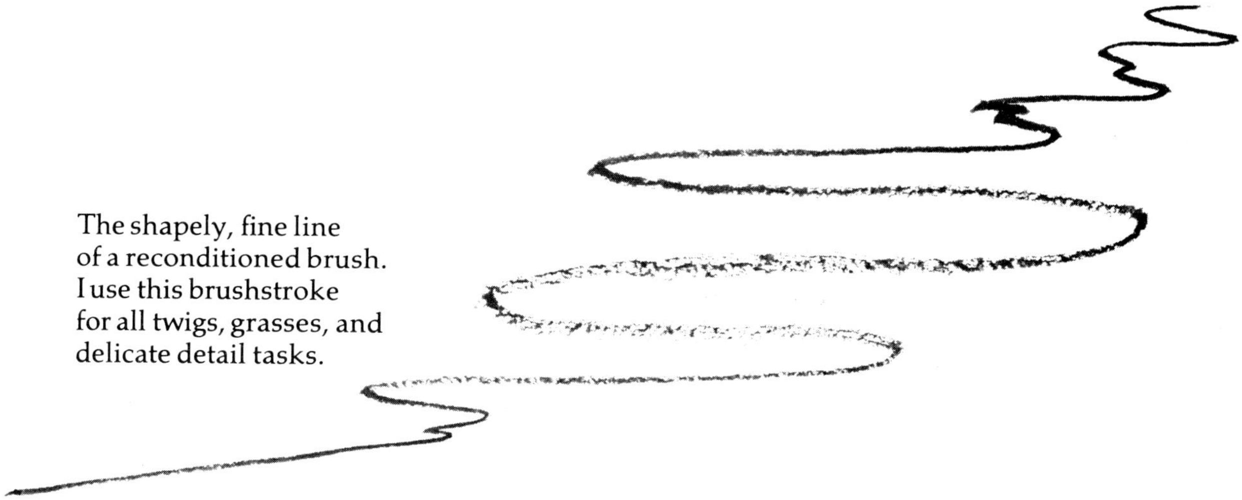

The shapely, fine line
of a reconditioned brush.
I use this brushstroke
for all twigs, grasses, and
delicate detail tasks.

The long, straight brushstroke, produced by laying the brush close on its side and gently running it along the paper.

Textural effects of the reconditioned brush.
This brushstroke is made by rolling the brush
on its side. Whenever I can, I avoid this
technique for the sake of the brush.
This kind of work wears it out in no time.

DRAWING
FOR WATERCOLORS

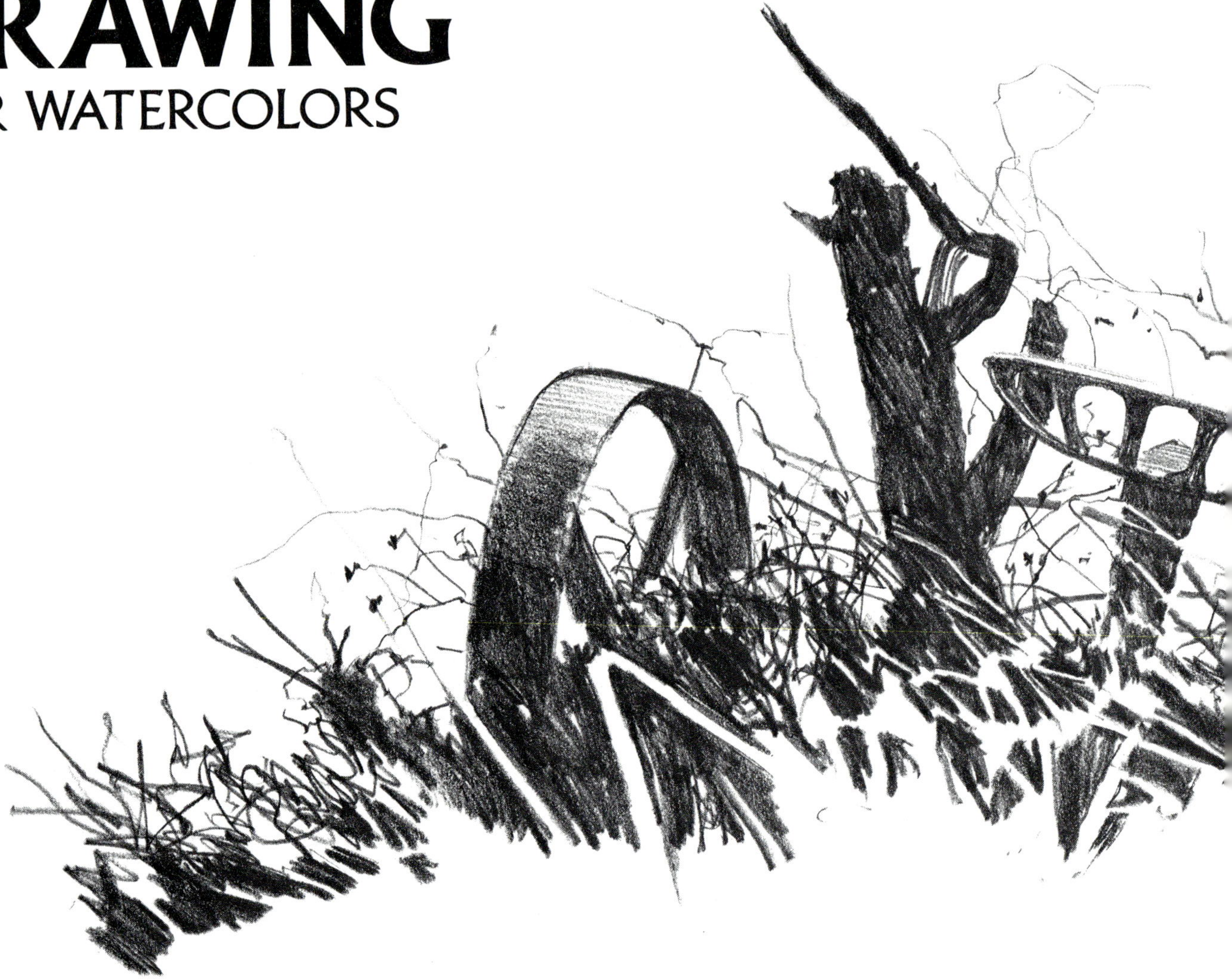

On the next twelve pages is a selection of drawings. I made them in different places, some quickly, some slowly, and each with a different purpose. Notice that every drawing contains just enough information for painting and that the arrangement of pencil or Conté lines tells me what to emphasize. Study each drawing with this in mind, and in your own work develop a system of noting shapes and textures, so that you resolve the plan for your painting during this stage. The excitement and vigor in your watercolor paintings depend on your ability to capture in pencil the very essence of a striking subject, so that you have a clear idea of exactly what you wish to paint and can work out a plan for rendering the key textures before you begin to paint.

The charm of drawing is that, like handwriting, everyone has his or her own different style that has developed with observation, concentration, and practice. However, with drawing, it is important not to be fixed or rigid. Varying the medium can make a difference, as can the speed at which you execute a drawing. With every drawing, spend a minute beforehand to decide whether you need a studious, highly detailed drawing or a swift set of visual notes for future reference. Sometimes I prefer to produce a tightly controlled, highly complex drawing and derive great enjoyment from observing and registering detail closely. At other times, when I wish to be more expressive, I dash down bold lines, using the side of the pencil and digging in the tip to create vivid linework. The most common drawing fault is an overtight line, which comes from the belief that everything should be stated in total on the paper. As an exercise, practice drawing in values alone, so that you suggest edges by changing light and value, rather than with line only. If your drawing or painting suffers from tightening-up, the best remedy is to allocate yourself a short time to work, so that you are forced to make quick decisions and cannot overwork certain passages with excessive detail.

I encounter a great deal of frustration in my painting, and many drawings and paintings are a battle in an attempt to capture some mystical effect. I often finish with a feeling that it could have been better and have learned to view this as an objective lesson in improving next time. In time, we all learn to make strong painting statements

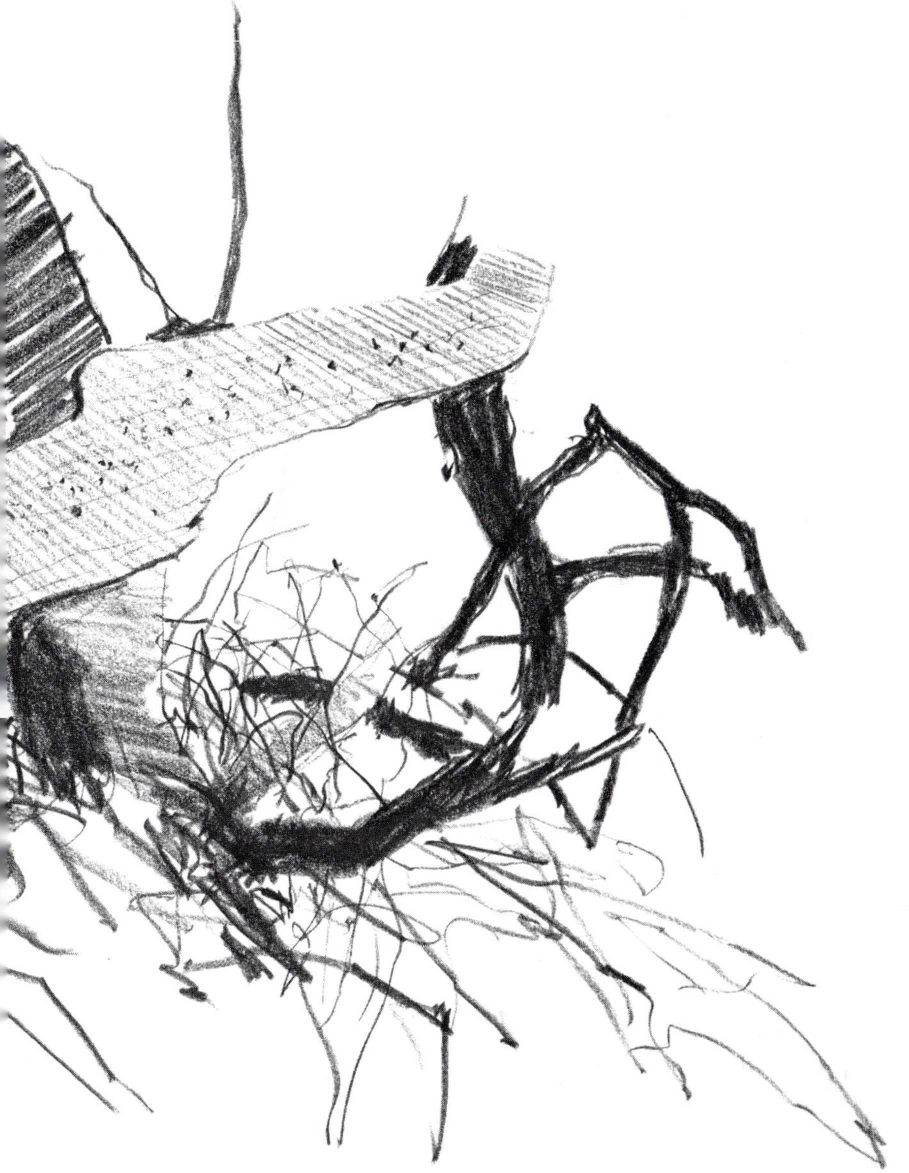

COMPOSITION

I found this old grass rake submerged in a tangle of dead grasses and weeds behind an old barn. The heavy steel wheel and seat had been carefully molded a long time ago, and their shapes and well-rusted surfaces made a great potential painting subject.

I made the drawing with Conté pencil and used very few mid-gray values, relying on a stark contrast of black and white to emphasize the smooth, round, symmetrical man-made shapes against the ragged, random natural forms.

I juggled the composition of the shapes and edited out many foreground details to make the preliminary design for a future painting. I toyed with the negative shapes of the foliage in the foreground, looking for a pattern of values that would offset the man-made seat and wheel above.

As I almost buried the rake in the long grass, this drawing demanded only a little technical drafting skill. It is quite easy to render seemingly awkward shapes in this way, without having to be highly proficient at technical drawing.

with a more economical use of pigment and water.

If you find drawing a struggle, choose a subject that does not rely on accurate technical draftsmanship. Remember that it is much easier to use a modicum of drawing and then depend on your skill and dexterity with watercolor to create textures that give character to a painting. The painting of the shed with pantiles on pages 72-73 needed very little technical drawing, and its strength is in its array of paint textures. The painting of half a tractor on pages 82-83 needed some technical drawing, but the traction engine on pages 92-93 was a tour de force in precision work. Or was it? Look at it closely through a magnifying glass and you will discover that there is little actual *drawing*. It is the careful application of paint that creates the illusion of precision engineering on the boiler, funnel, and wheels. If I had drawn the engine rather than painted it, it would have become stifled in technical accuracy and lacked any sign of my own interpretation of the subject. It is the color and texture of the rusty steel that produced such a striking painting here, and not the drawing.

Of course, you may prefer to do no preliminary drawing at all and go straight into a painting, which is fine if that is the best way for you. But in my experience, drawing is an integral part of the thinking process of watercolor painting, and without it, paintings sometimes lack structure and shape. They suffer from a lack of definite composition. So take the time to draw—you will never regret it!

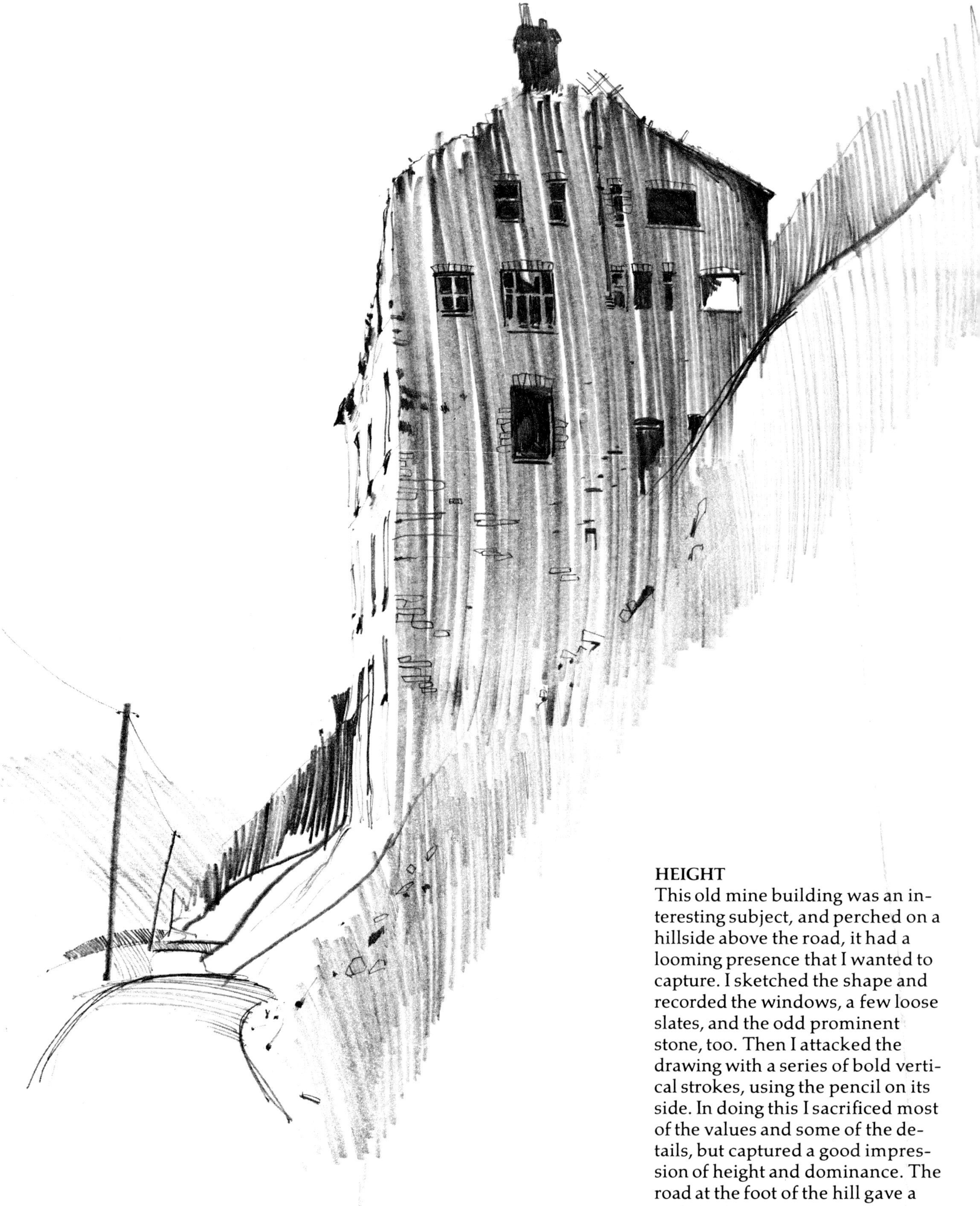

HEIGHT
This old mine building was an interesting subject, and perched on a hillside above the road, it had a looming presence that I wanted to capture. I sketched the shape and recorded the windows, a few loose slates, and the odd prominent stone, too. Then I attacked the drawing with a series of bold vertical strokes, using the pencil on its side. In doing this I sacrificed most of the values and some of the details, but captured a good impression of height and dominance. The road at the foot of the hill gave a scale to the scene.

SPEED

I didn't exactly dash off this drawing at great speed, but I concentrated hard on capturing the essential features of the dovecote, such as the doorway shapes, the roof angles and shadows, and the pole at the top. I used bland, horizontal Conté strokes across the face of the dovecote to suggest only its local values, and I was concerned with the density of the twigs and branches behind, rather than the exact character of each one.

This is not a great drawing—it was never intended to be that, but simply a set of pictorial notes that could be reworked into a painting later.

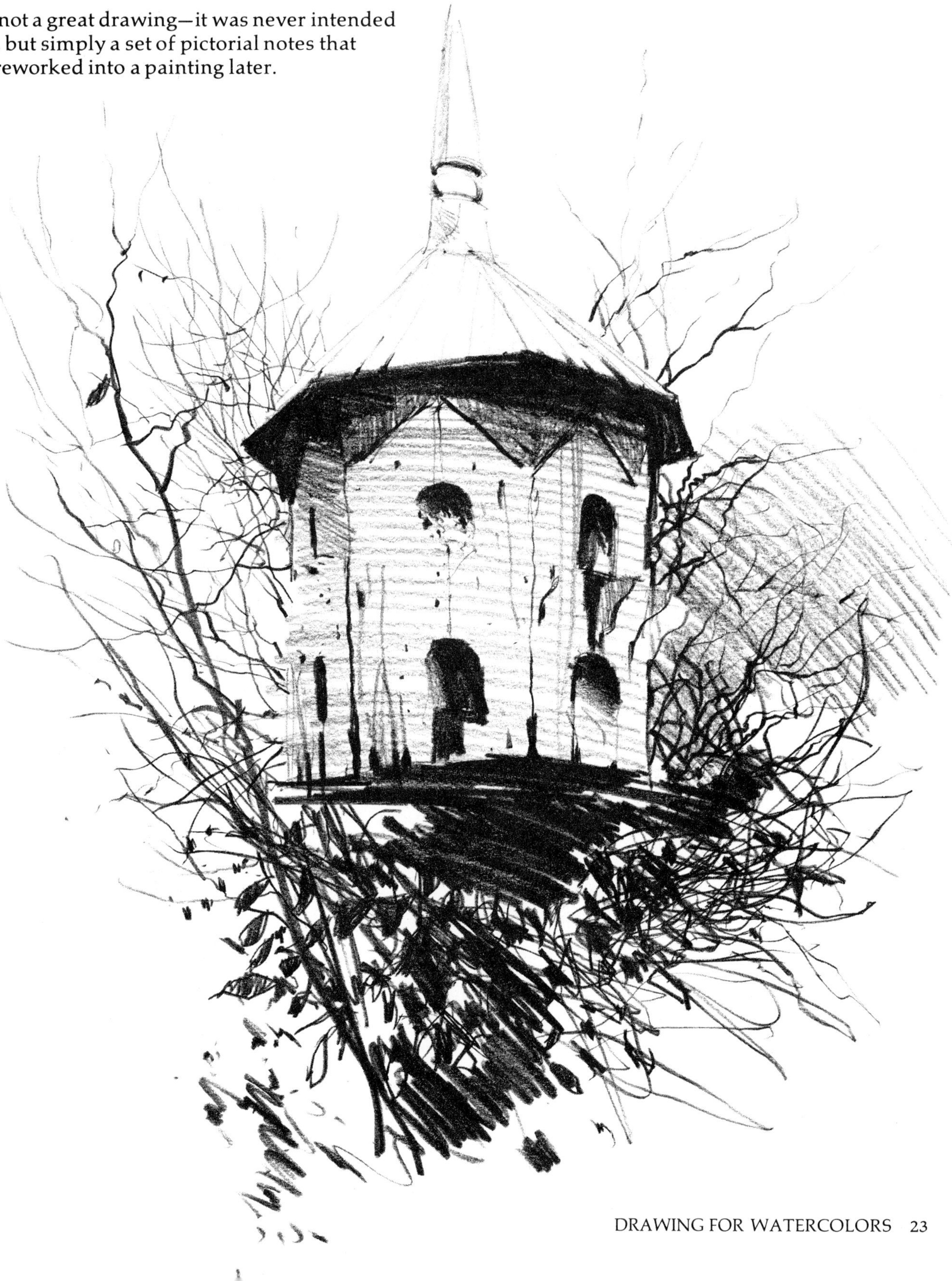

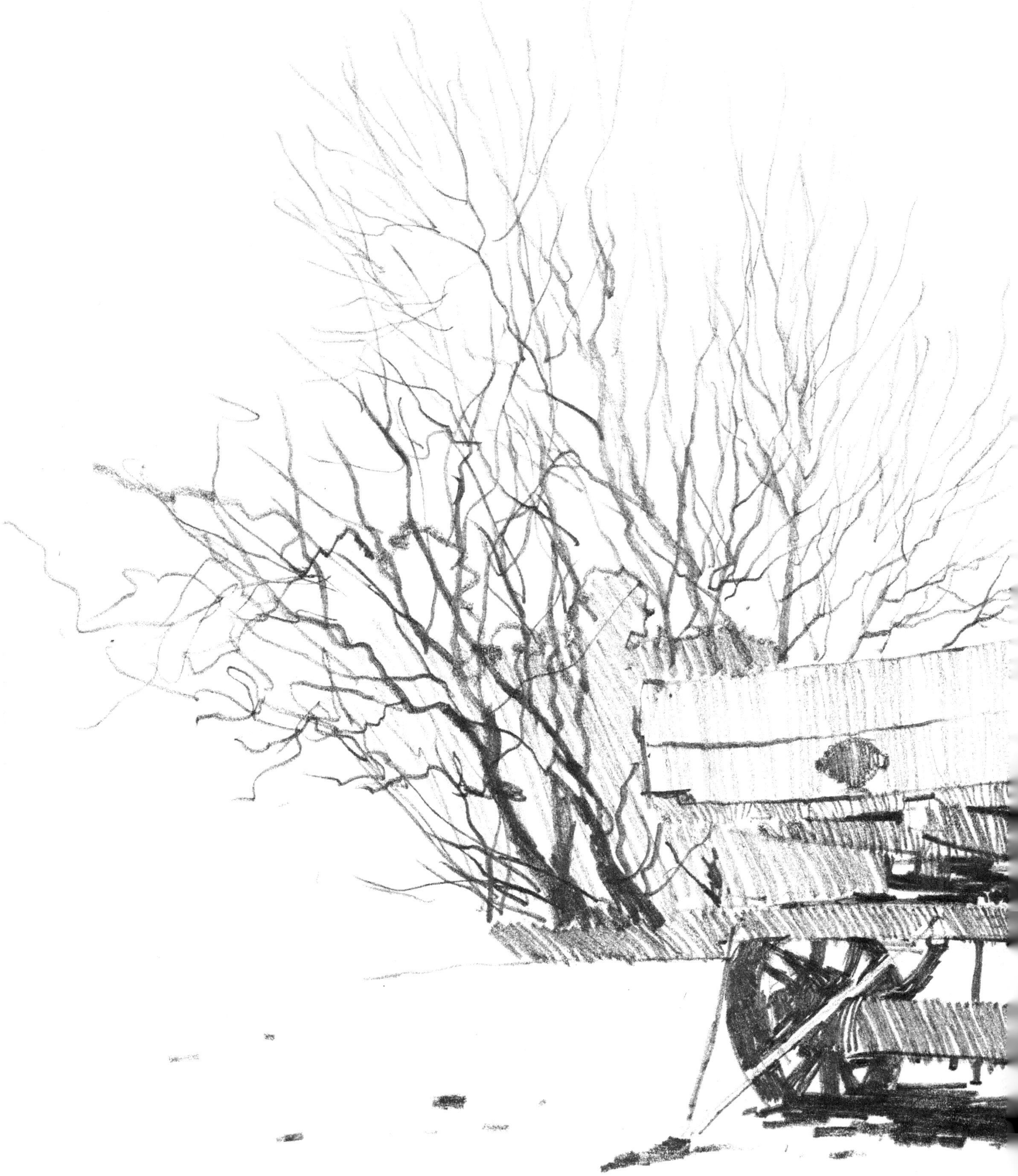

VALUE

Rather than become buried in a mass of technical details under the chassis of this old cart, I started this drawing by marking in lightly the basic features and then added those of less visual appeal with hatched-in values. Notice that the axles and cross members on the cart give the impression of being complicated in structure, but are only loosely stated. I may have left out altogether some essential load-bearing features: this cart could never function as a farm vehicle, but it is now easy for me to paint and *looks* like an old farm cart. I only suggested the shadows between the spokes on the wheel in the foreground, yet it has weight and that certain chunkiness, too. I relaxed while hatching-in the outbuildings and put in more values than really necessary, but I had time to doodle. I arranged the tree branches to form a satisfactory V-shaped composition with the cart and outbuildings.

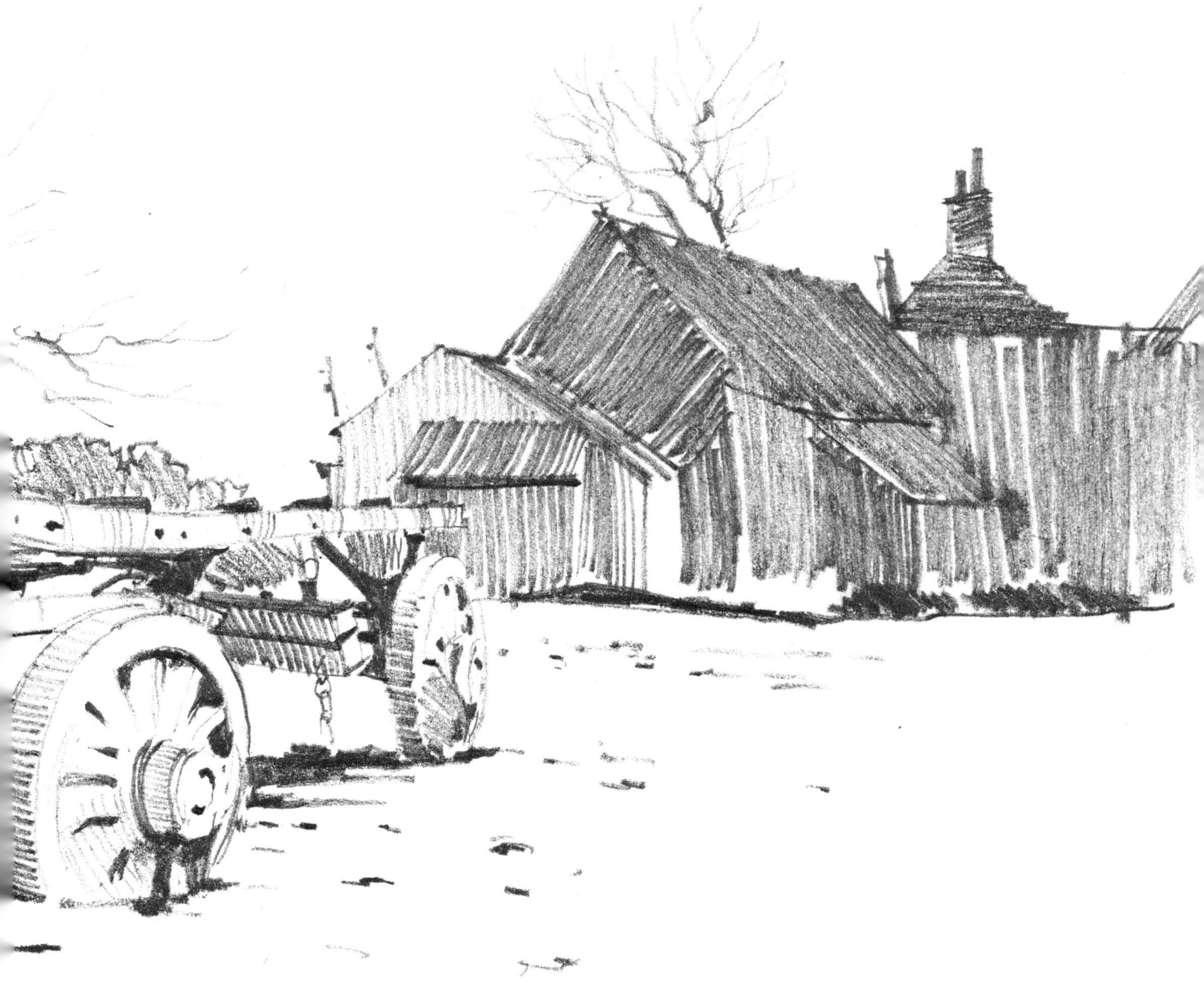

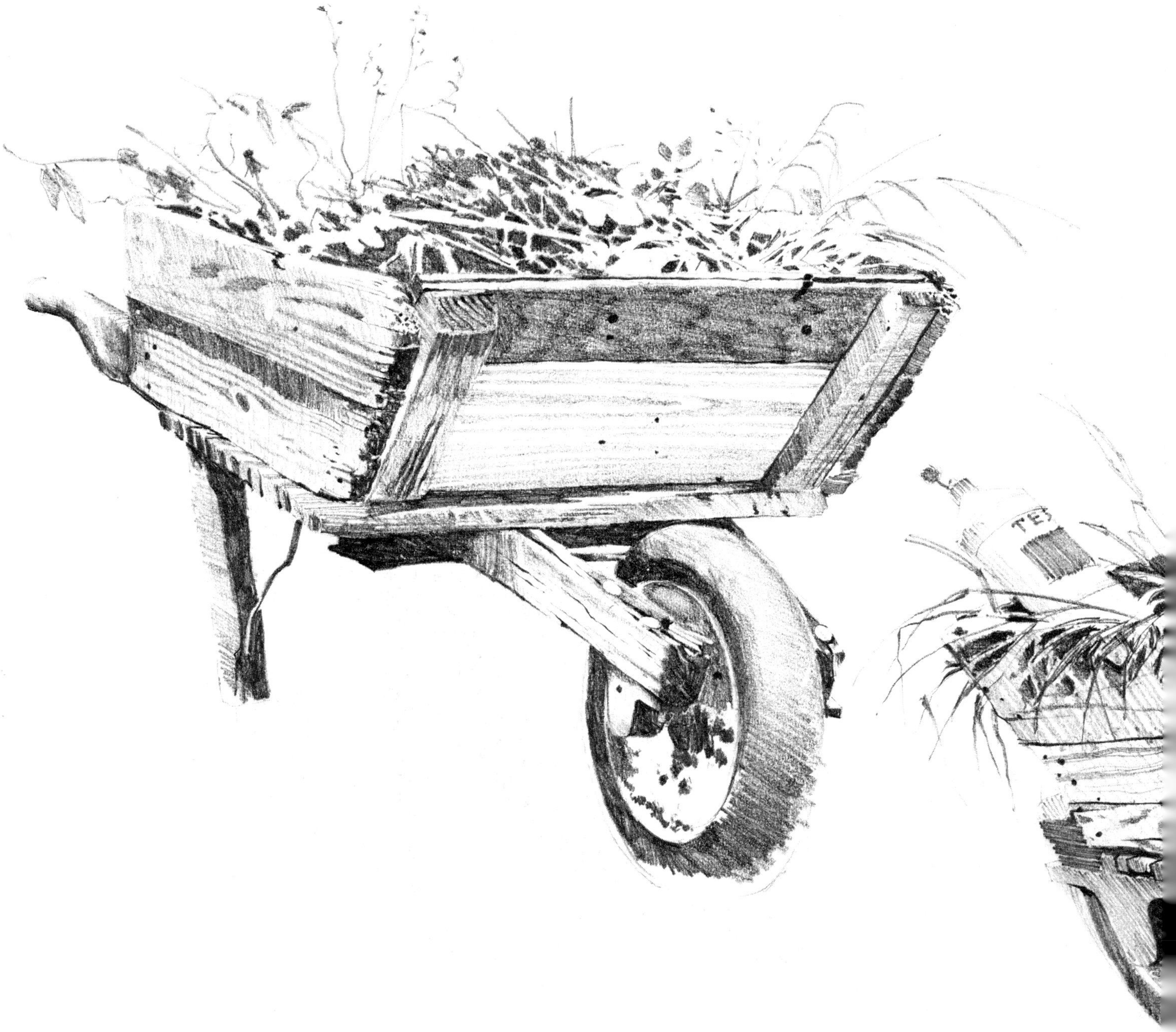

RECORDING CHARACTER IN DETAIL

There was nothing particularly magical about the shape of this battered, old wooden wheelbarrow, but the textures of the grain in the planks of wood were very clear and I set to work. I decided that this grain was just as effective depicted in pencil as it would be in paint, so I made a careful, studied drawing in pencil and left it at that. To do justice to it all, I ended up drawing it twice. The grain you see here is simply the result of study and carefully weighted values. This fine detail is easy to portray when you have an array of pencil drawing techniques and can vary the width and weight of each stroke at will. Take your time to draw a subject like this in as great detail as you can. The perspective is quite simple, and with care, it is difficult not to produce a really satisfying drawing.

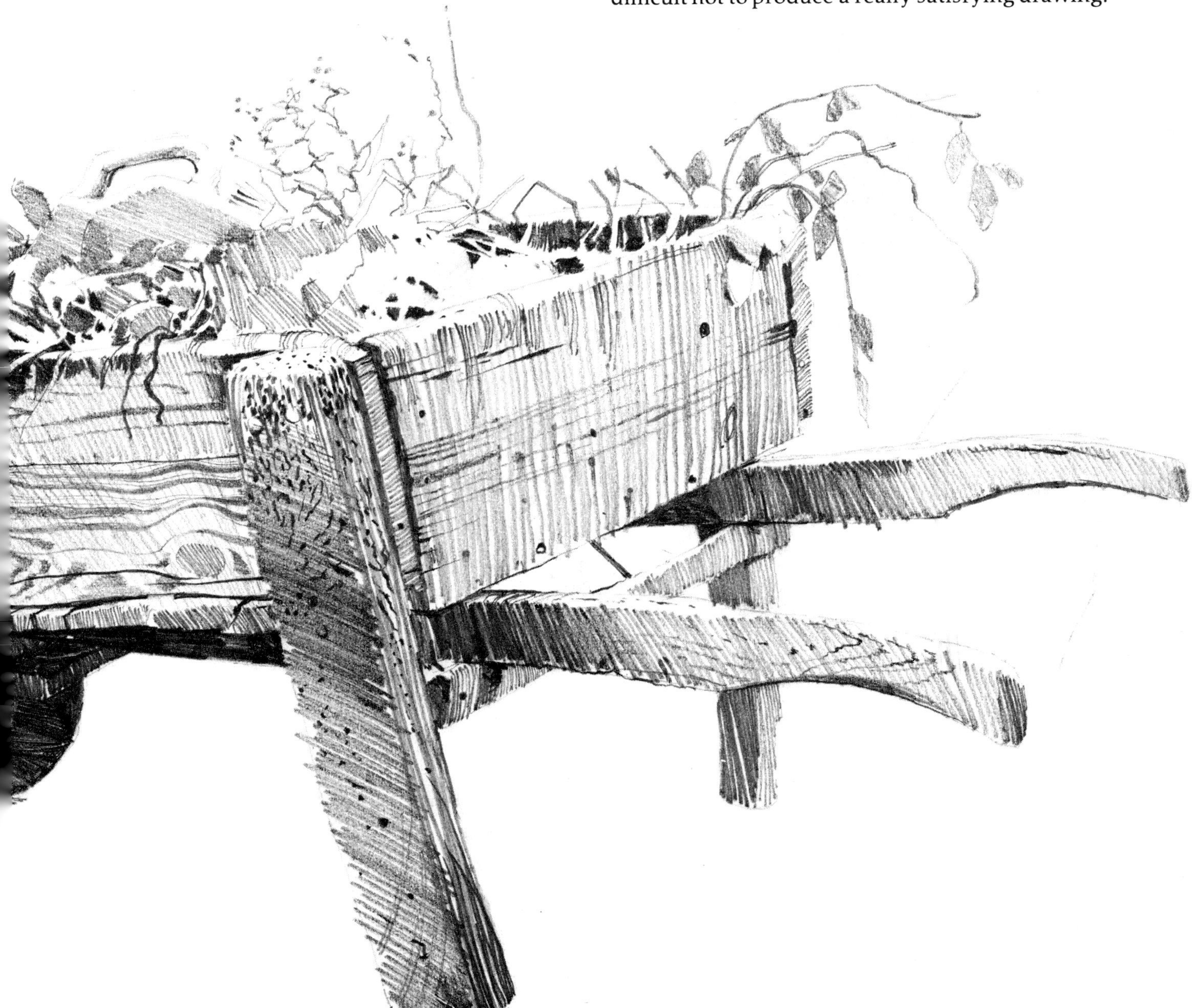

EVALUATING SHAPES

The key to this drawing was the shapes of the windows. As the car was beaten and bent, I could have arranged them to suit myself, but I chose not to do so. I concentrated on nothing but the outline drawing of the car and once it was right, I began to establish some values to give the correct planes to all the pieces of metal. The windows in this drawing are an example of when it is necessary to draw very precisely around objects rather than roughly suggesting them. Where the weeds covered the car, I relaxed and left some areas undrawn: so long as the focal point of the drawing—the windows—was established, everything else was less important and needed less detail.

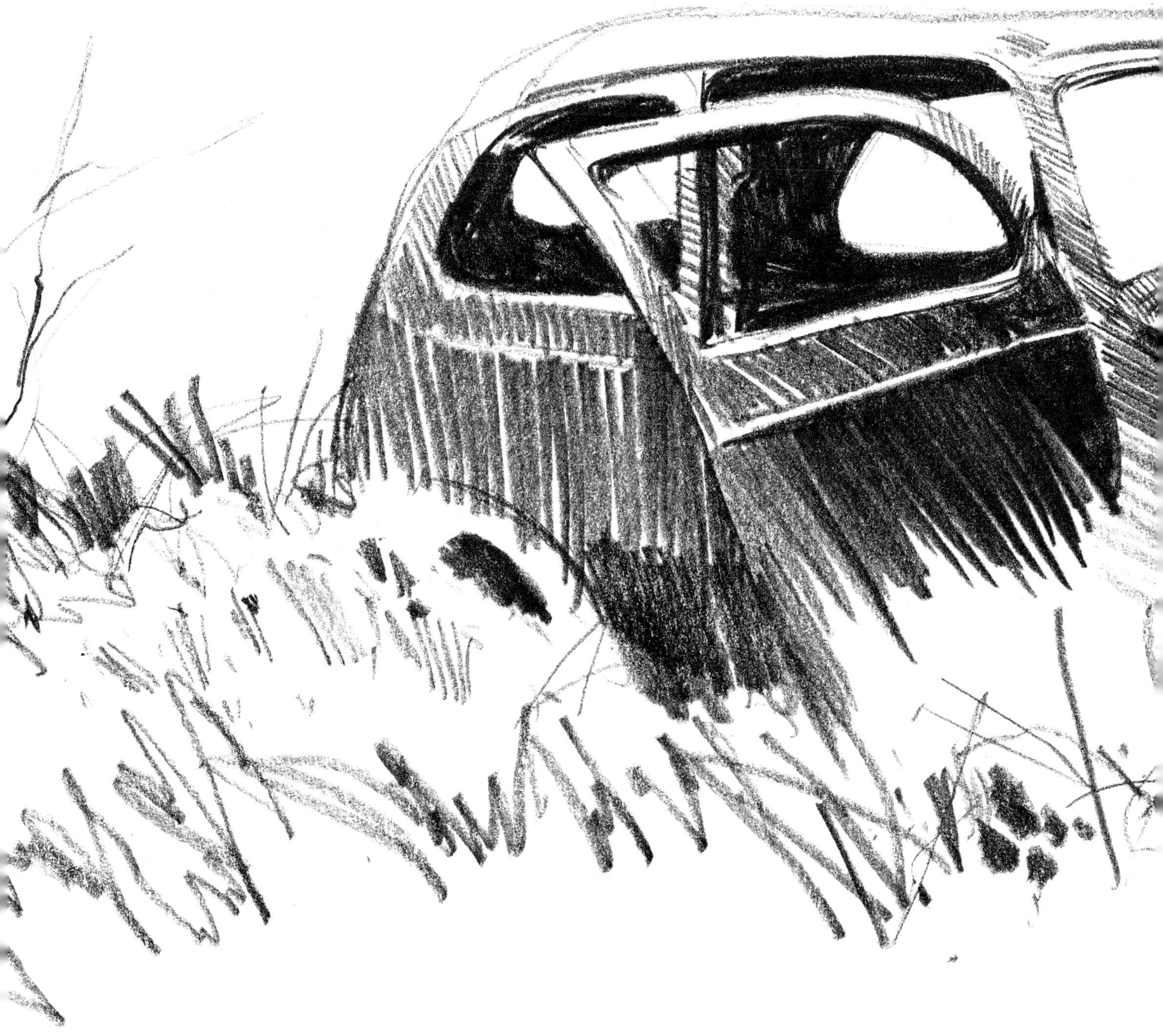

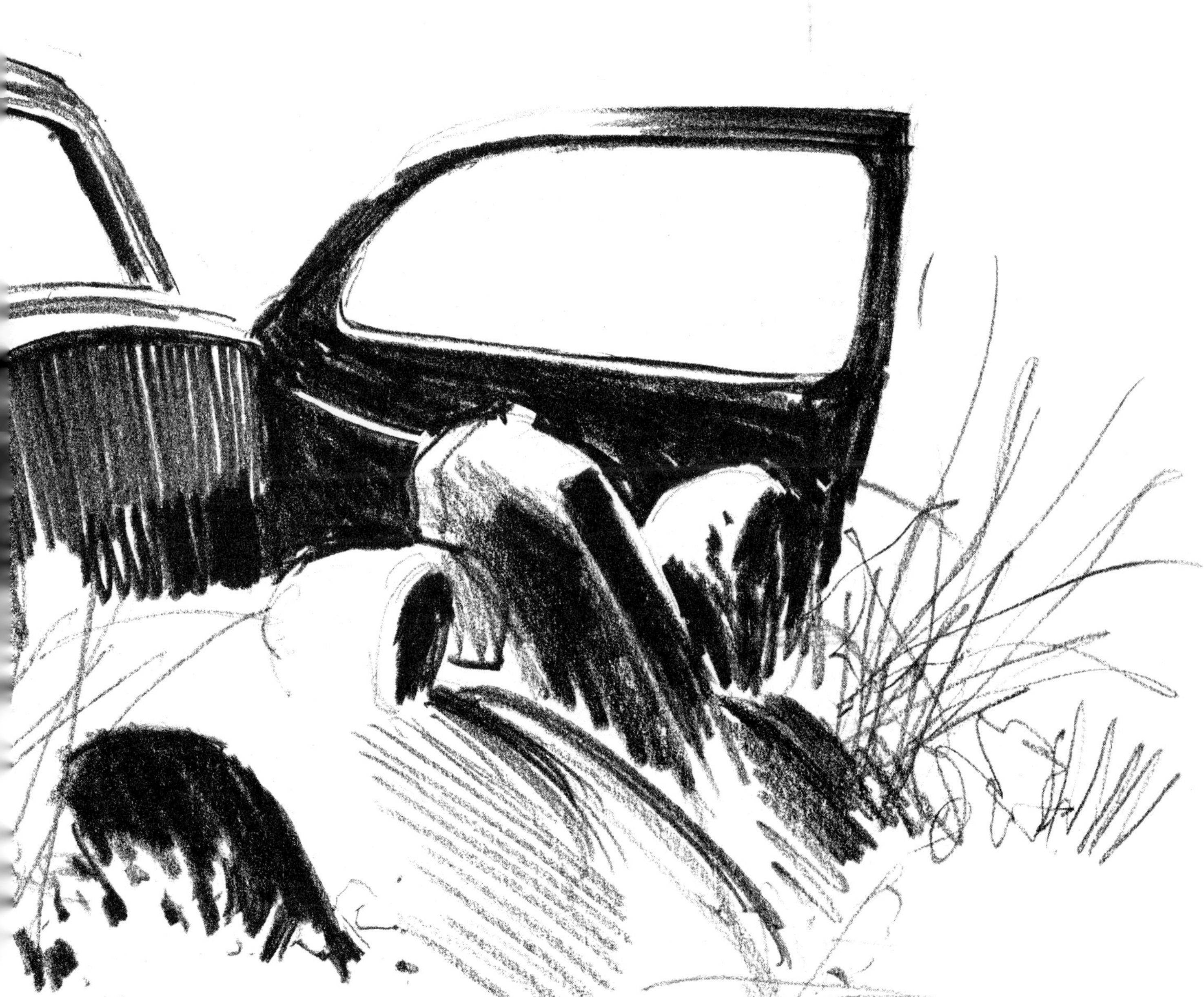

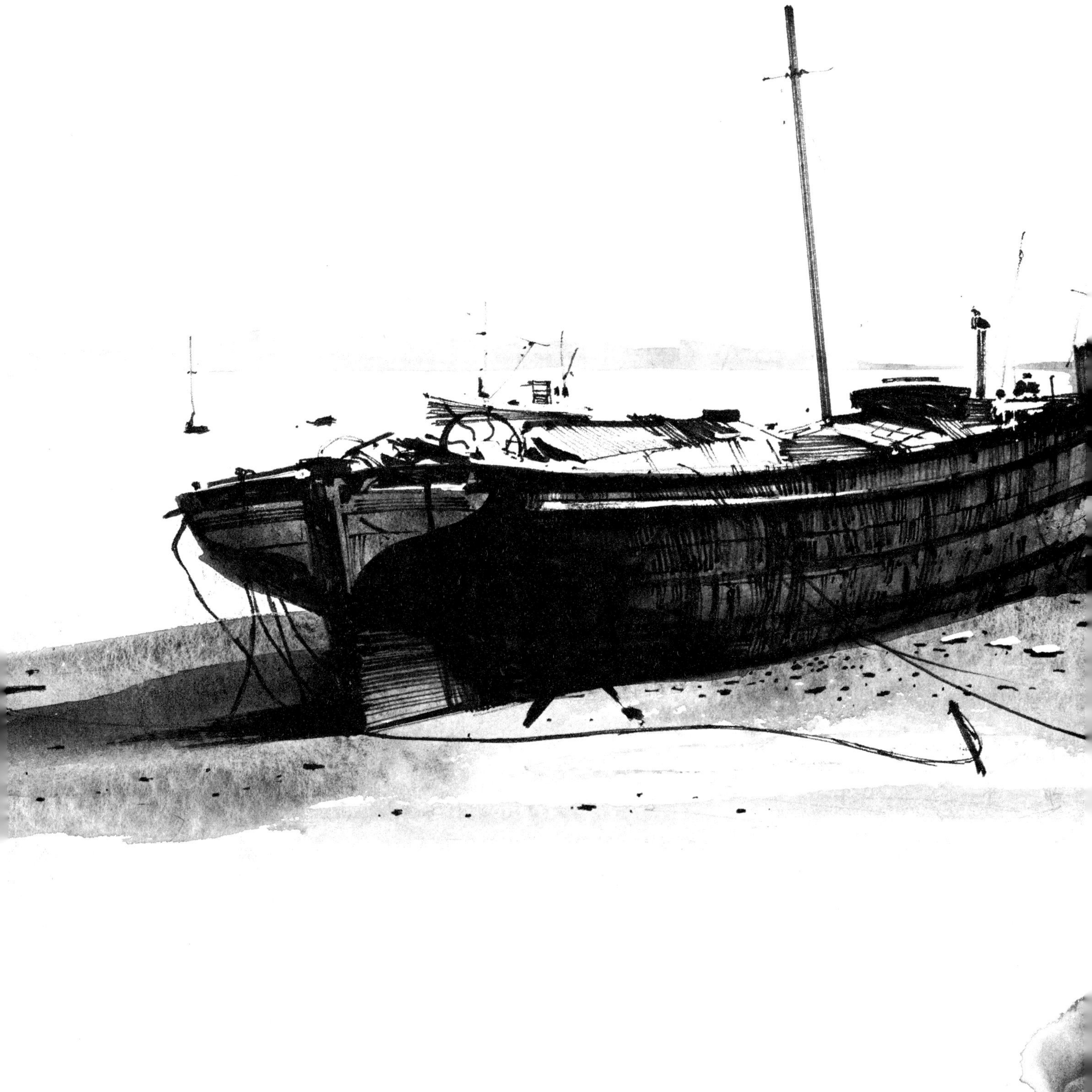

CAPTURING THE LIGHT

A trip to the boatyard at low tide never fails to produce a selection of hulls and boating paraphernalia that is great painting subject material. On this bright day, the shadows were dark beneath the boats and stones on the beach. I experimented with a felt-tip pen and an Indigo wash: first, I made the basic drawing with the felt-tip pen, ignoring fine details and darkest shadow areas. Then I masked out the stones on the wet sand, so that the subsequent wash would leave areas of white paper. The wash dried quickly on this hot day, and I removed the masking fluid and added shadows under the stones and all the other darkest details. The high contrast of values above and below the boats gives a strong impression of overhead light.

Although not a traditional "pen and wash" drawing, I find great satisfaction in this medium and advise you to try it for yourself.

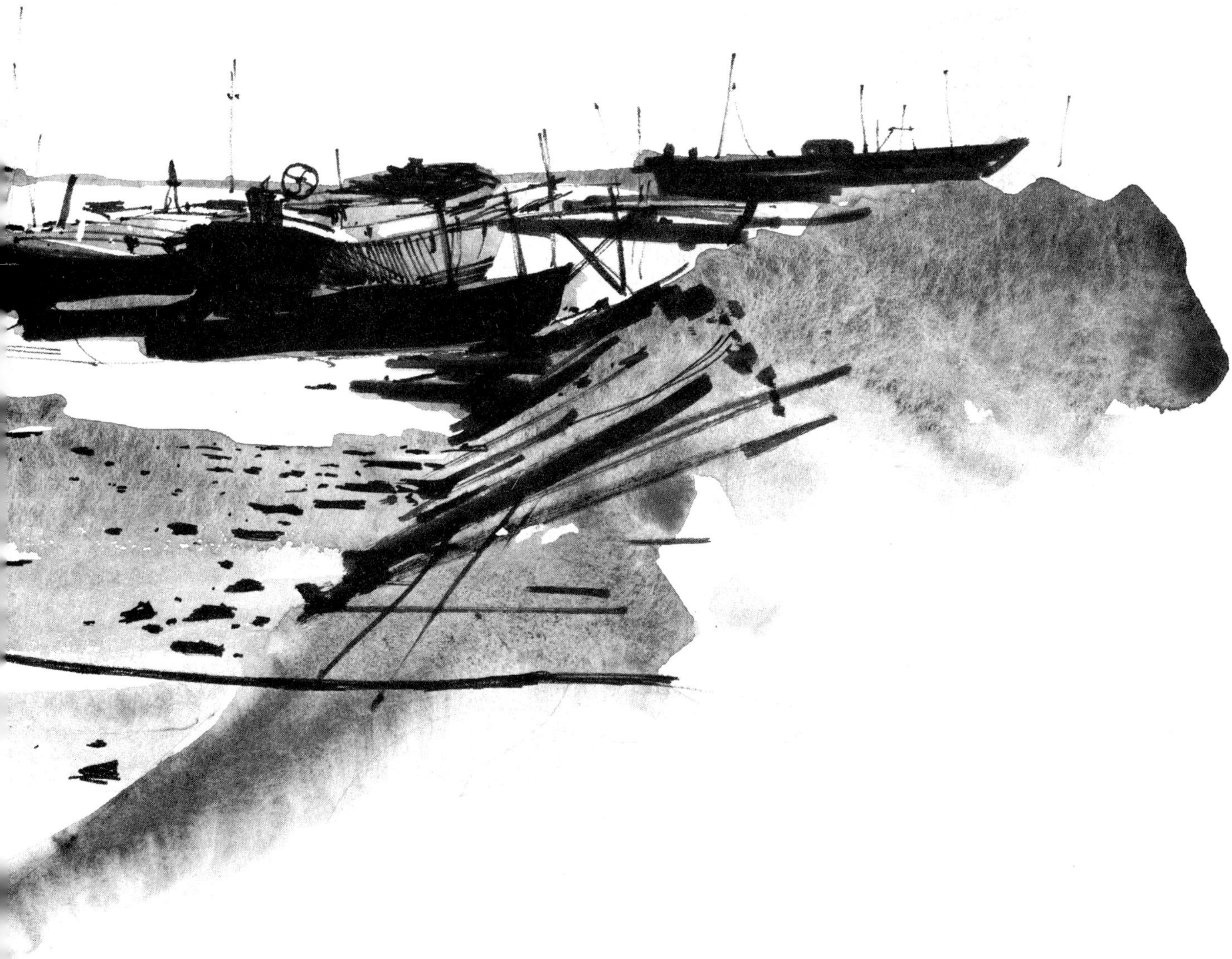

WEATHERED TEXTURE
DEMONSTRATIONS

This section contains seven demonstrations that show my working procedures. They are not the only way to paint these subjects, but they work for me. I can plan beforehand the process of painting a picture, so that I don't have to go back and lift out a lot of color or muddy-up some of the more delicate washes. Why seven demonstrations? No reason, other than the fact that these show some of the more important considerations that go into the planning of a painting.

There is no substitute for time spent in thinking out the order of working procedures for a painting. I still rush into some paintings because I am excited and want to get on with developing the idea and see it take life on the stretched paper. Often this leads to disaster, especially where I have made a commitment in paint that is irreversible, and the painting has to be scrapped and started again. No matter how experienced you are, always take time to plan the picture before you reach for the brush. What is the most important feature in the painting? Where is it going to be placed? What quieter objects will offset it and provide that all-important balance? If strong textures or rich colors are to be a main strength, how will you maintain control over them throughout the work? How will you cope with difficult structural drawing, and is the focal point of the painting to be tight and highly detailed or loose and more simply suggested?

There is a demonstration on each of the four most important points to remember. First, aim for an economic use of pigment, using just as much as you absolutely have to and no more. Always try to leave some quiet areas in a painting and preferably let some of these be white unpainted paper, so that the spaces where there is interest will stand out by comparison. Second, concentrate on keeping detail loose, so that pigment doesn't become muddy and there are no areas that are tight and tense. Third, use a limited palette to encourage yourself to become more versatile and adept at mixing colors and measuring the strength of washes. Fourth, take extra care when using rich colors: they need to be carefully controlled, or they can cause a violent upset in a painting. The other three demonstrations serve to show the order of painting the three most common weathered-texture subjects: wood, metal, and stone.

Don't worry about the specific textures in each demonstration, they are all examined in close detail in the workshop section. Concentrate on mastering the most practical sequences of working in watercolor; most important, change and adapt these methods to suit your way of painting and develop your own strong style.

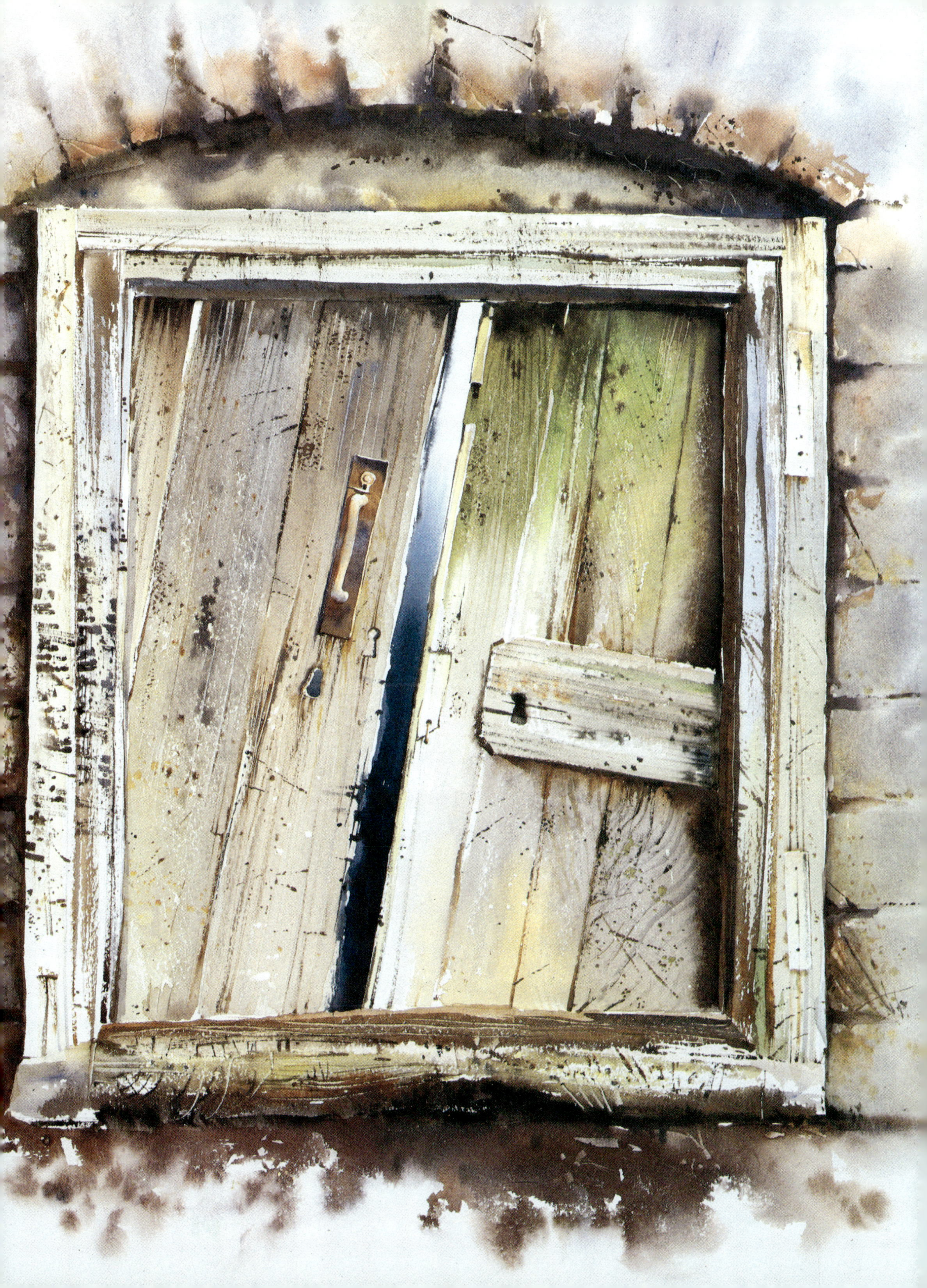

RICH COLORS

This abandoned lead mine, where a whole piece of mountainside has been excavated, presented such a strong statement about earth structure and colors that it seemed to lend itself to painting. The structure, sitting amid shale left from years of mining, has been derelict for many years and consequently it's covered with rust, giving me the opportunity to paint rich oranges and mauves.

The intense darks, like those in the foreground of the finished painting, give strength to the structure and tie the middle ground with the foreground. Watch the patterns of light to middle to very dark tones on the shed, as these variants help fit the shed into the picture by tying in with other similar tones. Otherwise the shed would be merely an isolated object.

Broad washes play an important role in this painting, with great sweeps of paint and water laid across the paper, capturing the feel of the hillside and the shale strewn across the landscape.

To make your washes work you need to be bold, using the brush across the surface in sweeping, generous washes. The speed with which color is applied, and the self-assured manner in which it is laid in, are both very important.

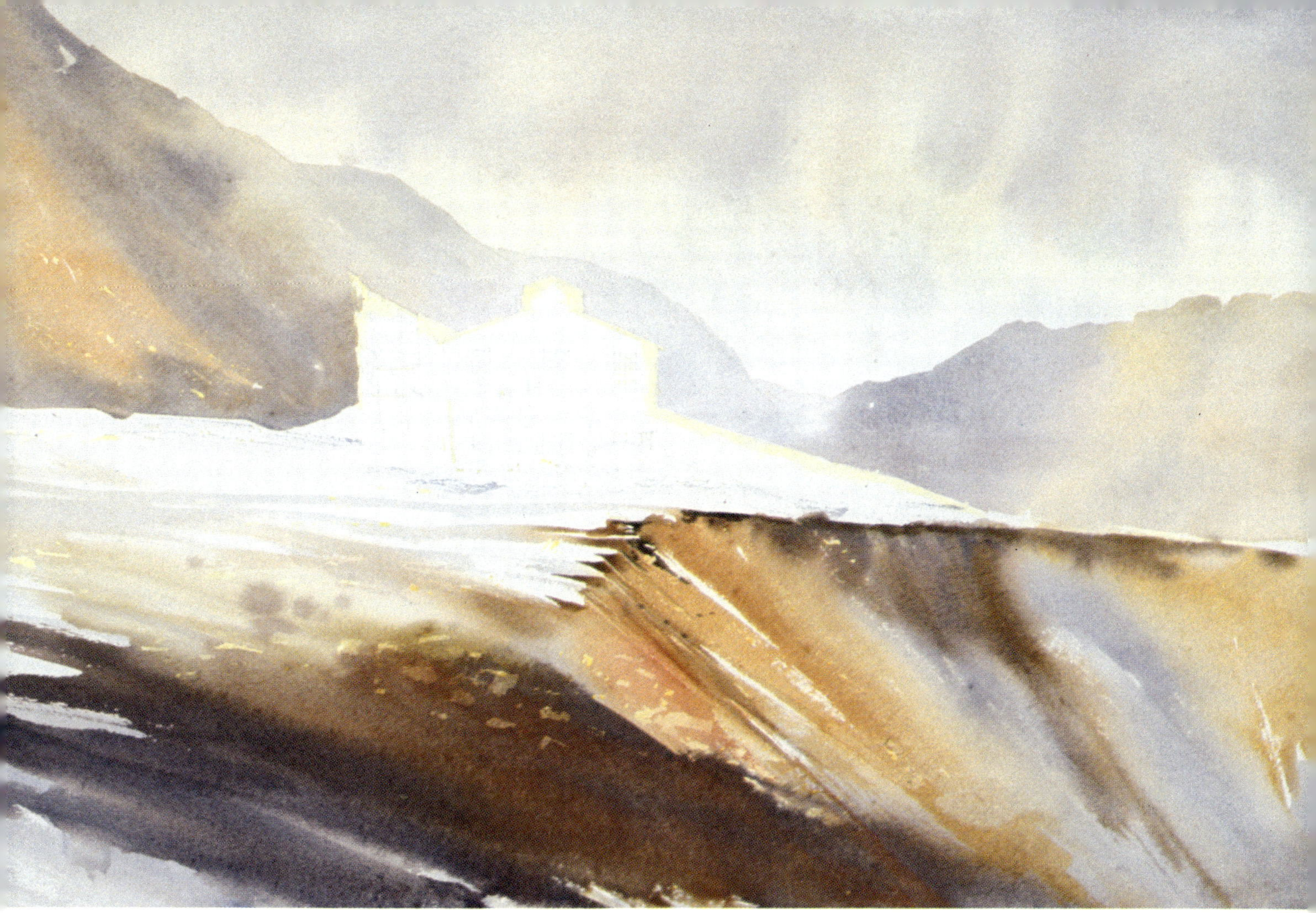

Stage 1. For a pale sky, one that wouldn't fight with the strong detail of the mine, I started with a thin wash of Naples Yellow and Cobalt Blue. While they were still very wet I introduced, in very diluted washes, Cadmium Orange, Burnt Sienna, and a little Sap Green, producing the delicate mottled effect. Washes can be altered by tilting the board back and forth to encourage the colors to run together. Further washes can be added if this seems too pale, but add them only when the others have dried.

I used an HB pencil to draw in the corrugated iron shed. Because it is so important to the picture I paid particular attention to it, even using a ruler to draw in the window frames. The mountains were mapped out simply as they will be treated with a broad wash later on.

The myriad stones were painted in with masking fluid, and I took care to vary the shapes and sizes, with the larger ones closer. A band of masking fluid around the shed and its windows kept them clear of paint when I later painted in the hills.

Stage 2. Defining the rugged contours, indicating large land masses and mountains and the shale breaking away in front of the shed, requires careful attention as each has its own feeling and texture. I painted in the dominant colors, the blues and rusts, with a broad, flat 1-inch brush. This is the stage of large washes. A wide brush helps to give you the feeling of the dynamic action of the earth upheaval you are painting. I applied a wash of Cobalt Blue, then Burnt Sienna, Alizarin Carmine, and Cadmium Orange, allowing the colors to run together. Creating a strong horizontal at the top of the shale helps me to see where I am going. This ledge, where the house is, must have solidity amid the falling slopes and rolling hills.

Stage 3. Before removing the masking fluid, I added the detail—the stones and shale working loose and tumbling down the steep hillside—to the previous wash, now dry. This creates a rough and uneven texture and the feeling of movement.

On the distant hill, the rocks were painted in Ultramarine Blue and Burnt Sienna. Because the foreground stones are bathed in sunlight, they are painted in warm colors, mostly Burnt Sienna and Bright Red. For the rocks in the immediate foreground, I used Indigo mixed with Burnt Sienna. These well-defined, hard-edge darks give an extra dimension of shale texture and vibrant darks. The white specks left when the masking fluid was removed revealed the highlights of the stones and increased the vibrancy of the painting.

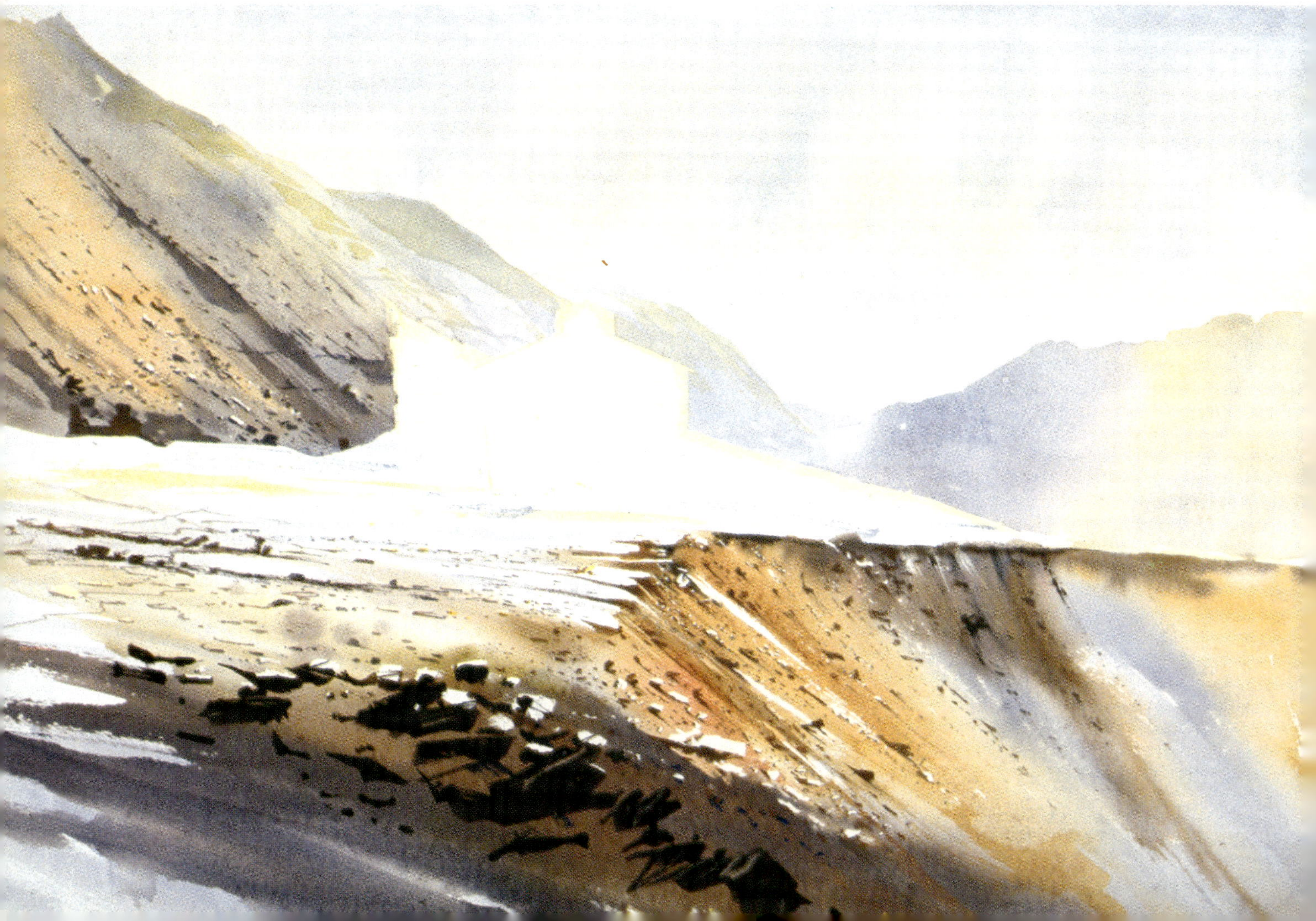

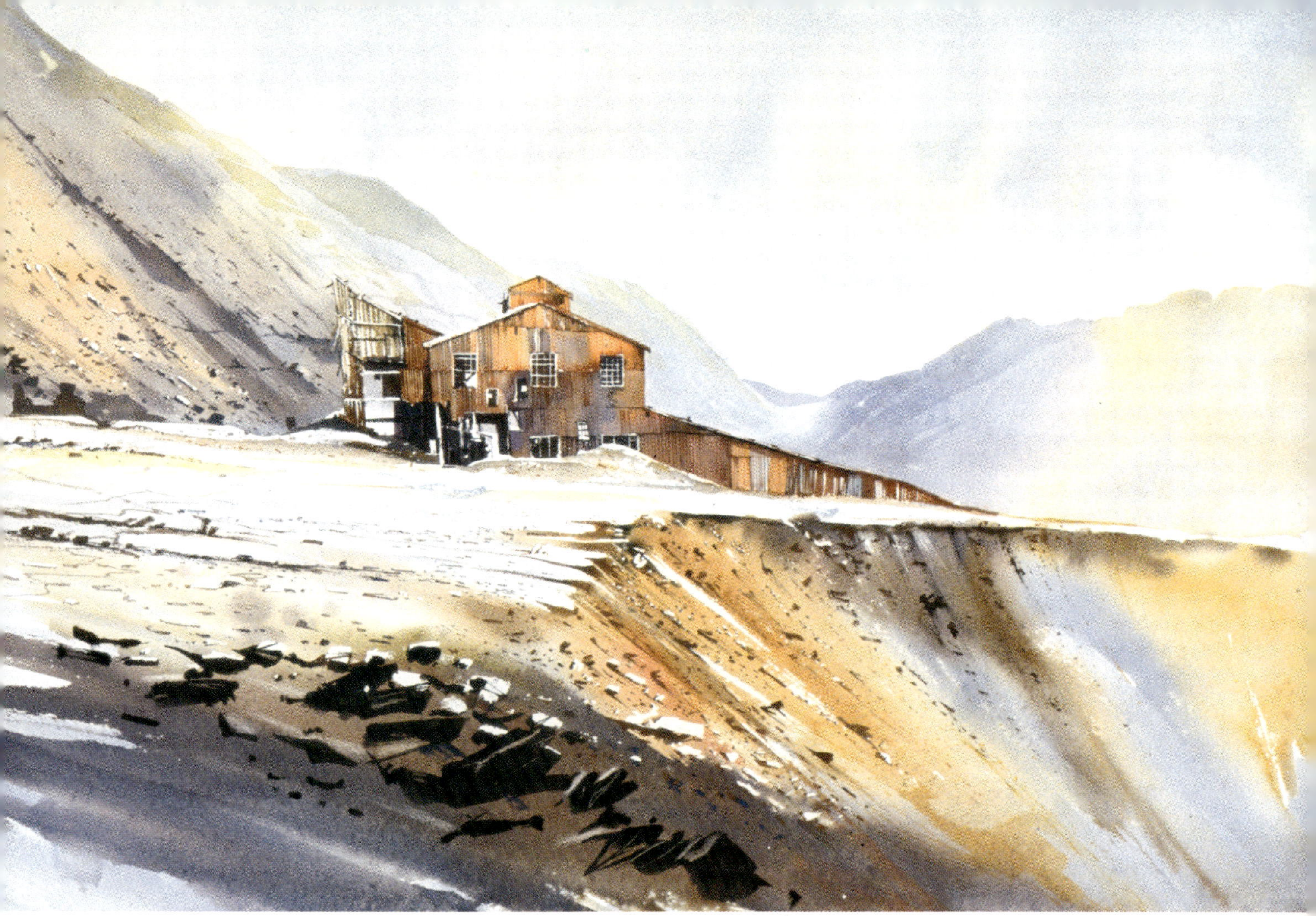

Stage 4. The shed form fits into the mountainside and its shute follows the land contours. To capture the rust colors of the shed, I used Bright Red, Burnt Sienna, Cadmium Orange, and Alizarin Carmine.

To create the effect of corrugated iron sheeting, I can either use a small brush and paint in the corrugations, or I can paint in the entire area and scratch in the corrugations with the edge of a razor blade. Lastly, when the masking fluid was removed from the window frames, their delicate outlines came through fresh and white.

KEEPING DETAILS LOOSE

Boatyards offer a chaos that I find irresistible. This one was full of odd shapes and multi directional lines, elements I always look for in composition. The problem is to make order out of the chaos, choosing the major elements of the composition and harmonizing the lesser, contributing elements around them. Otherwise the painting will fall apart with unconnected fragments.

This particular boatyard is a real, working yard and I wanted to reflect the energy and busyness it exudes. The boat in drydock, another already launched, cranes, winches, and barrels give the scene immediacy. Broad areas of color help to unite the myriad elements into a visually compact whole.

In the foreground, pools of reflected water keep the browns of the dock area from becoming monotonous and also break up the long vertical area that would otherwise overpower the horizontal structure.

Stage 1. Because of the intricacy of design here, I began with accurate drawings of the principal shapes using an HB pencil. I tried to be as economical as possible, avoiding the details that would later be obliterated by my brushwork.

When the outline was completed to my satisfaction, I picked out details with masking fluid. Look at the two ladders in Stage 4. Although they could be painted in carefully later with a fine brush, they would never have the crispness and seeming looseness of technique that I wanted. I also masked in bits of foreground stone to get a speckled effect when the masking fluid is rubbed away.

Now to the first wash of the sky. The idea is to keep the area simple, to contrast with the busy dock below. An extravagant sky would fight with dock patterns and reduce their vitality. I mixed this wash on the wet paper itself. I painted in the lower wash with Cadmium Orange and Naples Yellow, the middle with a very diluted Alizarin Carmine, and lastly Cobalt Blue. With a large 1-inch flat sable I brushed the colors onto the paper, allowing them to blend. Tilting the board backward and forward will help the colors run together, and a clear-water brush will help you guide the washes into proper blends.

Stage 2. The entire foreground was painted in loosely with Cobalt Blue and Naples Yellow. Each wash has a touch of the other in it, and all the objects will reflect one or the other of these colors to promote an overall harmony that prevents the painting from breaking up into isolated elements.

I started to build up the main boat forms with color, establishing their weight and prominence in the picture and making sure to leave large white areas to retain an openness to develop later. At this stage I planned to break the picture into four planes that repeat both a light-dark pattern and a warm-cool pattern from foreground to background. These large organized bands help to keep the diverse elements in perspective. Knowing at least in part what you intend to do is essential to most kinds of watercolor, where areas cannot be reworked successfully later on.

Stage 3. When I was fairly clear about what I wanted, I began to lay in the darks and paint in some of the delicate verticals where the masking fluid was. The strong patterns on the left will need to be balanced with similar volume and tone on the right later on. Ultramarine Blue and Burnt Sienna make up the dark shapes to the left, with the darkest areas picked out with Indigo.

The boats at the center must remain the focal point. To do this I kept that area solid, free of the clutter suggested to the right and left. While it was tempting to jump into all those fascinating details at this stage, I kept the overall composition in mind, making sure that the major areas were well defined first.

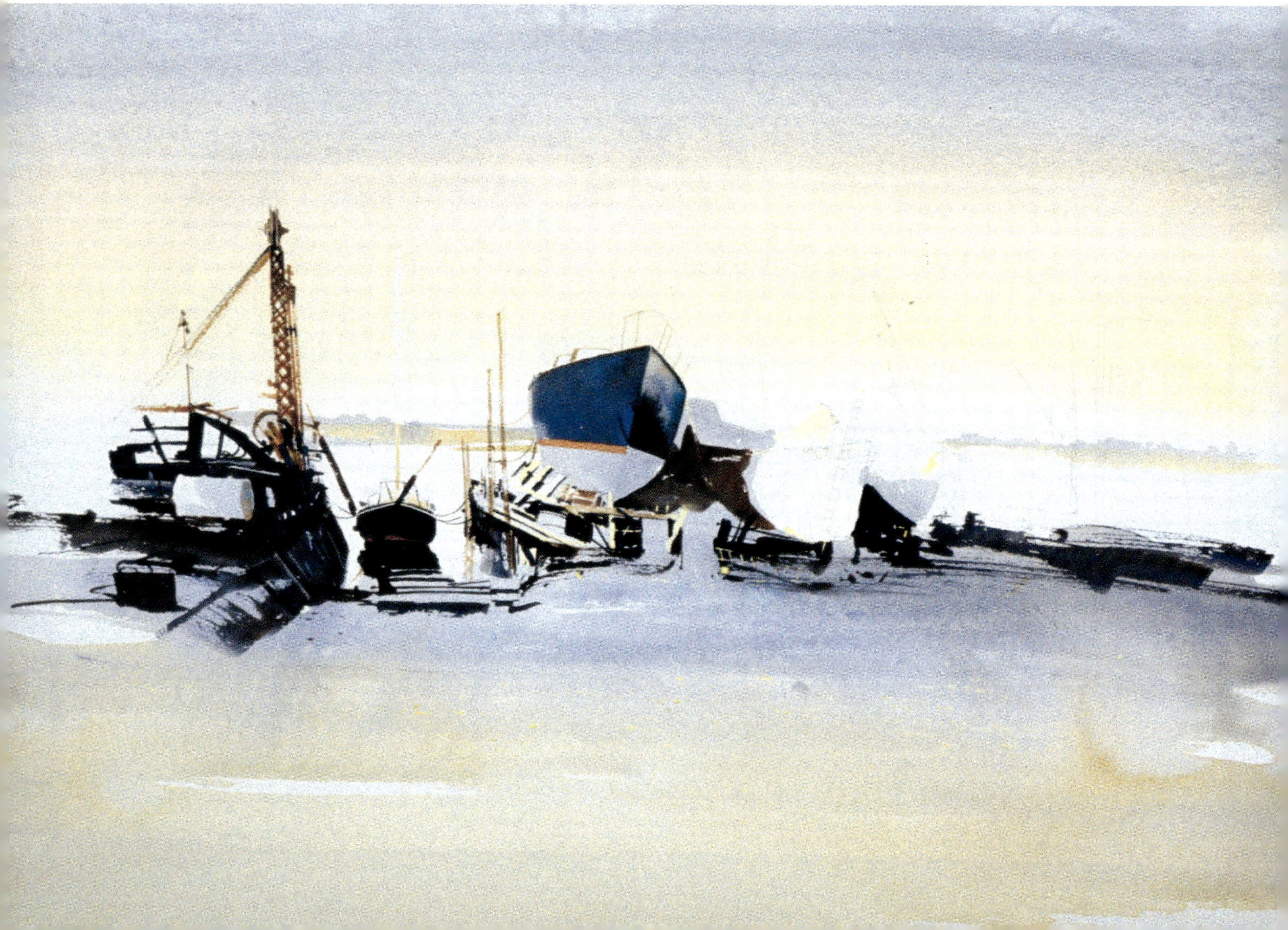

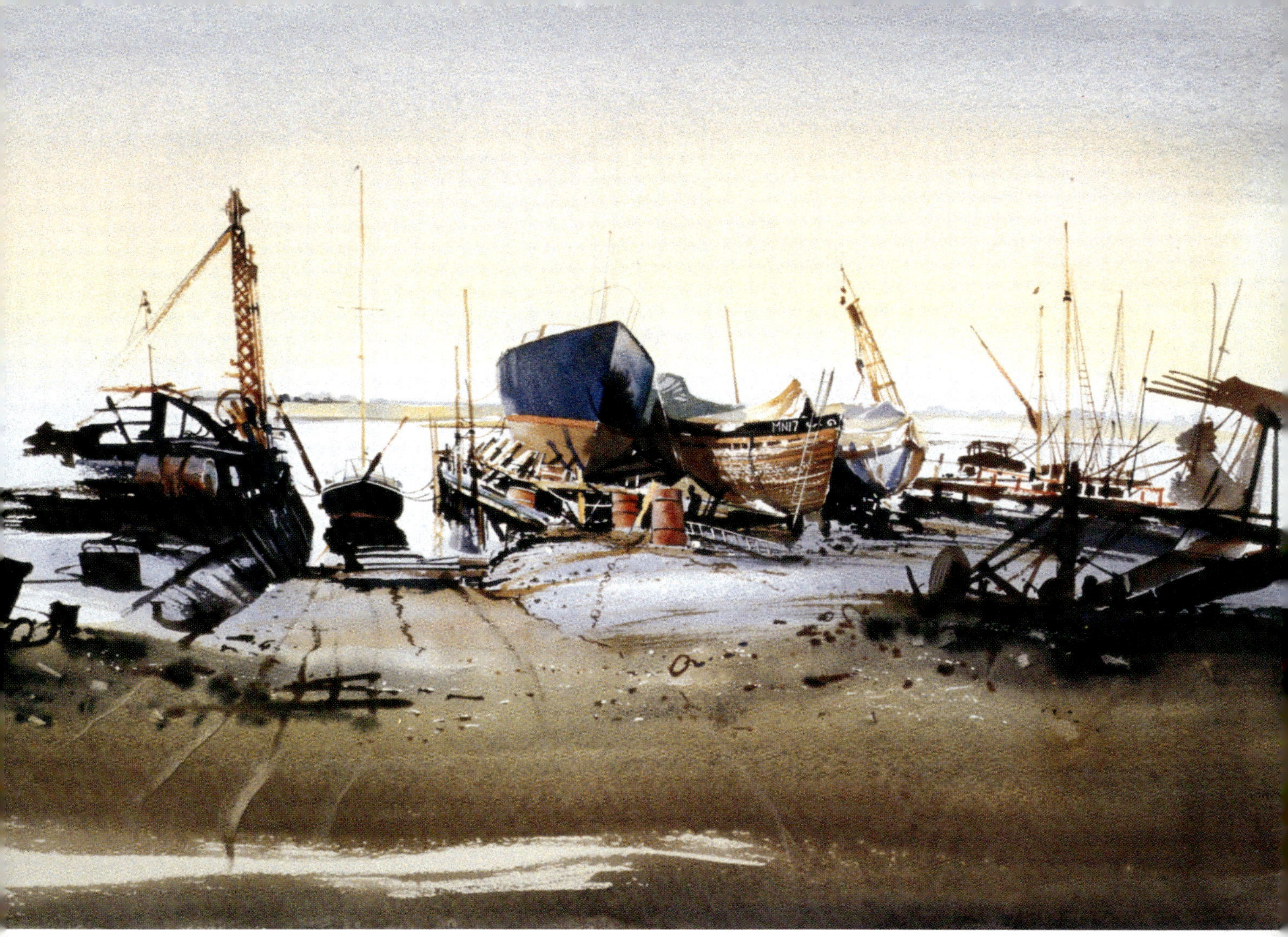

Stage 4. This is the part I like best: details and textures. But again, every line and form must contribute to the whole. Composing a picture like this one is a good way to appreciate the abstract principles that underlie successful representational painting. Attention must be given to volume and form and to the direction and vitality created in each area—and these elements should also work as abstractions.

The center forms need to be modified slightly to create more interest. Red barrels, texture marks on the brownish hull, and the crane that moves the eye to the center do the trick. The pale road emphasizes the forms above it, giving perspective. The track lines of the launching area also give depth and guide the eye to the water beyond.

Standing back from the painting, I could see that the light tones in the foreground would have to be changed to enhance the subject area. A broad wash of Raw Umber and Ultramarine Blue accomplished this and also gave a dockside wavy irregularity to the whole scene. Along the upper edge of this wash I ran a brush of clear water to avoid a hard edge. While the wash was still wet, some more delicate detail was added to the right. This was kept rather airy and loose as I did not want it to fight for attention with the central boats.

Removing the flecks of masking fluid revealed speckles on the stones, and I added bits of dark debris to play against these white specks. When painting a scene as involved as this it is easy to get so preoccupied that the water gets muddy. Clean colors and fresh brushwork are essential, or the picture will become grimy instead of sparkling.

WOOD TEXTURES

What has always fascinated me about willow trees is their sheer endurance. They can be chopped down to mere stumps and burned by the farmers, and yet they manage not only to hang on to life but even to produce a few new branches.

The rough treatment they receive causes them to grow into unusual shapes, and it is this warping, by man and nature, that is the sort of thing I love to spend time developing in line and color. I have the chance to paint swirls and cracks and build up textural effects in the bark and dead wood. Besides the close sharp detail there are free-flowing shapes that allow for broad, graceful sweeps of the brush and spontaneous movements of natural growth, as in the outgrowth. Here the buds of early May can be seen bursting open despite the unconventional source. If you develop a keen eye you can see subjects as prosaic as spring buds in a new and evocative way. Here both the seeming deadness of winter and the regenerative spring can be depicted in a fresh, dramatic mode.

Stage 1. In this first stage my chief concern is the central stump shape, which I drew in lightly with an HB pencil. Those areas I wished to keep clear of paint I covered with masking fluid, which can be rubbed away later.

To keep the sky simple I mixed two washes on my palette—one of Naples Yellow, one of Ultramarine Blue. These two washes were painted in briskly with a 1-inch flat brush. Then I tilted the drawing board forward to allow the colors to merge on the paper itself. If too much blue ran into the yellow, I used a brush of clear water to absorb it. Before the sky was completely dry I added a hint of background trees, using a strong mixture of Sap Green and Indigo, which yielded a good dark green. I let this mixture become absorbed into the paper, blending softly into the sky.

Now is the time to start to create a strong pattern of darks and lights. Care must be taken to continue this balance in tone and form. Soft edges here will contrast nicely with the fine detail I have planned for the stump itself.

Stage 2. Next comes what is perhaps the most important stage of the painting—the time to make a definite statement, which everything else depends on. First I built up the willow stump with strong strokes of Ultramarine Blue and Burnt Sienna, touched with Sap Green and Cadmium Orange, for highlights at the base.

For the tree's hollow center, I used black ink, Burnt Sienna, and Alizarin Carmine. The red warms the black and gives it more depth. The white under the masking fluid will create a more vibrant contrast, emphasizing the burned center of the stump. When the ink mixes with the rest of the trunk it lends a natural touch as it spreads, much like that of fire-charred wood. When the ink was dry, I mixed a very thin wash of Naples Yellow with a touch of Indigo and laid it across the cut surface of the stump. When completely dry, I made some fine, quick strokes with the same wash across the top of the stump, to show the natural cracking of the wood. I also used ink to indicate the texture of cracks and dark knots. A hard dry brush creates the jagged splinters of wood against the sky, which contrasts with the soft wash of the distant trees.

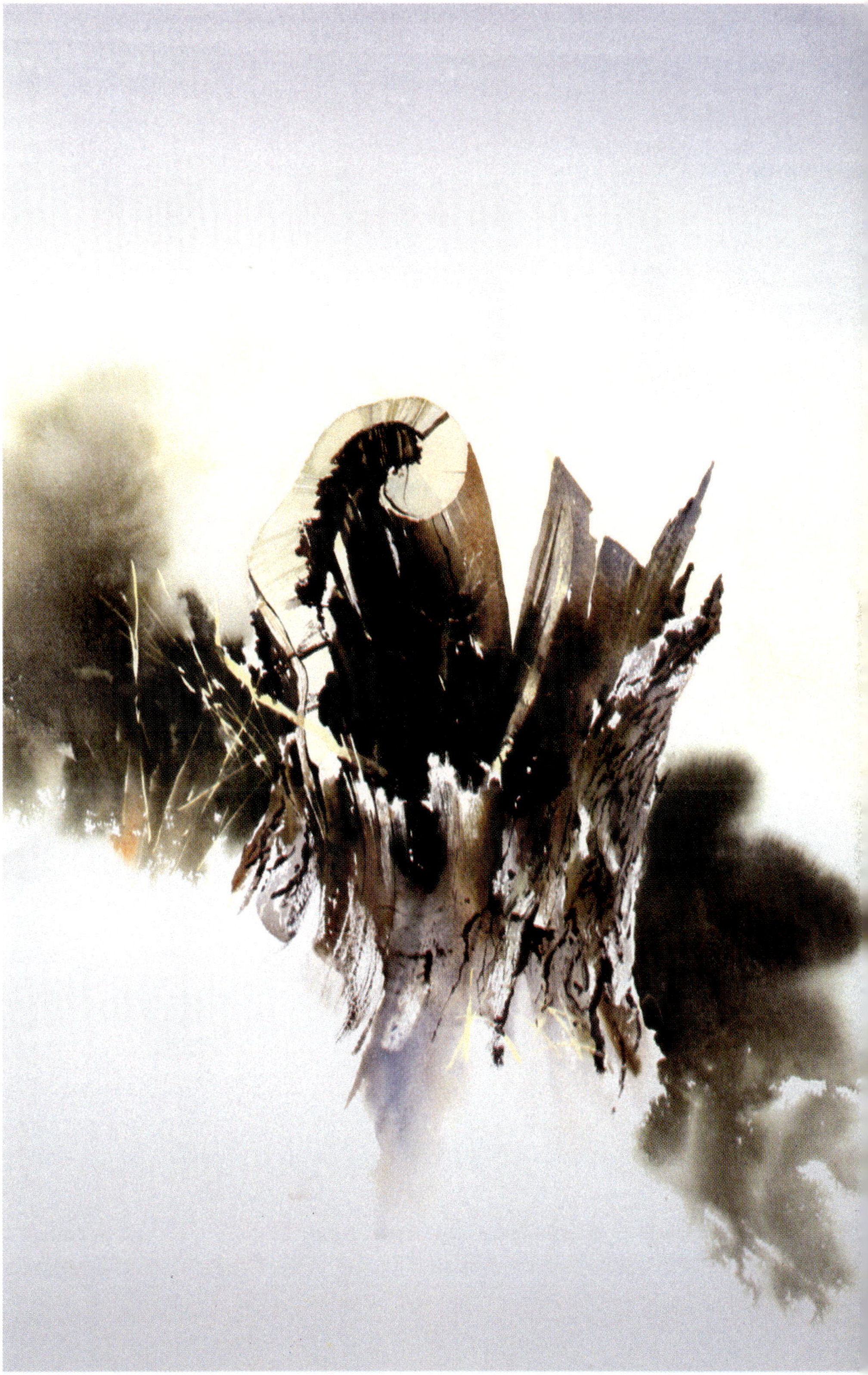

Stage 3. At this stage I built up the previous brushwork, filling in the detail on the bark. I mixed a strong Burnt Sienna-Indigo combination to bring out the delicate texture, the cracks and fissures of the trunk. Keep the paint fairly dry to facilitate drawing in the fine lines you need. What I have found works best are a bamboo brush and a size 2 sable. If there is excess water on the brush, I used a paper towel to remove it. To create the kind of textures that I want I am very hard on a brush. Sometimes I scrape the brush on its side, leaving a speckle of paint behind on the paper, or I jab it straight into the paper and rub it around until the worn mottled effect I want appears. Anything goes to get the effect I want. For the finer touches and the surrounding twiggery and grass I used another, finer brush which I treated more gently.

In planning the pattern of the emerging willow shoots and buds across the old stump, I was careful to take into account the entire composition, letting the curve of the largest shoot reflect the curve that the stump base and shrubs follow below.

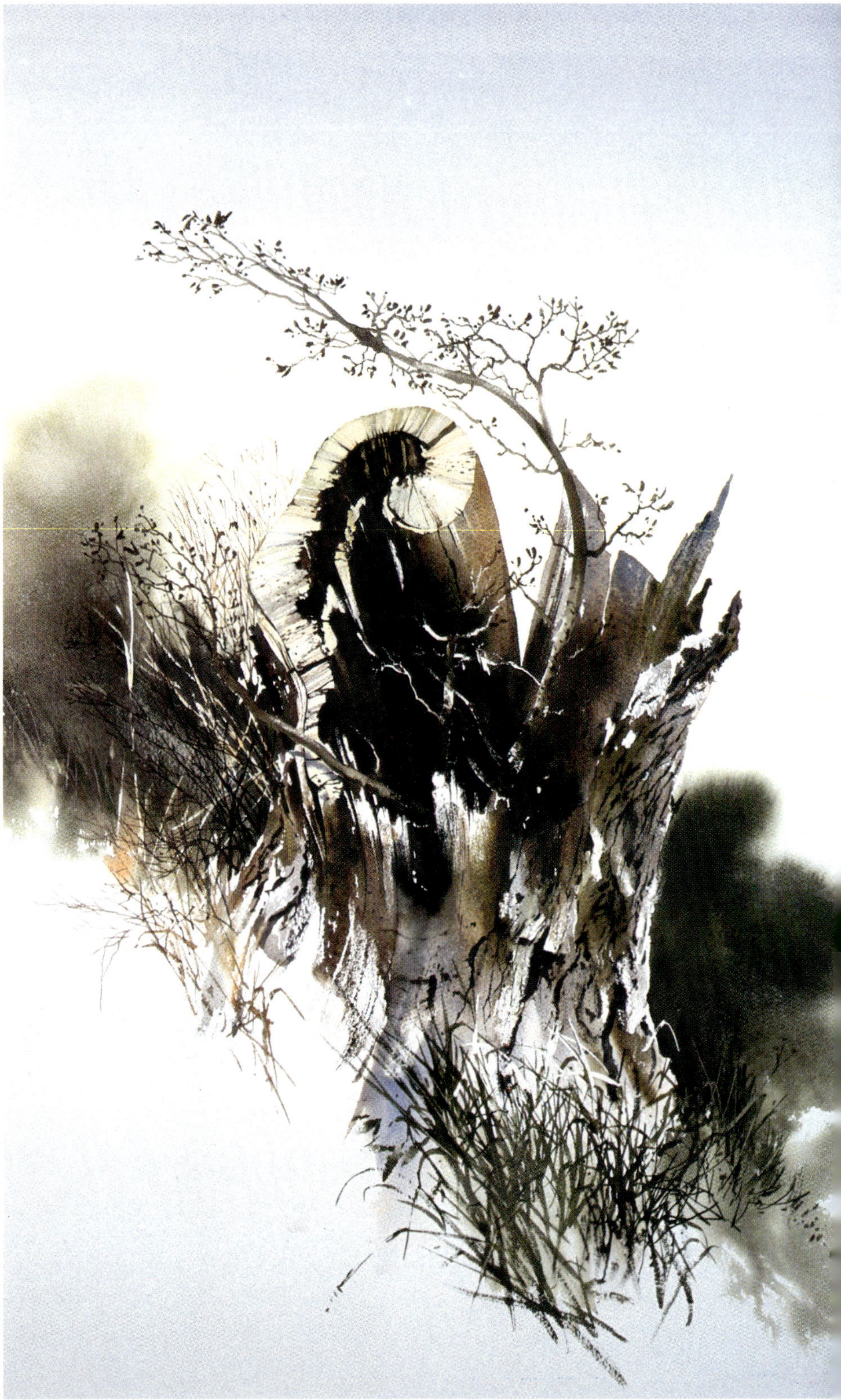

Stage 4. Because I wanted to create a complete painting and not just a sketch, I began to build up the undergrowth, using a fine brush and keeping the detail close to the base of the stump to keep the eye from straying out of the picture. Beneath the willow stump I rubbed wax into the paper, to create an irregular surface for the next wash. I totally ignore the dictum of some watercolorists who insist that the brush and only the brush must be used. I use anything I need to create the effect I want, which often the brush alone cannot do.

Underneath the stump I used black ink again, running it into Raw Umber and Bright Red. I then spread clear water over these dark colors to prevent hard edges from forming. All these colors were allowed to run together, leaving nothing more than a suggestive haze of hidden detail. While the paper was still damp, I used the corner of a razor blade to dash in the suggestion of grass in the foreground.

The band of white that bisects the painting just above this dark mass creates both a feeling of distance between the grass and the stump and a more harmonious blend of lights and darks in the watercolor. Otherwise, there would be two masses, one dark and one light, with little relationship between the two.

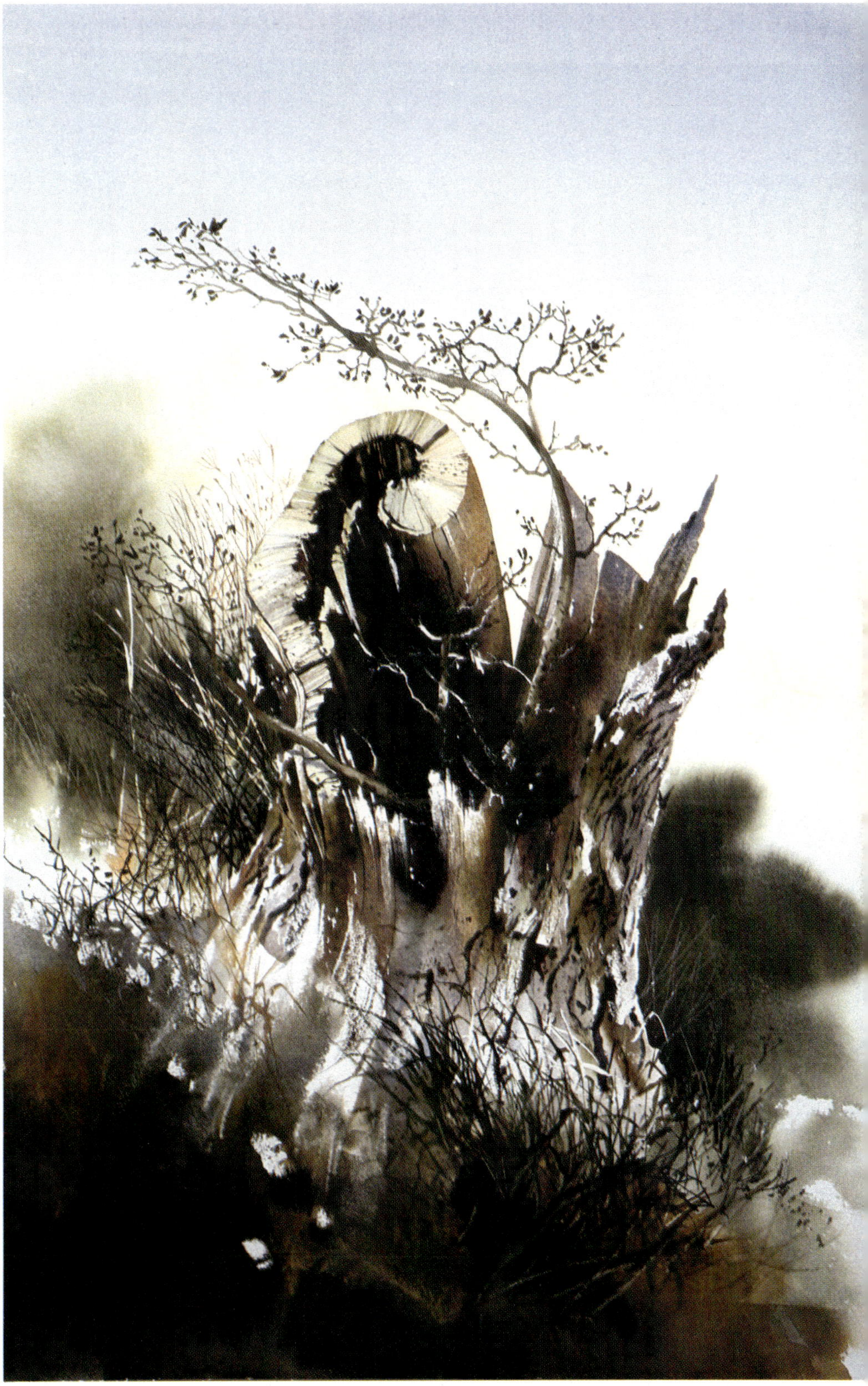

FADED AND PEELING PAINT SURFACES

I saw an almost lyric beauty in this well-worn building, the result of pastel tones and powerful textures. The powerful forms of door, window, and base supports are softened by the light colors and mottled effects of the wall. This light effect can be ruined by overworking, which is another reason why preplanning is essential to the desired result. Patterns of darks and lights, color harmonies, and varied shapes are essential to the most successful paintings, be they abstract or strictly representational.

An interesting and often helpful way to get new ideas for composition is to isolate individual elements of the whole, either by creating a square shape with your fingers and looking through this frame or by cutting a square or rectangle out of the center of a piece of paper and moving it about as if it were a camera lens. Try it on buildings, for example. Take each element individually; roof parts, door, window, decoration, drain pipes, anything that the building offers. The abstract composition that results may suggest a painting or a whole series of paintings, whether you are looking at St. Peter's in Rome or the shed down the road.

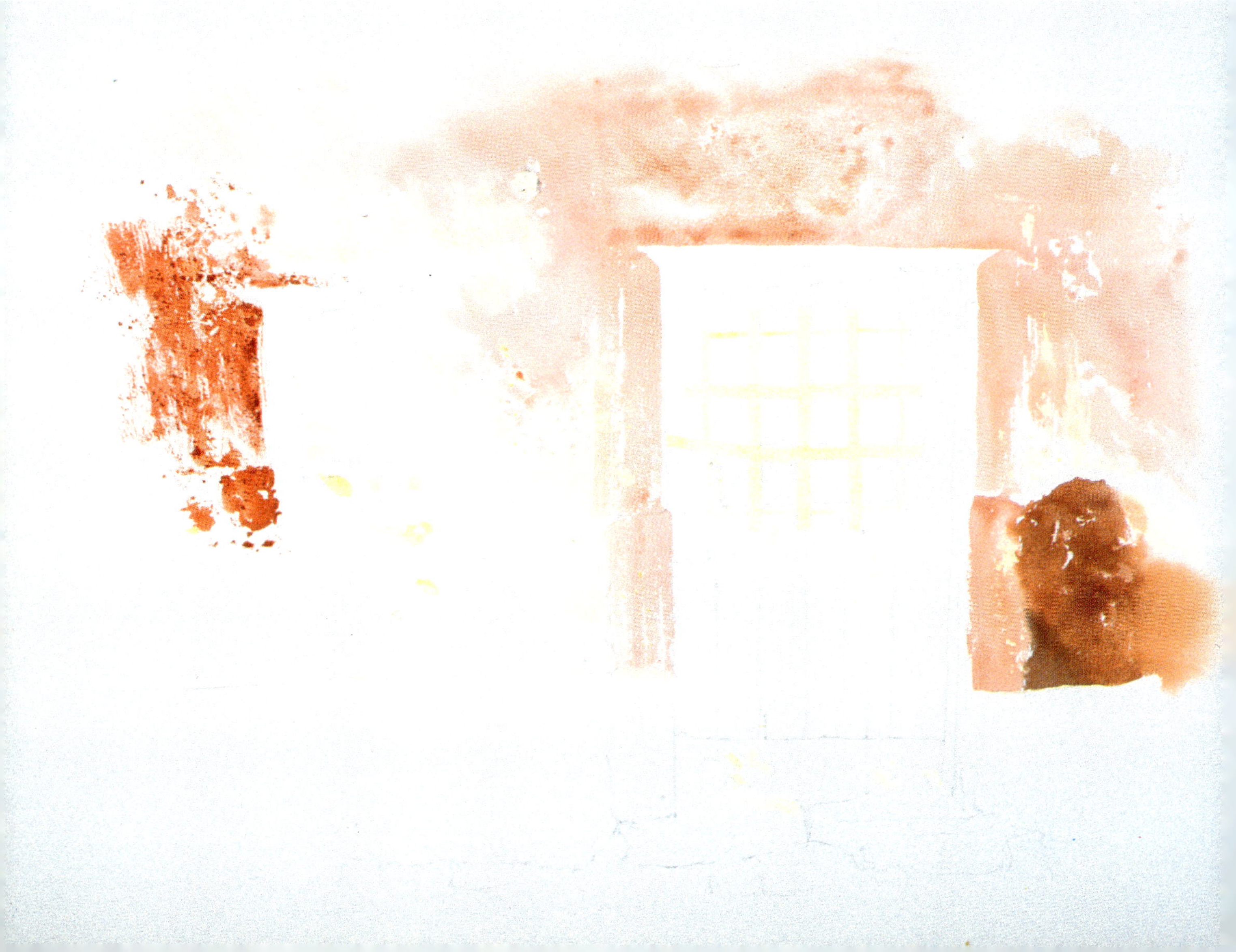

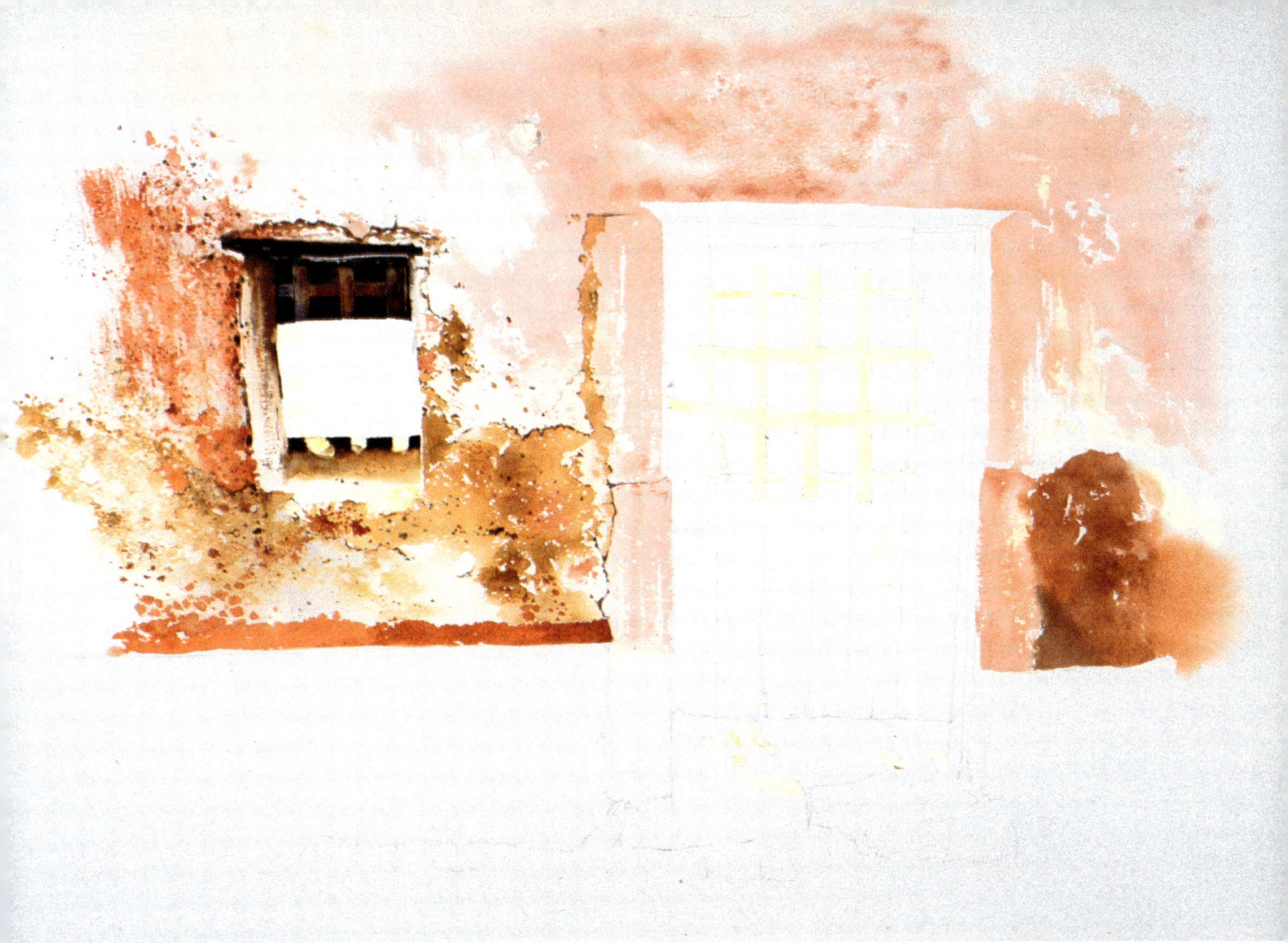

Stage 1. After lightly drawing in the principal elements, I rubbed clear candle wax gently over the paper to create a speckled texture. Then, using a dry brush, I showered fine drops of masking fluid to enhance the mottled texture of the wall. Masking fluid was used to enhance the crumbling stonework beneath the door area. In some areas I painted the fluid on with the side of the brush pressed against the paper to create more prominent textural effects. I painted out the window bars with masking fluid in order to maintain their sharp edges while overpainting the area.

Turning my attention to the wall, I could see that it had been built up with layers of cement and paint. In some areas weathering had worn away the surface through several layers, sometimes to a deep red-brown. The surface is quite an irregular mix, full of cracks, pinpricks, and gaps of missing cement. They all add up to an interesting subject, though a tax on painting skills. I picked an area to the left of the window as a trial patch, to test out colors and techniques. The first washes above the door are composed of Naples Yellow and Alizarin Carmine, applied briskly over the wax and masking fluid.

Stage 2. I built up on the first washes with a fine brush, stippling in dots of Ultramarine Blue and Burnt Sienna. Cracks were painted in with the same brush, producing the rugged irregular lines characteristic of cracks in plaster. I then began to create the patterns of light and dark. As I already knew that the window's interior would be very dark, I stabilized this dark with an Indigo and Bright Red mixture, which created a vibrant black. After rubbing away the masking fluid from the bars, I painted them in with a fine brush, blending Cobalt Blue and Cadmium Orange together on the paper. For the section beneath the window I mixed Yellow Ochre and Raw Umber and washed it in loosely, adding another wash of Cobalt Blue while the paper was still wet. The texture of the wall was continued slowly, building up cracks and dots, varying the shapes, sizes, and colors to avoid any pattern emerging. Small areas of cement that have not yet fallen away were painted in and some areas were left as white paper.

Stage 3. Now to the major task of the door. The wood effect is rendered with Cobalt Blue, Burnt Sienna, and Cadmium Orange. Loosely brushing in the basic tone of the wood, I left highlights of white paper showing through to add vibrancy to the grain. The rusty color at the base of the door was brushed in with Burnt Sienna, using an almost-dry brush in an upward movement so that the paint is applied in a speckled manner. As the upper part of the door is in shadow, I darkened the wash to reflect this. Here and there a razor blade is effective at picking out the grain of the wood in this dark area. After rubbing away the masking fluid, I painted in the iron bars of the door as I did the window, mixing blues and oranges. Firmer shapes were created by adding dark shadows after the bars are dry and also outlining with a dry, pointed brush the bolts that hold the bars in place. The black interiors behind the bars were built up with Indigo and Bright Red. Rubbing the masking fluid away beneath the door created an interesting strong texture.

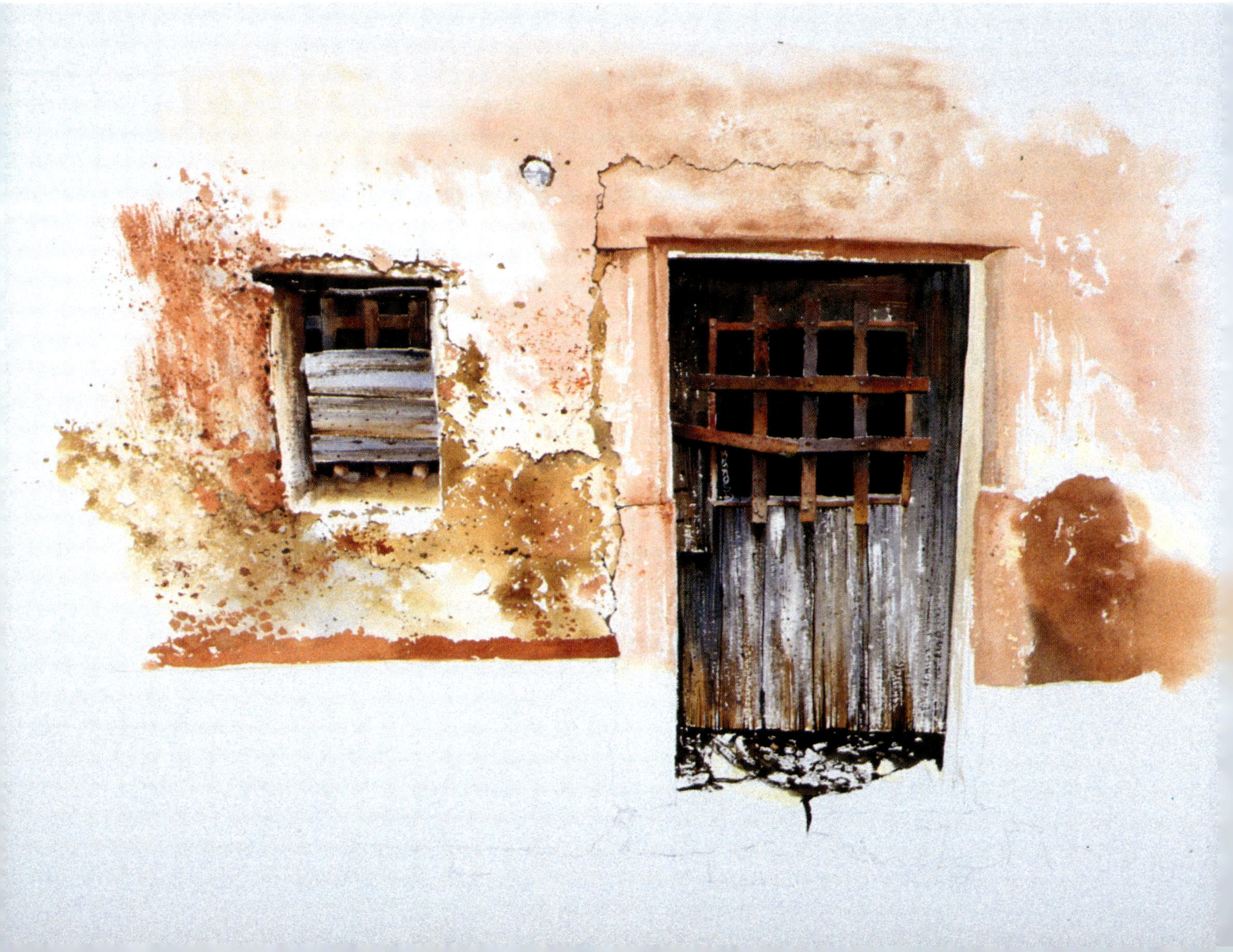

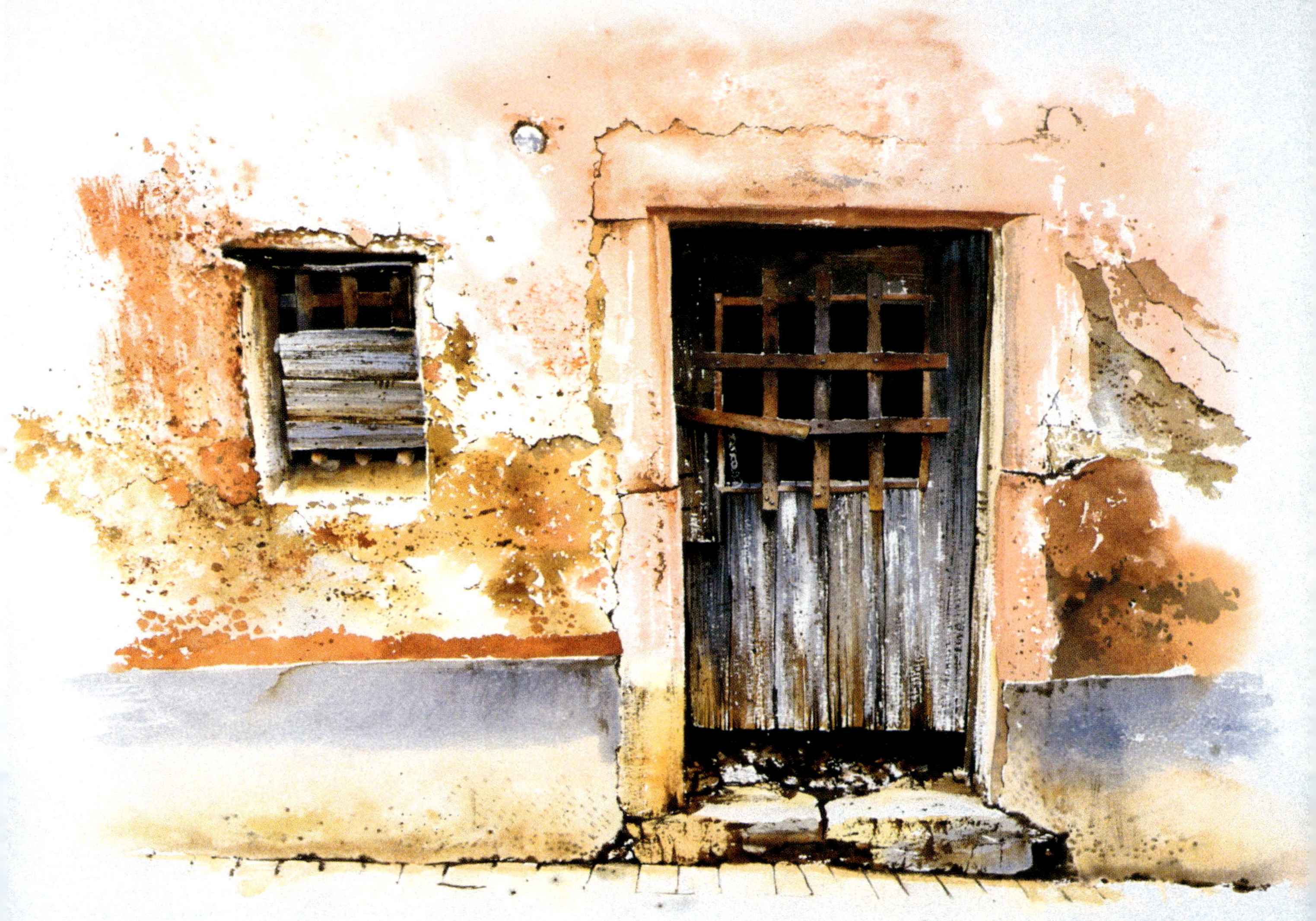

Stage 4. When the masking fluid was removed from the stonework, lots of small highlights appeared. I overpainted some of them in other colors, and some I turned into holes in the wall by dabbing dark colors on top, leaving a rim of white highlights. Continuing like this, I added tones and colors until I felt I had caught the texture of the wall.

Until this stage the predominating colors are warm, and I felt that the lower sections needed a cool Cobalt Blue. The strong, red horizontal works well in contrast with the blue, and I paralleled this red along the bottom with a pale band of Raw Umber. To emphasize the dark shadows beneath the door, the light area was touched with bits of color and repeats the door colors on the front of the step. I also suggested a few cobblestones at the base but allowed the edges to fade off softly, in contrast with the sharpness of the rest of the picture.

Notice the overall pattern of whites that have been created. Checking against earlier stages of the painting you can see how preplanning was essential in its development. This is one of the chief problems in creating successful, bright watercolors, for you must develop an eye that sees the white or negative areas as you visualize the color pattern. The use of masking fluid can help you to develop these areas with more confidence earlier on as its yellow color gives an idea of the pattern of lights that you want.

USING A LIMITED PALETTE

Boats and their watery reflections present an ever-changing, rich source of painting material. Their colors and shapes lend themselves easily to a harmonious composition, as they do here at Haybridge boatyard. I was particularly attracted by the cans, ladders, and pieces of wood that repair yards collect.

My main concern was to capture the clutter of the yard and yet retain the easy flow of the medium, which is all too easily lost when too much attention is paid to detail. I tried to look at the details in terms of patterns and shapes rather than trying to make them recognizable objects in the picture. I just chose a few pieces and defined them more closely, letting them represent others just hinted at. The area on the horizon has been painted as a silhouette with wooden posts and derricks building a pattern of shapes. Masking fluid is a great help here, enabling me to leave thin white lines and dots amid the brushwork.

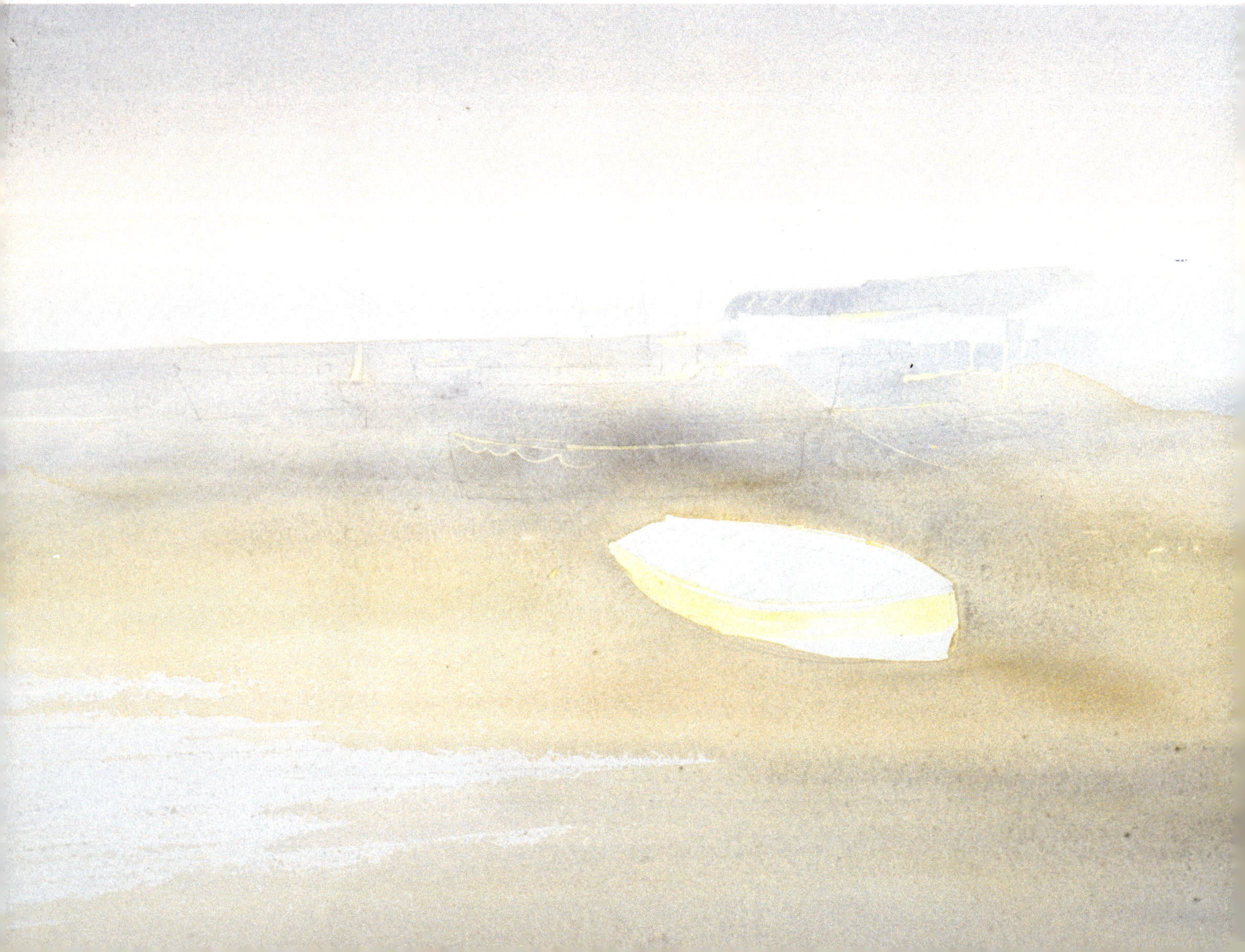

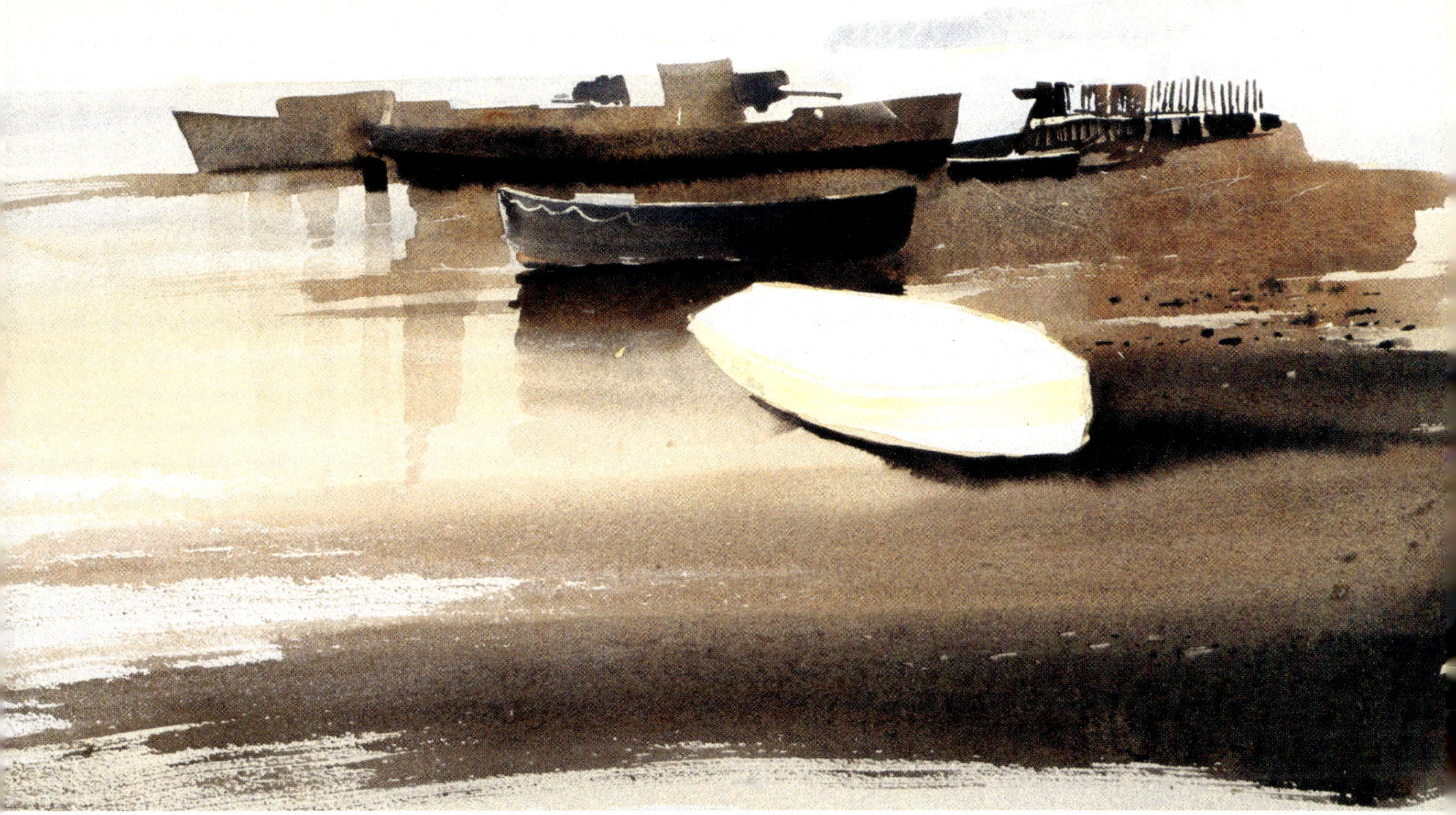

Stage 1. I decided to use a very limited palette for this painting, mainly Indigo and Bright Red. A very strong, dominant color in a painting like this has the advantage of uniting all the elements of the composition. It's easy for a painting to become very stilted and cautious. I've tried to make a strong statement in paint, using the brush quickly and freely to develop a quality of loose freedom in the strokes.

I have held off painting detail to the last in an effort to keep the free feeling. Once you start picking out details the broader issues tend to get neglected.

The rowboat in the foreground is important to the overall success of the painting, as a solid form and as a strong light area. I drew in the form lightly and then painted out the boat's hull with masking fluid. I also masked out such details as ropes and pebbles, because these smaller forms would be impossible to paint around later.

The sky consists of broad bands of color that I have blended together on the paper. Cobalt Blue, Bright Red, and Cadmium Orange washes were followed by Naples Yellow. They were all painted in very thinly, merely to tint the background.

For the mud flats below, I painted in a wash of Cobalt Blue and then Burnt Umber, tilting the board slightly to encourage the colors to run together. However, I was very careful to paint around the rowboat, letting that area dry to keep a sharp outline. I left a light area of water to the left of the rowboat that I would complete later.

Stage 2. This is the most important stage of the painting, for the broad values are created by boldly constructing with large brushstrokes the mud flats and background jumble of boats. I have allowed the brush to run dry at the right edge, creating a highlight on the still wet sand. The only colors I have used, in varying strengths, were Indigo mixed with Bright Red and Burnt Sienna to give the sand a rusty look. The boats were painted in the same colors as the washes, to contribute to the overall harmony. After the washes were dry, I removed the masking fluid around the poles in the background and painted them in carefully with drybrush.

The boat reflections were painted on a wet background with a mixture of Burnt Sienna and Ultramarine Blue. I used a great deal of water, painting them in loosely to add a watery look to the mud.

Stage 3. The rowboat at center will draw the viewer's eye, so I was careful to give it interesting tones and depth. I let the white of the paper act as the white paint on the boat. The interior sides and seats are a pale gray, created from a wash of Cobalt Blue with a touch of Burnt Sienna. This was darkened for the shadows and the bottom is a warm Burnt Sienna to contrast. Interior details around the seats and oar-locks were filled in when the paper was dry with dry-brush. But I took care not to overwork it, for the boat's main function is to act as a white area against the dark background of mud and boats.

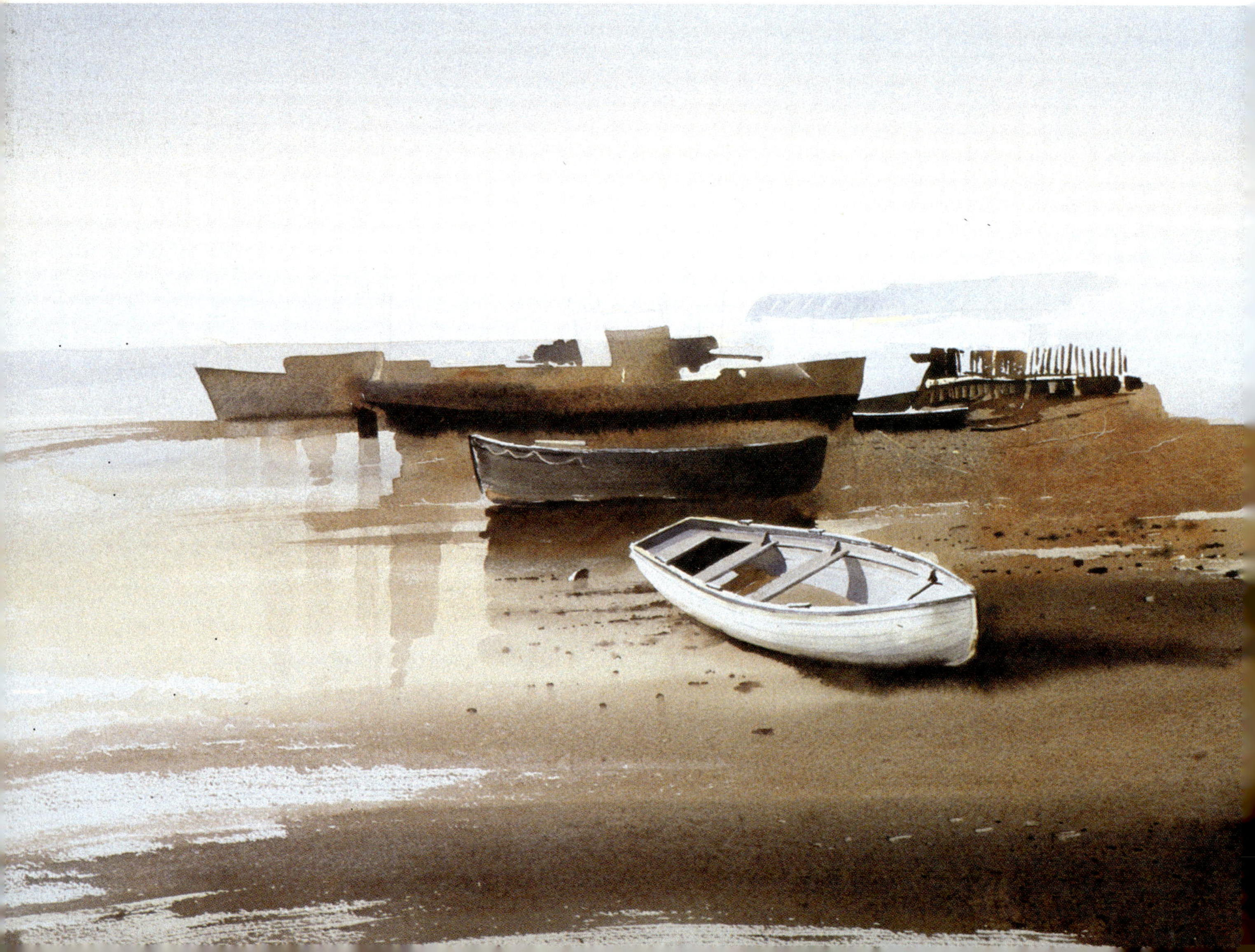

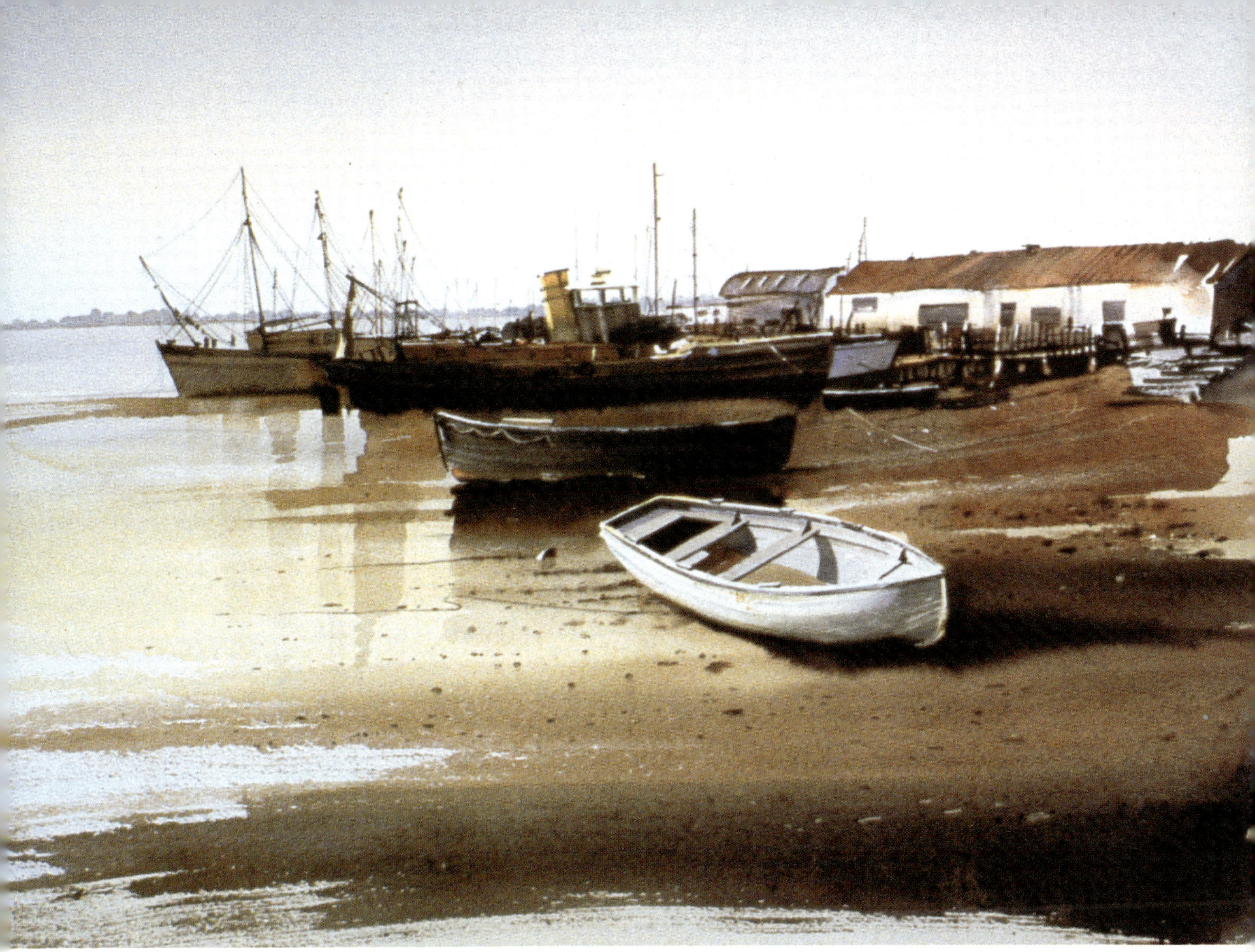

Stage 4. In this final stage, I removed the bits of masking fluid to give highlights to the muddy foreground. There are a lot of stones in the mud. I did not attempt to paint them all in, just enough to add texture to the foreground. I used the same basic Raw Umber, Burnt Sienna, and Ultramarine Blue to develop the [illegible]sheds. Their flatness contrasts with the complicated [illegible]es and masts at left, and by creating a light-dark pattern, I tied in the darks and lights of the surrounding patterns.

Although the boat forms in the background are essentially dark, they are relieved by light texture highlights picked out with a brush of clear water. The dark boat at center is a simple link between the light rowboat and the background boats in its simple style and dark colors. Looking at the overall rhythms of the painting, they are typical of many seascapes. The wet horizontal washes and zigzag patterns of light and dark give a buoyancy and an energy to what could have been an uninspired boatyard scene.

STONE WORK

Outlined against the sky, this rugged stone pillar caught my eye immediately. The loneliness of the setting and the complexities of the irregular stonework were the elements I wanted to capture in the painting. The column's simple form, the way the stones were coming loose and weeds had taken hold provided the detailed visual drama that intrigues me. But solitary, simple forms require as much care in composition as a complex work of many elements.

The negative space that surrounds the pillar is as important to the overall design as the form of the pillar itself. The moody darkness beyond must have its own interesting shapes and tones and not merely outline the stones. I wanted a somewhat vague and mysterious quality that would evoke the romance of ruins that so many painters have been drawn to. The pale gold and blue of the sky emphasize the essential melancholy of the scene. Blurring out the distance in contrast to the carefully drawn stones and weeds emphasizes both the pillar's age and its enduring strength. By modifying its whiteness with soft blue tones and allowing the reddish-brown weeds to almost blend with the distance tones, I suggested that the pillar was returning to the natural world from which it was created.

Stage 1. When I began to lightly draw in the pillar's outline, I kept in mind the importance of negative space and that as I developed the form of the pillar I was at the same time creating the form behind the pillar. The composition has to hold together as an abstract pattern first, then the details that evoke a specific image can be added.

I drew in the individual stones at this stage not only for later use but also to give myself a clearer feeling of direction, an indication of the kind of spatial relationships that the final version would have. In order to retain the crumbling edge of the stonework and not let the background washes destroy it, I first outlined the pillar and supporting beam with masking fluid. I filled in the background sky with a wash of Naples Yellow and Cadmium Orange, blending it upward on the wet paper into another wash of Cerulean Blue touched with Cobalt Blue. I always try to keep all the colors fresh and clean and to start with bright colors. Brights can always be toned down, but muddy colors remain muddy throughout. The less you tamper with colors once they are on the paper the better.

Stage 2. Before beginning to work on the background bushes I let the paper dry completely. For the rich background tones I first laid in a wash of Cadmium Orange and then added Ultramarine Blue on top of it, allowing the blue to mix in some areas and not in others. Clear water was painted over the wash in order to encourage the color to creep up the paper. Leaving the stonework for later I concentrated on building an overall pattern that would support and complement the pillar, which was to be the center of interest. On the completely dry sky area I drew in the weeds that have taken hold in the stone with a fine brush. Their upward movement also helps to link sky to column. Because the edges remain hard, the sky and column do not merge, but still have a strong visual link.

Stage 3. Now the masking fluid can come off and more of the grass can be added to the dry background. This takes time. I used a thick mixture of paint with a brush starved of water to paint in both heavy tufts of grass and fine blades, building on the essential structure and also connecting it further with the sky. As this pattern began to form I started to create rhythms in the pillar, which suggested the loose stones and the feeling that the whole structure was disintegrating, literally going to seed.

The success of this painting hangs on capturing the texture of the stone, keeping it sharp and the colors clean. All the stonework was painted with a fine, size 2 sable. This brush took a lot of punishment, sometimes being scrubbed sideways to produce the grass or pushed and scraped around to capture the texture of the stonework. This is not the place for delicate brushstrokes. The kind of texture I like requires that I use my brush as a tool. Needless to say, brushes do not last long this way and since they are so expensive I set aside one for this kind of treatment. When a brush is no longer good for painting it gets demoted to a masking fluid brush. I keep another for its fine point and use it here for delicate blades of grass on top of the stone. While the paper is still damp, I scratched in the thin white lines with the corner of a razor blade.

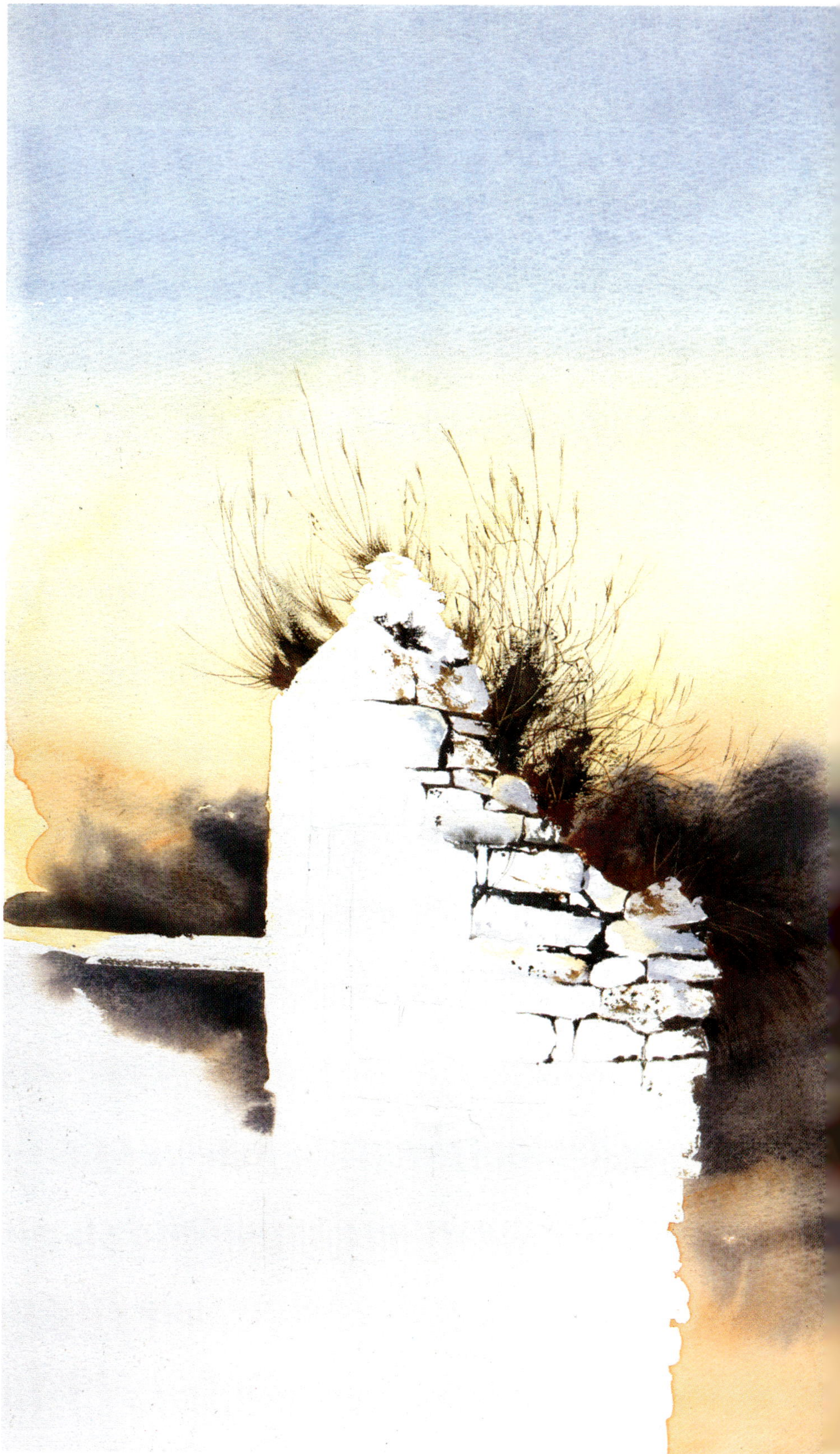

Stage 4. In this last stage all the elements come together. The stonework is built-up with a mixture of thin washes and dry brushwork. I use the paper's own texture to help capture the rough stone surface. Rough watercolor paper can be the basis of a number of textural effects. A heavy grade, such as 300 lb., is admirably suited to these effects, although its price is often a bit steep.

Practice creating rough surfaces on less extravagant paper. Dragging the brush over the rough surface of the paper, rolling it on its side, and stippling with the point are all techniques that you need time to learn. Lay a wash on practice paper and then try out as many brush effects as you can think of. Use a razor blade to make fine and rough cuts in the paper before laying in the wash and then paint over the cuts to see what happens to the surface as a result. I finished painting the pillar one stone at a time, giving each its individual characteristics and building up the washes and brushwork carefully until I reached the desired texture. Small washes were added last to create a harmonious tonal pattern between pillar and background. Where the horizontal supporting pole was joined to the column I emphasized the verticality of the surrounding stones and added irregular surface shapes to vary the horizontal stone patterns. The pillar has been allowed to fade off at the base, as a slightly unfinished look adds more contrast and interest to the picture.

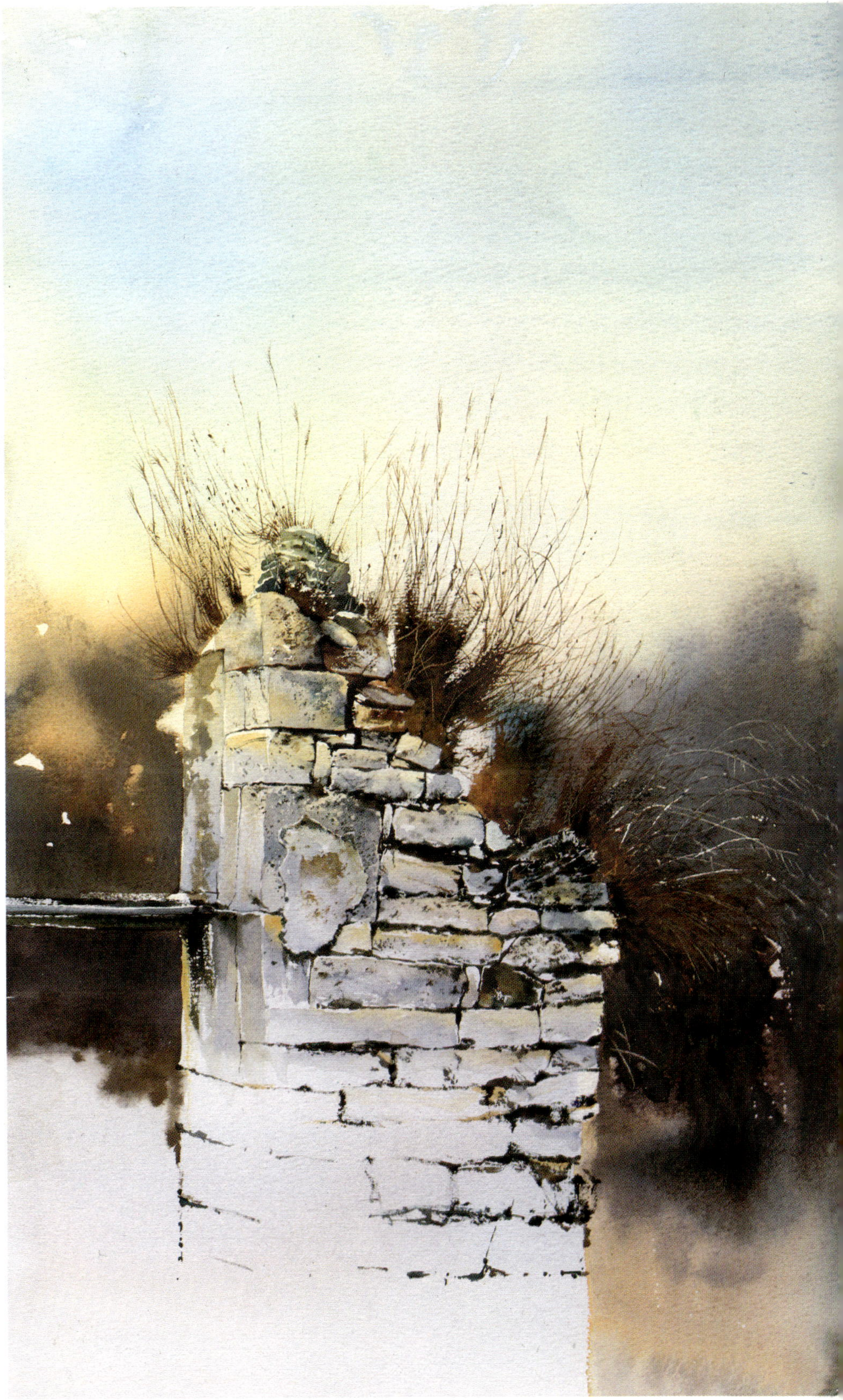

USING WHITE SPACE

The part of the country where I live is mostly farmland, and I've developed an affection for the tractors, trailers, and other tools of the trade that get abandoned at the sides of fields or are left cluttered around unused farm buildings. Their sharp angular forms contrasting with the soft textures of the countryside make beautiful compositions. This effect is heightened when there is snow on the ground, and makes an ideal subject for a watercolor.

I like putting together the elements of a painting like this: a sweep of sky, an indication of background, an overgrown tree reaching out in all directions, and, in the midst of all this, the very precise form of a tractor. Not the usual subject for a winterscape, but that is why I like it. A few curious crows add movement and immediacy. The soft blues of the winter palette are effective overtones, creating the heavy sky and the lightly tinged blue white of the snowy ground.

Stage 1. The tractor and tree are lightly drawn in, with highlights on the tractor outlined with masking fluid, so they won't get lost during painting.

The sky is a series of horizontal washes, blended together across the wet paper like the bands of a rainbow. At the horizon I used Cadmium Orange, then Winsor Red and Ultramarine Blue.

I left the snow area alone for the present. It will be developed as a negative area by creating the positive forms. Even leaving something alone is doing something to it in watercolor. That's the wonder and the frustration of the medium.

Stage 2. The area where I live is famous for its skies and many artists devote their work to that alone. Here a streak of clouds was used for some early evening drama. First I laid in, over the dry washes that preceded it, a wash of Ultramarine Blue and Winsor Red.

With the same palette, adding only a touch of Burnt Sienna, I painted in the distant trees. You may need to rewet the paper here to let the colors disperse softly into the sky.

By completing just this half of the painting I have a good idea of the finished composition. The sky has created a mood that will spread to the scene below.

Stage 3. Since detail is a passion of mine, I take a lot of time painting in trees, and enjoy working in all the twigs and tiny branches. This attention to the particular means that paintings can be appreciated close up as well as from a distance.

These trees are actually willows, but because of pollarding (cutting back) their useful branches, which were once used for basket weaving, the trees have taken on strange shapes. Burnt Sienna and Ultramarine Blue make up the trees. For the branches I chose a long-haired, size 1 sable brush. Nearly all the branches sweep upward in a curving line, which is easily produced with a flick of the wrist. I then started on the gas tank area of the tractor, using Cerulean Blue with traces of Cadmium Orange and Ultramarine Blue.

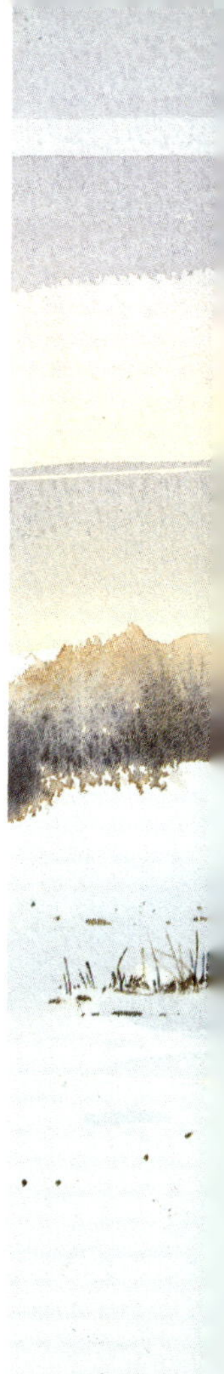

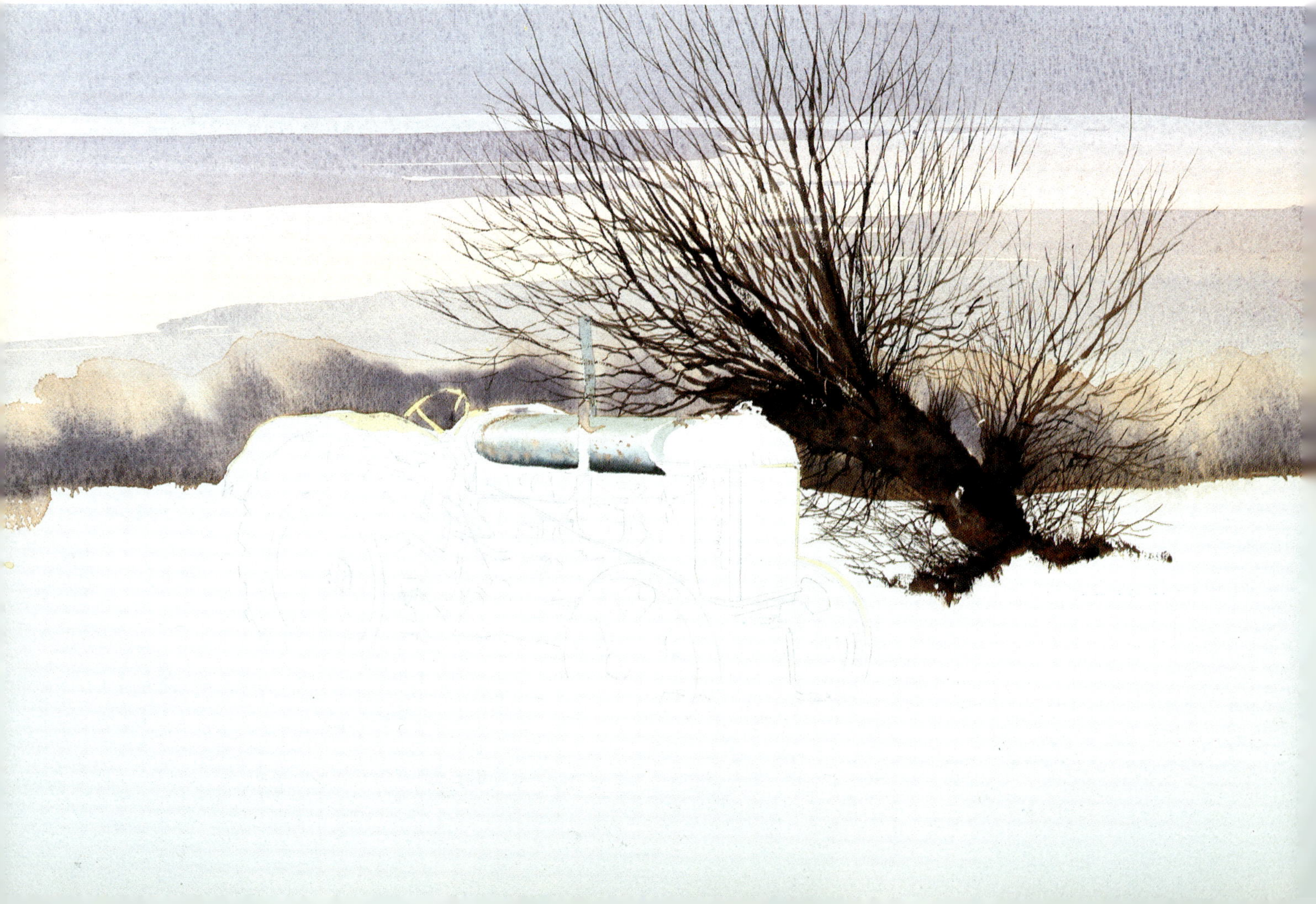

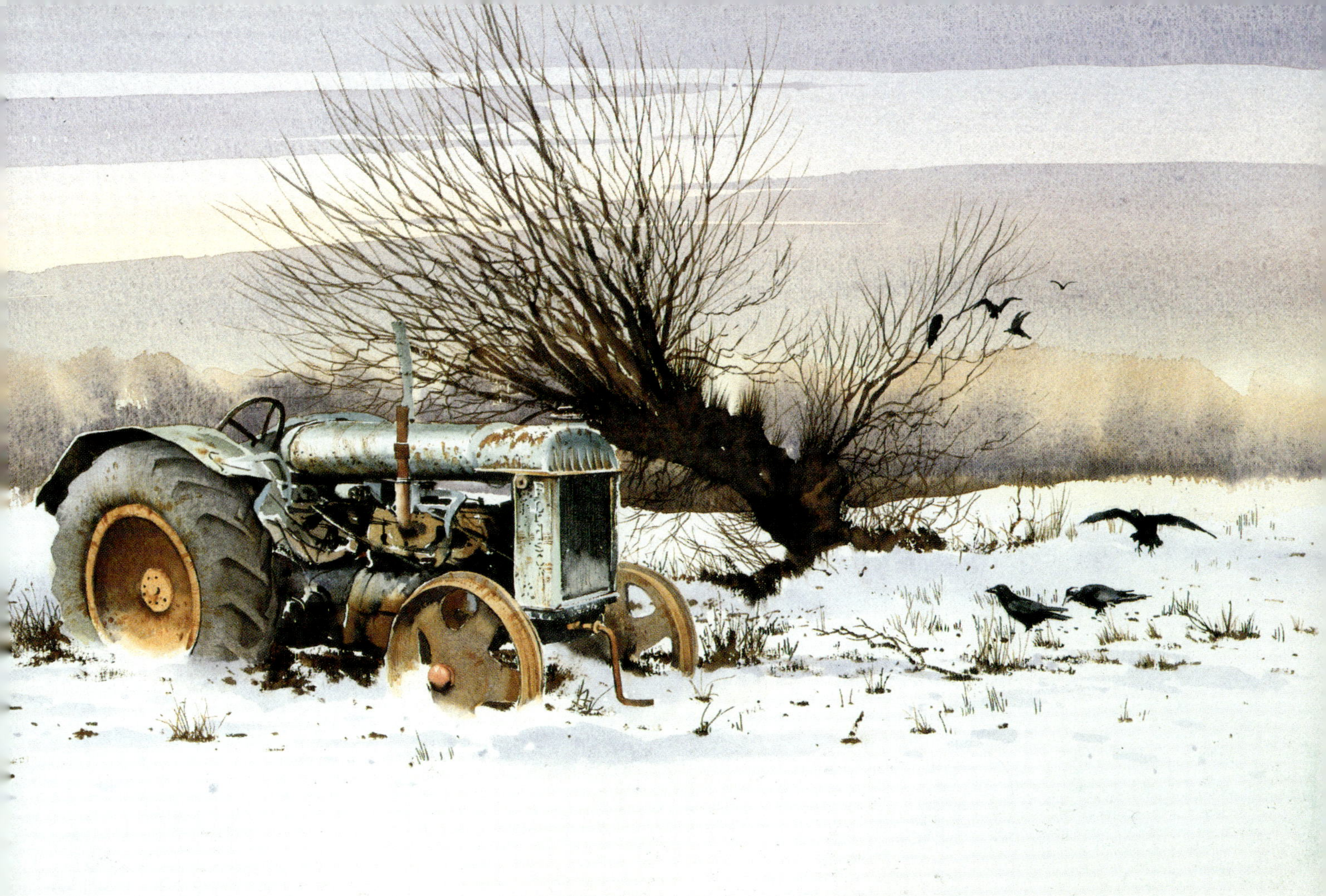

Stage 4. I find that the best way to paint a piece of machinery is to treat it as a jigsaw puzzle, taking one section at a time. After finishing the gas tank I used those colors for the other metal areas that require the same colors, adding spots and patches of rust with Burnt Sienna. The front wheels were also painted with Burnt Sienna, the shadows with Ultramarine Blue. In these dark areas I used a fine, dry brush to create the patterns of rust after the blue had dried.

You don't really have to paint in every bit of detail. Just suggesting it, as here around the engine, will often do, unless that detail is a critical part of the painting. I used Burnt Sienna again here, and in the dark areas a mixture of Indigo, Prussian Blue, and Cadmium Red. I often mix Cadmium Red and Prussian Blue to get black, and find that I have no real use for black as a separate color at all.

Tires are always a tricky subject and care has to be taken not to overwork them. Here I chose Gamboge, Ultramarine Blue, and Burnt Sienna. I painted the tire in a single wash, let it dry, and then returned to paint in the complicated tread with the same colors, using clear water to prevent hard edges from forming in the wrong places.

Around the tractor, patches of ground showing through the snow add a nice touch and provide some warm tones in the vast cool area. They can be dabbed and flicked in with Ultramarine Blue and Burnt Sienna.

Snow in the evening light takes on the color of the sky. A light Cobalt Blue painted freely behind the tractor and in patches in the foreground gives it form. I used a brush of clear water to blend off the edges and to give the snow a soft appearance.

As a final touch, some crows add life and a bit of humor as their tiny forms contrast with the layer of snow.

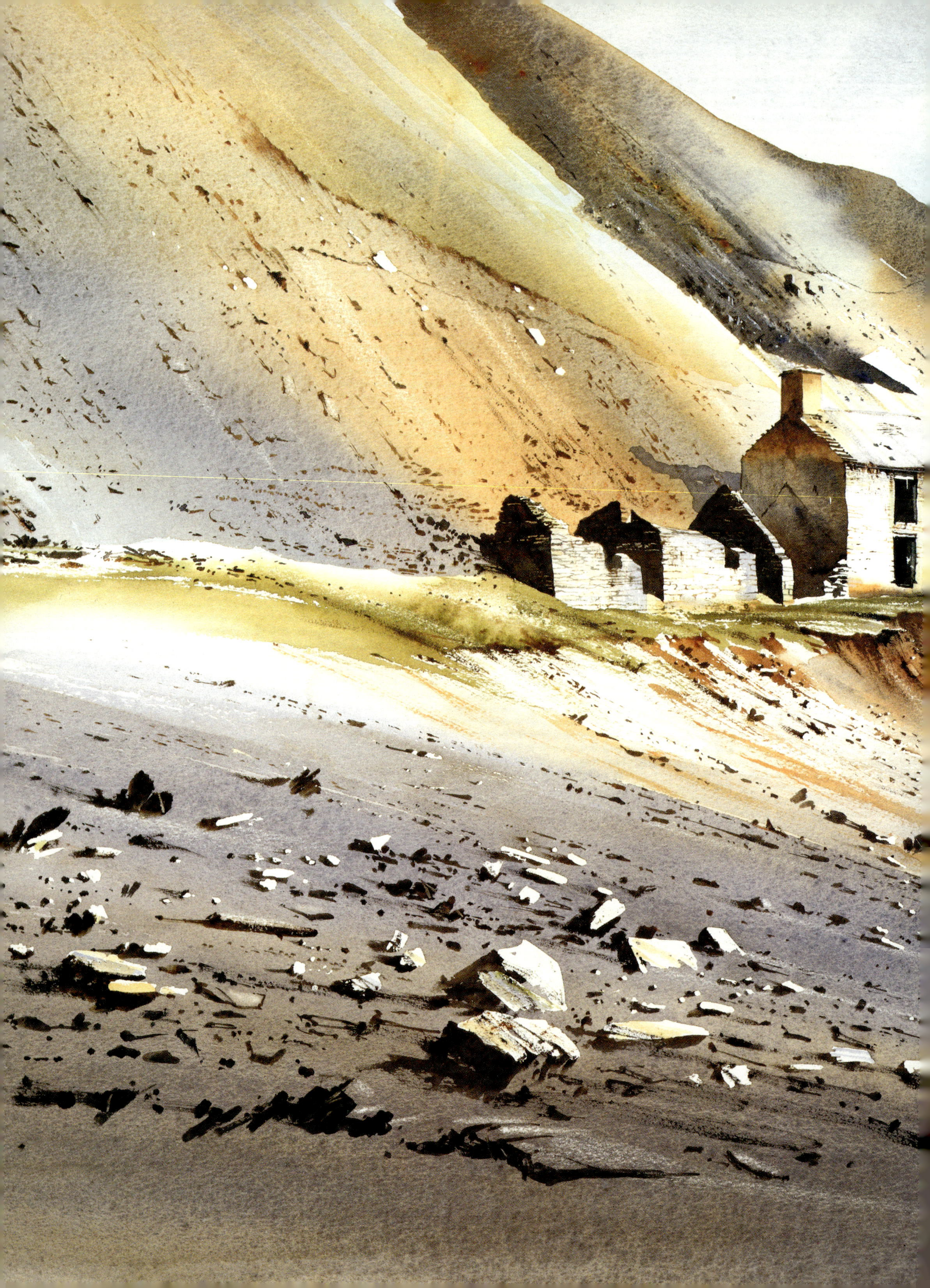

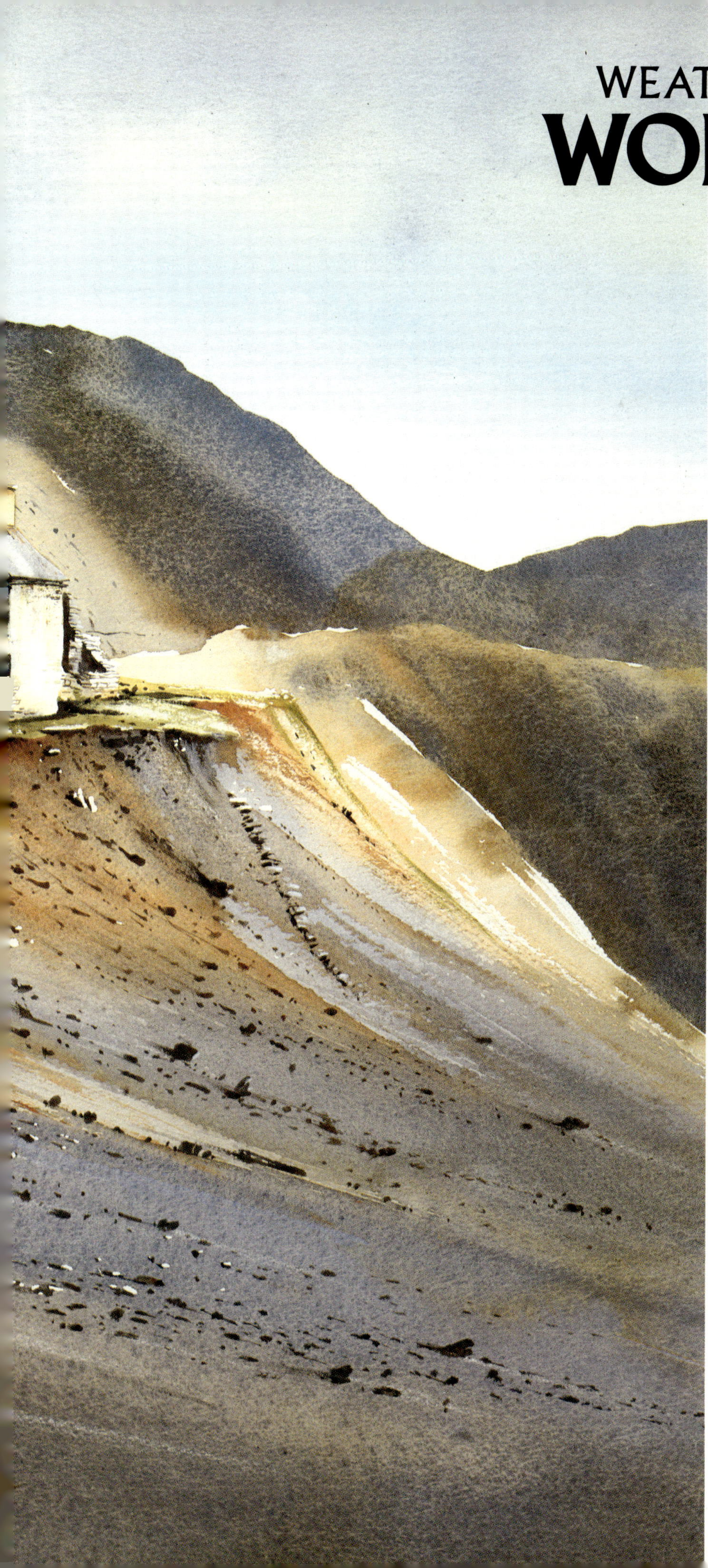

WEATHERED TEXTURE WORKSHOP

This section is divided into five parts, each one dealing with one loosely defined subject area. There is no development in the complexity of technique throughout this section, and some of the paintings are no more than successful watercolor sketches that have a loose, relaxed air to them. There is nothing magic about the painting techniques used here; they are all quite simple. What is important is the dexterity and confidence with which they are used. Start by going quickly through all the paintings and idenifying all the major brushstrokes that make strong statements in each painting: you should be able to trace them back to the brushwork section at the beginning of this book. Aim at becoming a detective, so that you can discover instantly how these and other paintings have been worked. After a while, painting techniques will become easy to identify, and some of the so-called "mysteries" of watercolor painting will seem quite ordinary.

Each painting has details taken from it, to help you see how the pigment takes to the paper. Some details have been enlarged many times, so that the character of pigment on crisp, pitted paper can be easily recognized and the drybrush detail understood. Other details stand out in color against a gray tint of the overall painting: the purpose of this is to show how centers of interest and visual activity fit into the context of the complete painting. Try them out and make them work for you—none of them is difficult.

A WORLD OF TEXTURES

My studio windowsill, in pale morning light, provided an easy still life, rich in textural effects. Though the palette is limited, the surfaces are not. Tall brushes play against cow parsley; shimmering finishes react with rough fabrics. The range of texture and shape is vast, as vast as that in many landscapes. Developing an eye for contrast is an essential part of painting, as is learning what variations most effectively lend more structure and depth to the visual experience you are creating.

The four shapes are different in form, size, and texture, each complementing the other to make an interesting cameo of a picture. The general tone remains the same and a pattern of highlights helps to unite all four. The highlight areas were decided on in advance as I had to use masking fluid to keep them white. I started with a pencil drawing because of the intricacy of some of these forms, such as the ink bottle and the rim of the gravy bowl. The soft brush tips contrast with the spiky cow parsley, and the straight center brush repeats the rhythm of the parsley stalk and the vertical window on one side. To both unite the objects and provide a strong contrast with them, I've added a powerful black (a combination of Ultramarine Blue and Burnt Sienna) border surrounding the windowsill. Wax has been rubbed lightly onto the paper from an ordinary wax candle. This gives the darks a rich, rough, finished look. The prosaic ink jar with its printed label plays with the mystic moon and cloud effect of the bowl. I like objects to enjoy each other's company.

The gravy bowl, tall jar, and wide-mouthed bowl present contrasting textures but harmonize because of a similar tonality—the Burnt Sienna theme that is obvious in the pottery and more subtle in the gravy bowl. I also used it as a connective in that small piece of windowsill that lies between jar and gravy bowl. Notice that on the other side of the tall jar, I used a cooler brown between the two warm colors of the larger objects. Little color touches such as these are not obvious to the viewer, but help to develop the overall harmonies in a painting.

In creating the feeling of real worked pottery in the large bowl and jar, I used the rough surface of the paper, adding pit marks and irregularities when the wash was dry to suggest a rustic charm. I also suggested the potter's hand in the curve of the jar's rim. Once I had begun to create the surrounding patterns, the bright highlight on the stoneware bowl at right began to look more and more like a moon partly hidden by a swirl of clouds and I played up this romantic aura.

The bowl is painted in Indian Red, with Cerulean Blue, Ultramarine Blue, and Burnt Sienna blended into it when very wet and pushed into cloud shapes. For the jar I used a Cerulean Blue wash, with Naples Yellow and Burnt Sienna over it with a dot of Indian Red. The right side reflection is Indian Red, the left Cadmium Orange as are the two top bands.

The gravy bowl, with its familiar willow pattern, needed just a few easy strokes to suggest the intricacies of the design, which the viewer automatically supplies. A very thin Naples Yellow wash touches the left side, and the rest is in light and darker Cobalt Blue. Burnt Sienna outlines the handle and the bottom rim of the bowl.

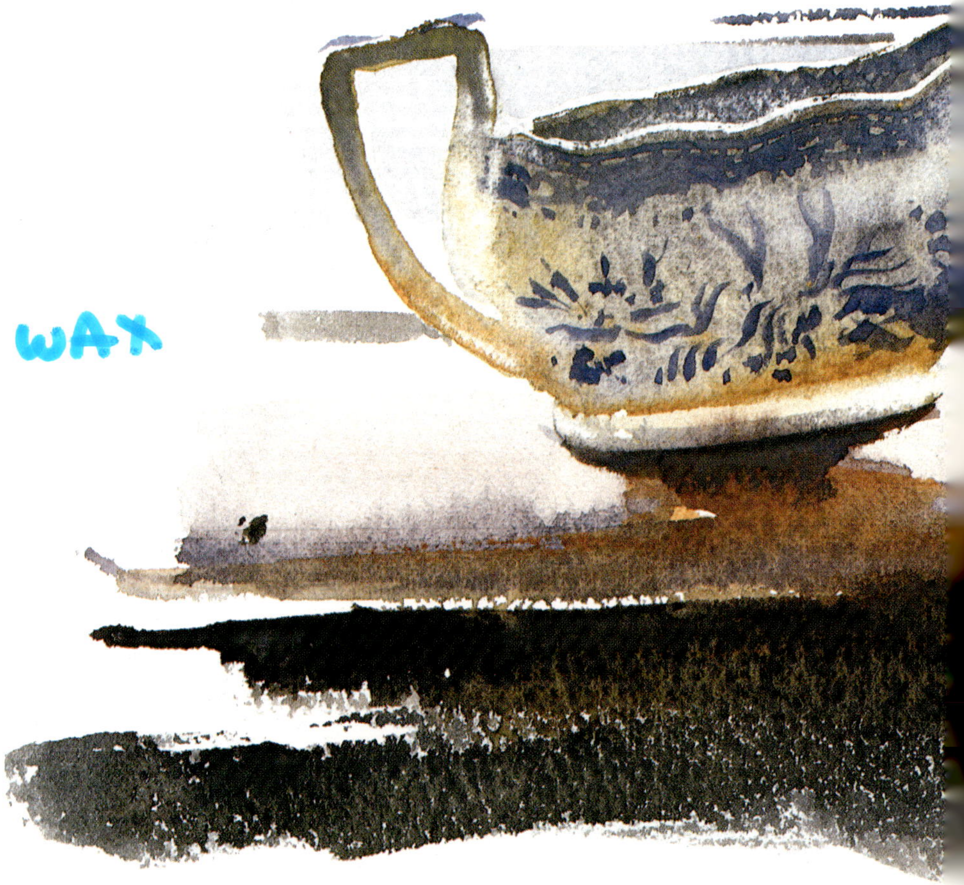

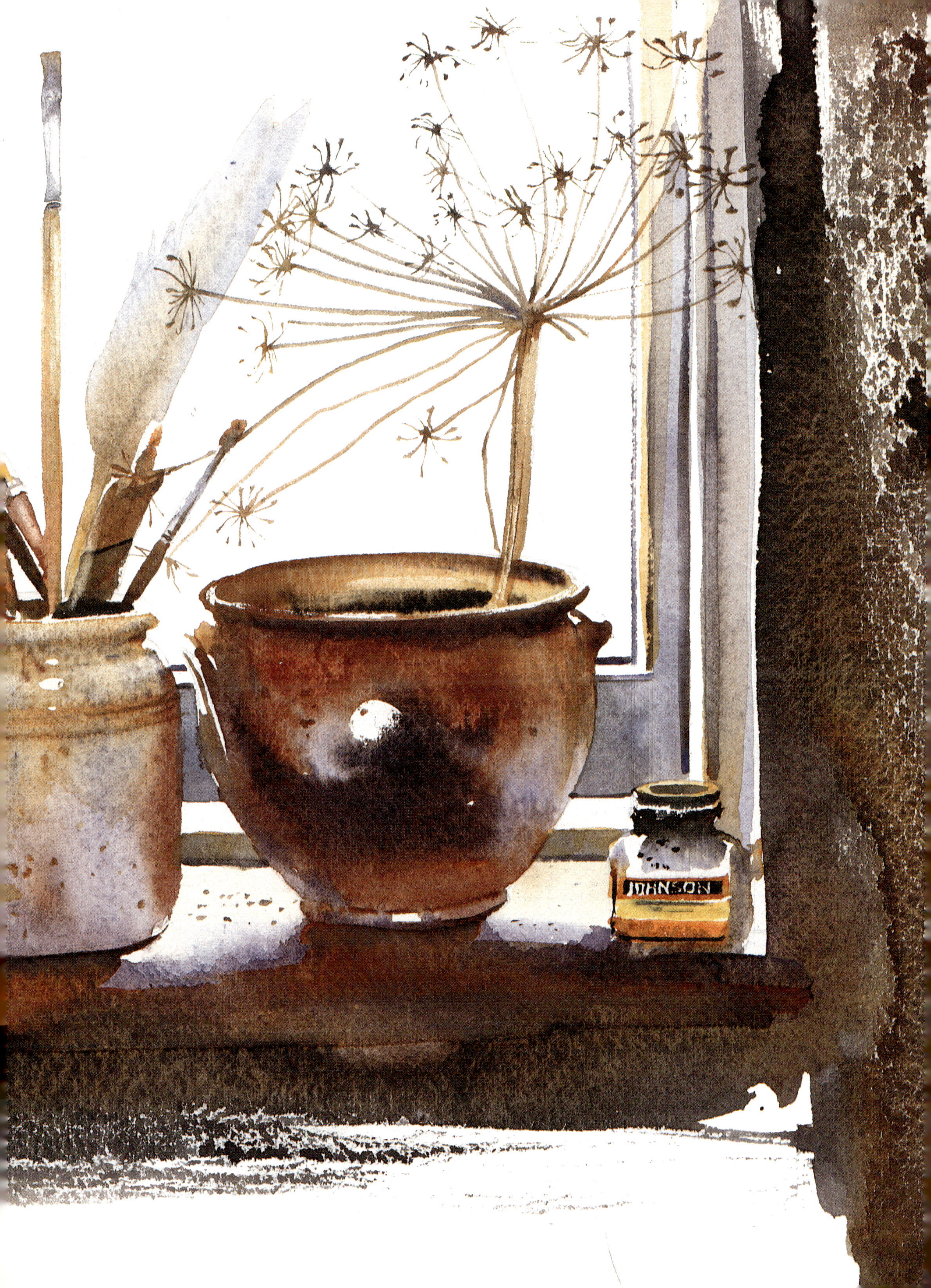
JOHNSON

WOOD AND IRON

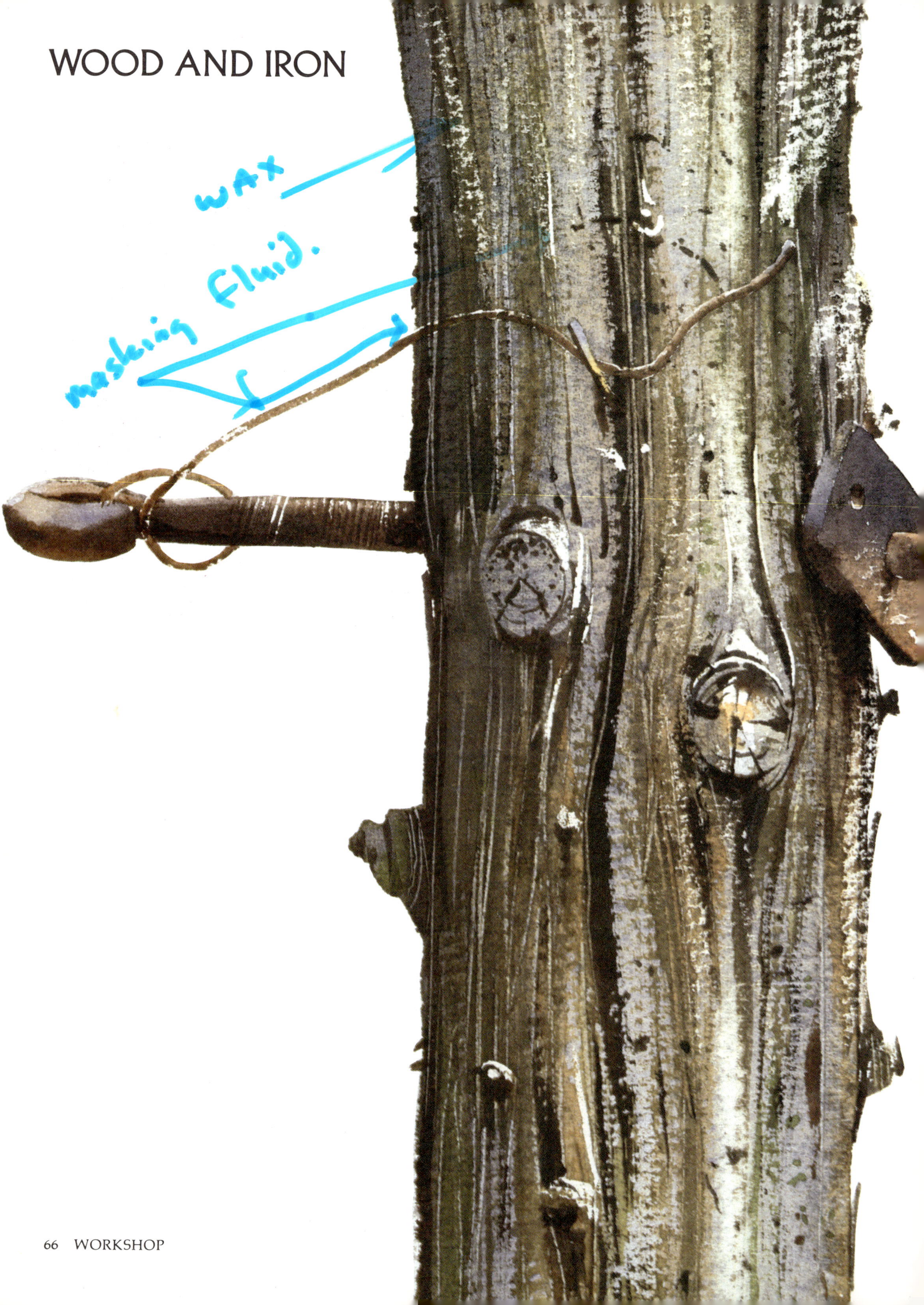

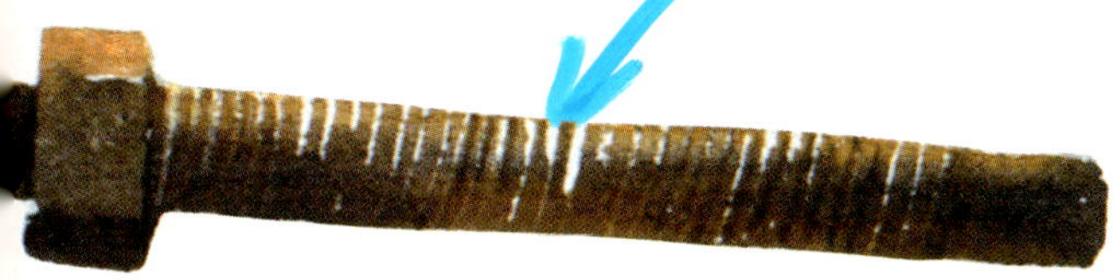

ROUGH WOOD GRAIN

It was the knots and cracks that attracted me to this piece of wood. I like the way the grain flows around the knots, causing them to move in a wavy line down the wooden post. The nature of the subject lends itself easily to watercolor, as the appearance of grain is easily achieved with a sweeping motion of the brush over candlewax. You need it only in places where you want a natural-looking highlight that blends in with the grain. Masking fluid would create too harsh a contrast for a wide area, but it can be quite effective for tiny highlights in the grain, to indicate worm holes or an irregular surface. I used it here also for the piece of wire bent across the post and the thread on the bolt.

The horizontal bolt gives a new direction and color to the vertical post. Combining metal and wooden surfaces can lead to interesting effects. The wire unites the two objects with a diagonal, reducing the impact of a single cross form. The post and bolt have obviously been connected for a long time and have the look of one object, accentuated by the wire.

For the wooden post, I first rubbed in candle wax and painted in small grain lines with masking fluid. I then used a weak overall wash of Cobalt Blue with streaks of Cadmium Orange and Burnt Sienna. For color accents on the wood, I used a mixture of Burnt Sienna and Ultramarine Blue, and Sap Green gave a realistic look of mold to the greenish patches. These colors were applied using as few brushstrokes as possible, and I tried to vary the color and tone subtly with each stroke. I then began to build up the texture of the wood by painting in all the dark streaks of grain, using as little water as possible. Keeping the paint dry on the brush but wet enough to apply smoothly to paper is critical.

Further thin white highlight lines were achieved by dragging the corner of a razor blade in the direction of the grain. In order to create a clean white line with the razor, the paint and paper must be damp. If too wet, color runs into the groove, creating a dark line. If too dry, you have to press down too hard on the paper and risk tearing the paper or making too coarse a line. The final step is removing the masking fluid.

For the metal bolt, I used masking fluid for the threading and also for the wire as it crosses the post. I then laid in thin washes of Winsor Red, Burnt Sienna, and Cadmium Orange, letting them blend into one another. When the washes were dry, I carefully picked out the lower edge of the bolt and the nail hole in a darker value, making the bolt a strong presence in itself. It is important to show here that metal is harder than wood, so I painted the bolt with sharp-edged washes in order to achieve a more angular shape. However, its rusting deterioration also gives it a harmony with the more rounded quality of the wood; it too is subject to the elements and the workings of nature. The askew aspect of the plate with its missing nail and loose nut makes a more interesting composition and emphasizes the worn quality of the subject.

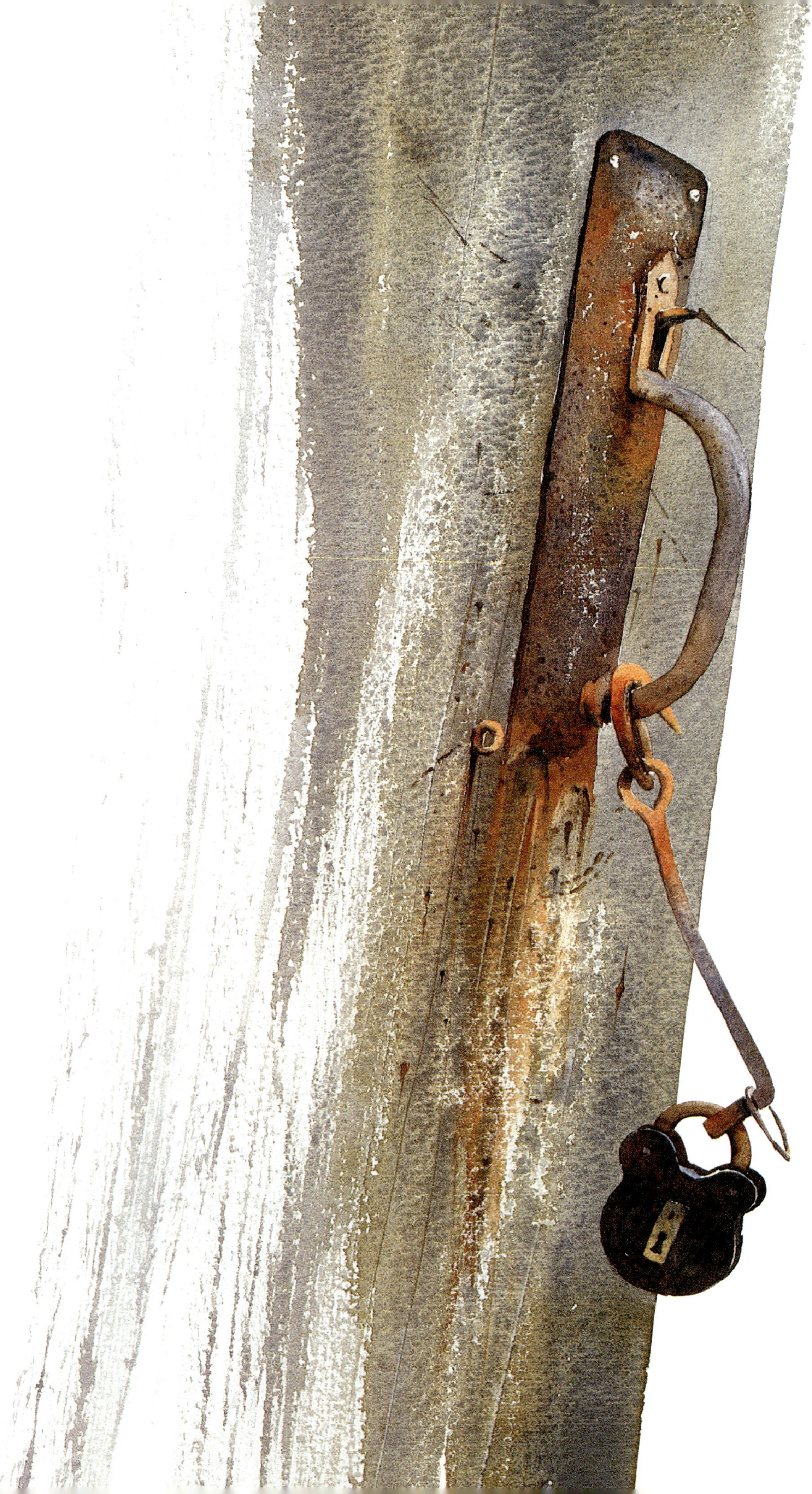

RUST-STAINED WOOD

The charm of this study lies in the contrast between the casual, loose approach of the woodwork and the tightly controlled painting of the door latch and padlock. The door had been broken off its hinges and bent forward, giving the painting its unusual perspective. Without the clearly defined handle, there would be no way to determine what the surface was. The handle defines it and gives it meaning.

The handle, hook, latch, and padlock were completely masked out with masking fluid first. That way I could paint the wood freely without worrying about painting over the fine details. To paint it in later would lead to a muddy look, and I wanted the crispness of finely drawn detail. Since I did want some feeling of texture in the wood, I first rubbed the paper with candle wax, which causes it to resist paint in places and adds to the overall surface interest. The paper must also have the correct surface to give the rough, granulated effect. I used the reverse side of the paper because I didn't like the regular surface pattern on the right side.

I then added a loose, watery wash of Cobalt Blue, Cadmium Orange, and Burnt Sienna, which I briskly applied with a 1-inch flat sable, letting the half-waxed pigments streak and marble on their own. I let the brush run dry on the left, suggesting further woodwork. The right-hand hard-edge is achieved by one quick stroke, insuring a straight line. I also wanted rust stains and flecks of granulation, which I picked out when the wash was dry.

I really enjoyed fussing with this padlock, and I think that pleasure shows through. After drawing it carefully in at an interesting angle, using the suspending hook to push it away from the door, I used the masking fluid to keep it and the highlights that form the curving top clear of paint. To get the very dark color I wanted, I used two coats of Ultramarine Blue, Burnt Sienna, and Alizarin Carmine together. For the keyhole, I used Cadmium Orange with Ultramarine Blue near the top to give it shadow. The keyhole shape is an interesting contrast to the overall shape of the lock, especially as it is shown here, framed by the rectangular plate that surrounds it.

I continued to use the same limited palette for the other hardware details. At the top of the latch plate is a patch of Ultramarine Blue. It is blended with Burnt Sienna at the sides and as I worked downward. Cadmium Orange appears just below the top part of the handle, and Alizarin Carmine and Ultramarine Blue are added and blended further down the plate. For the door handle, I used Cobalt Blue running into Burnt Sienna; the Cobalt is continued down the arc of the handle, until it fades again into Burnt Sienna. For the most precise details on the metal hardware, I again used Burnt Sienna and picked out the dark-toned nail holes, knife marks, and random indentations with a quick brushstroke. As a final touch, the edge of a razor blade was used to scratch in highlights.

Anything this carefully detailed needs to be drawn in first in pencil, then masked over. Use your finger to remove the masking fluid when you are ready, as an eraser or sponge will take the pencil lines with it. Don't put wax over the masking fluid or you'll not be able to remove it. I painted the hook in masking fluid, then the screw heads and bits of highlight. The brightness of Cadmium Orange gives a good rusty look. Alizarin Carmine creates the dark effects. The interplay of curved and straight lines, the variation in textures and colors, and the shift from the vague to the very specific are all operating here to give strength and interest to this vignette.

Don't put wax over the masking fluid or you won't be able to remove it

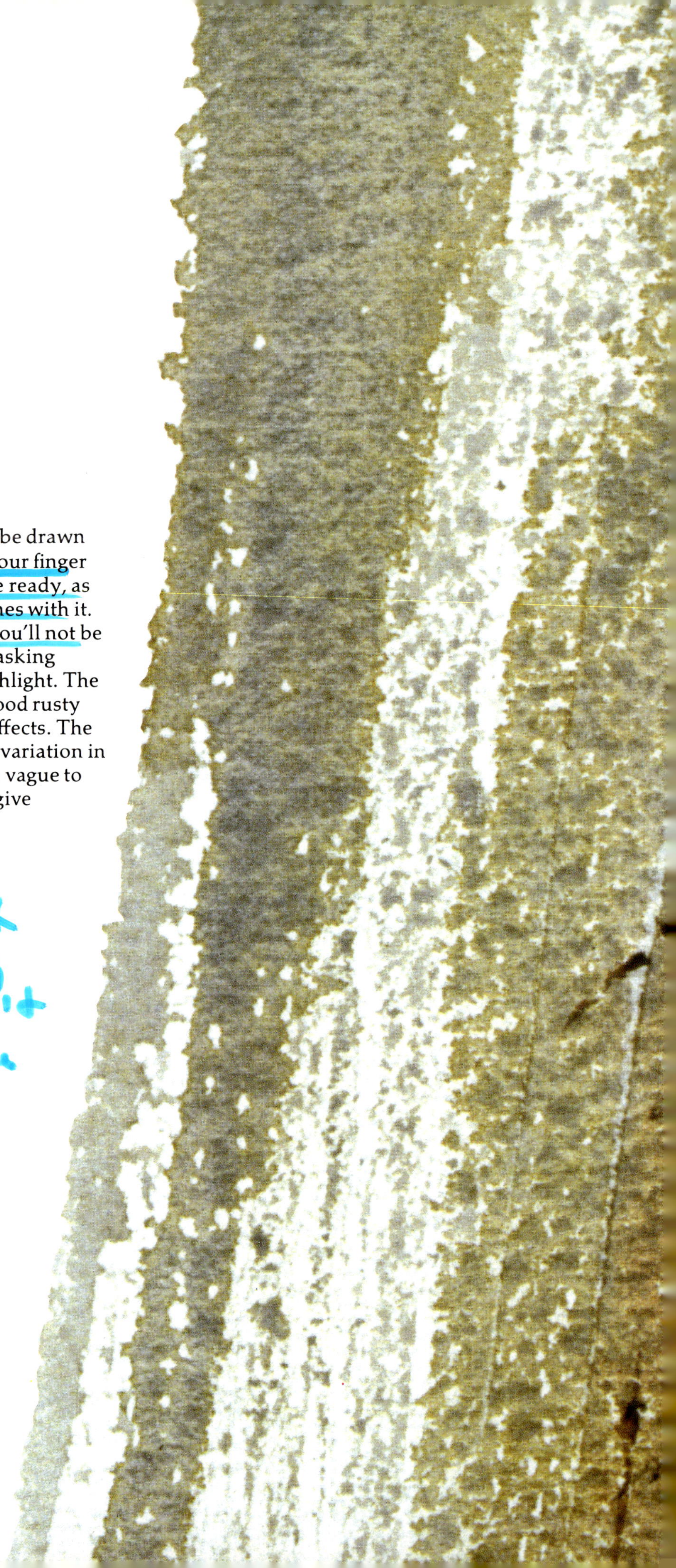

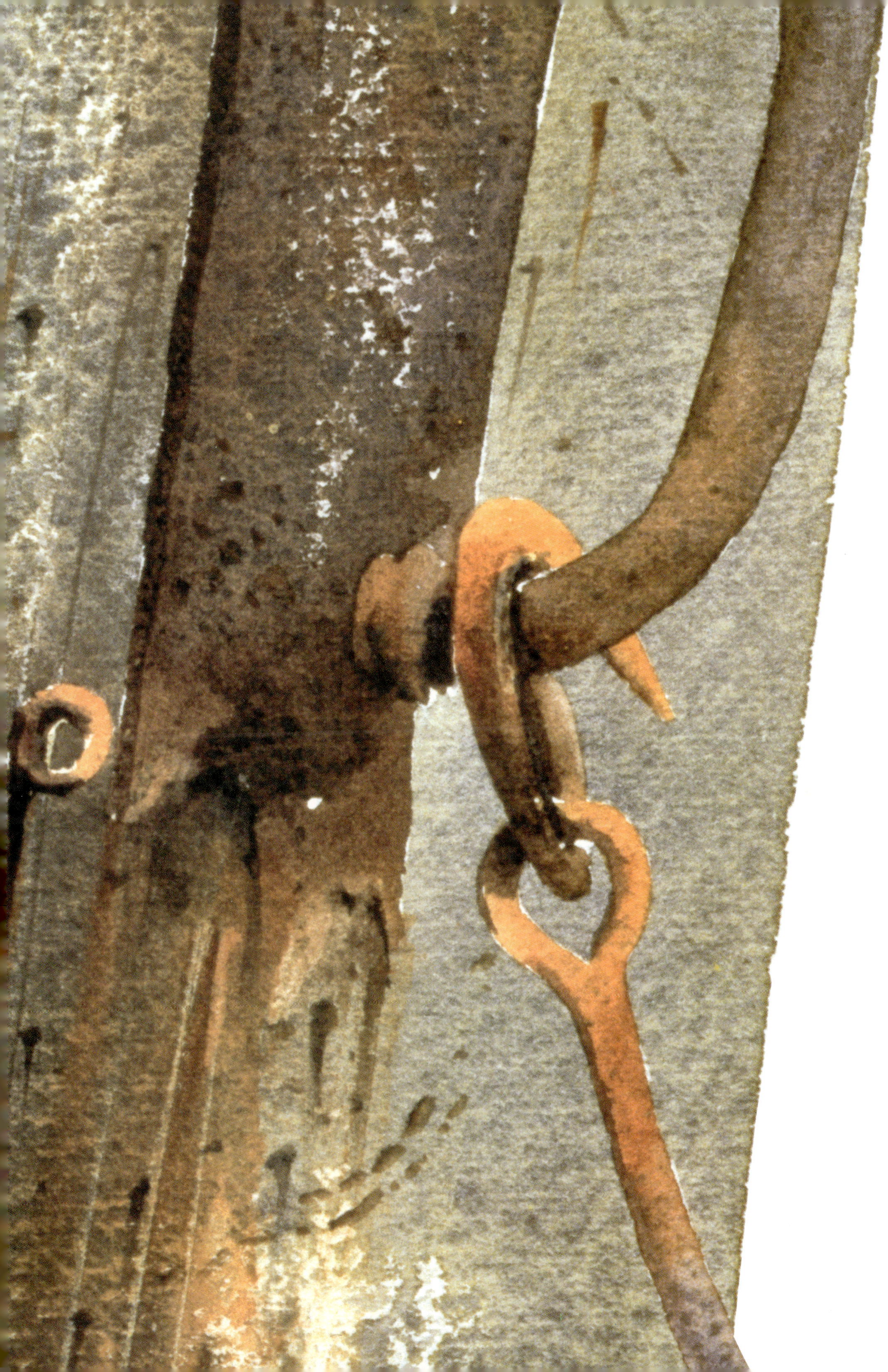

STRONG SHAPES AND HARD EDGES

It was the patchwork quality of this old shed that originally attracted me to it. The slabs of wood nailed here and there to cover up weathered places form an interesting irregular pattern, and a surprisingly varied array of colors give the structure an intensity all its own. It's the sort of place you may walk by every day without ever seeing its potential as a subject for a watercolor.

In order to give strength to what could have been a weak structure, I decided to emphasize the strong horizontals and verticals created by the patched wood. A strong color contrast, created with drybrush technique, would give vitality to the form. I also wanted to create a feeling of the special texture present in the decaying wood with its wormholes, flaking paint, rust, and cracks.

While the original structure would have had an ordinary horizontal and vertical pattern, the wood patches and weathered colors have now created a dynamic design that keeps the eye moving about the shed. To anchor the right side of the shed, which seems about to collapse off the page, I used the pitchfork, bucket, and the surrounding weeds, to balance and soften a rather stark composition. I wanted hard-edge lines to create a strong contrast between the boards, so I used drybrush to avoid the blurring effects of softer techniques. The darker colors are more forcefully separated by hard-edge darks, sometimes against a band of light wood, for further emphasis. These strong edges are made more powerful by using finer, lighter-toned, blended edges for the light, low-key colors.

Getting down to work, I first painted in light base coats to indicate the planks. Cobalt Blue and Cadmium Orange were the colors I used most frequently, although some of the timbers are almost a pure Sap Green. To keep the colors vivid and fresh, I changed the

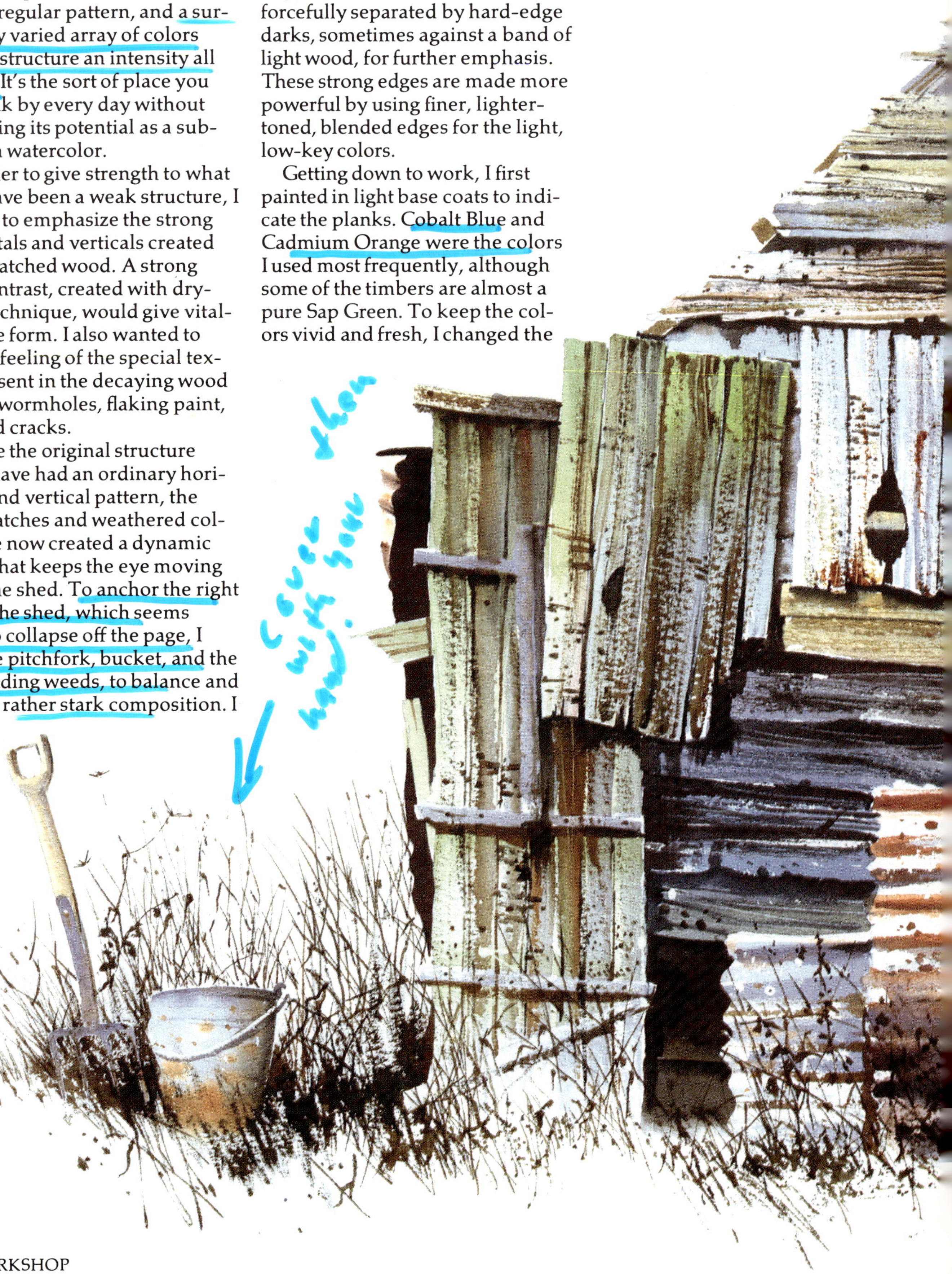

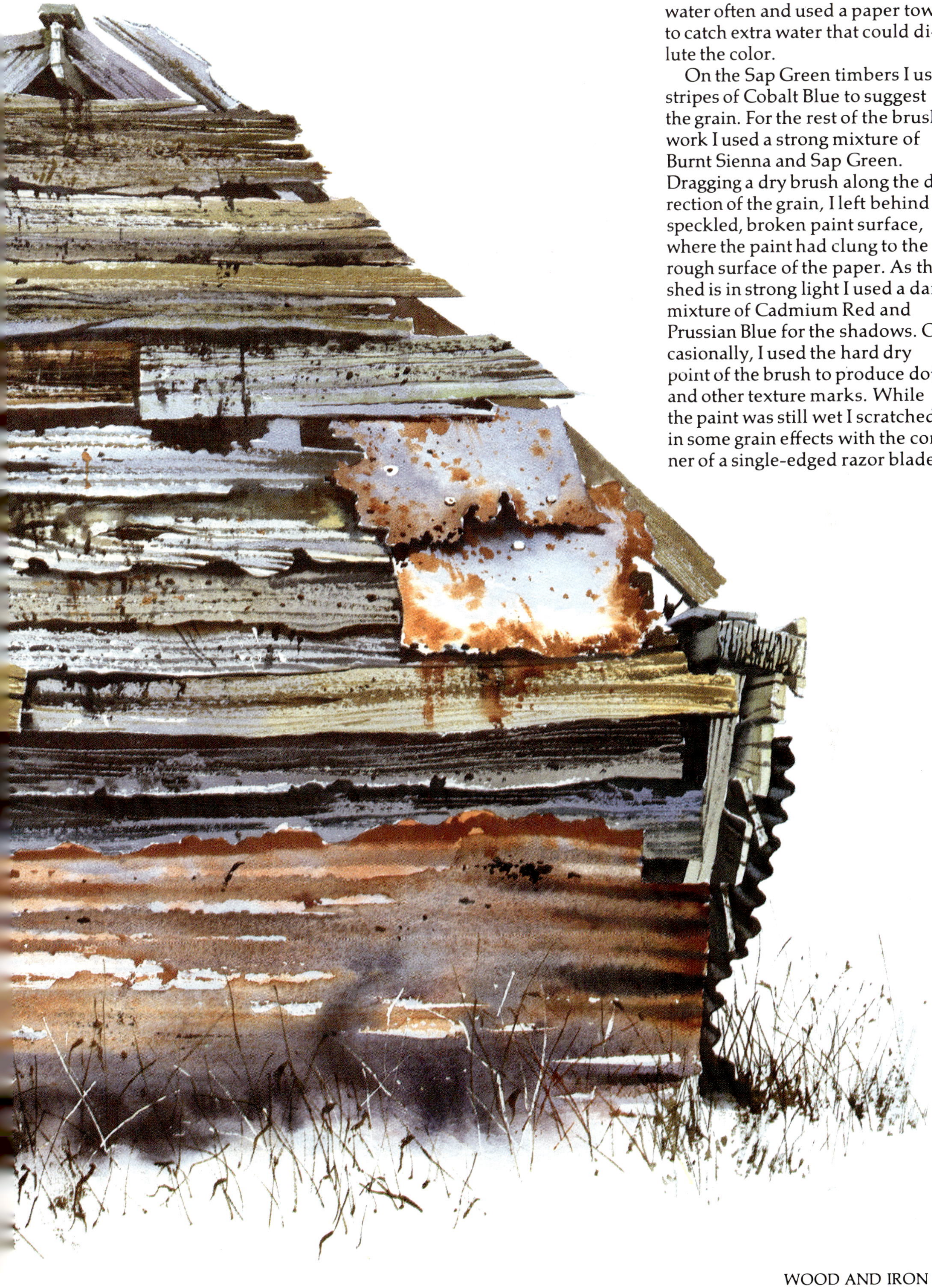

water often and used a paper towel to catch extra water that could dilute the color.

On the Sap Green timbers I used stripes of Cobalt Blue to suggest the grain. For the rest of the brushwork I used a strong mixture of Burnt Sienna and Sap Green. Dragging a dry brush along the direction of the grain, I left behind a speckled, broken paint surface, where the paint had clung to the rough surface of the paper. As the shed is in strong light I used a dark mixture of Cadmium Red and Prussian Blue for the shadows. Occasionally, I used the hard dry point of the brush to produce dots and other texture marks. While the paint was still wet I scratched in some grain effects with the corner of a single-edged razor blade.

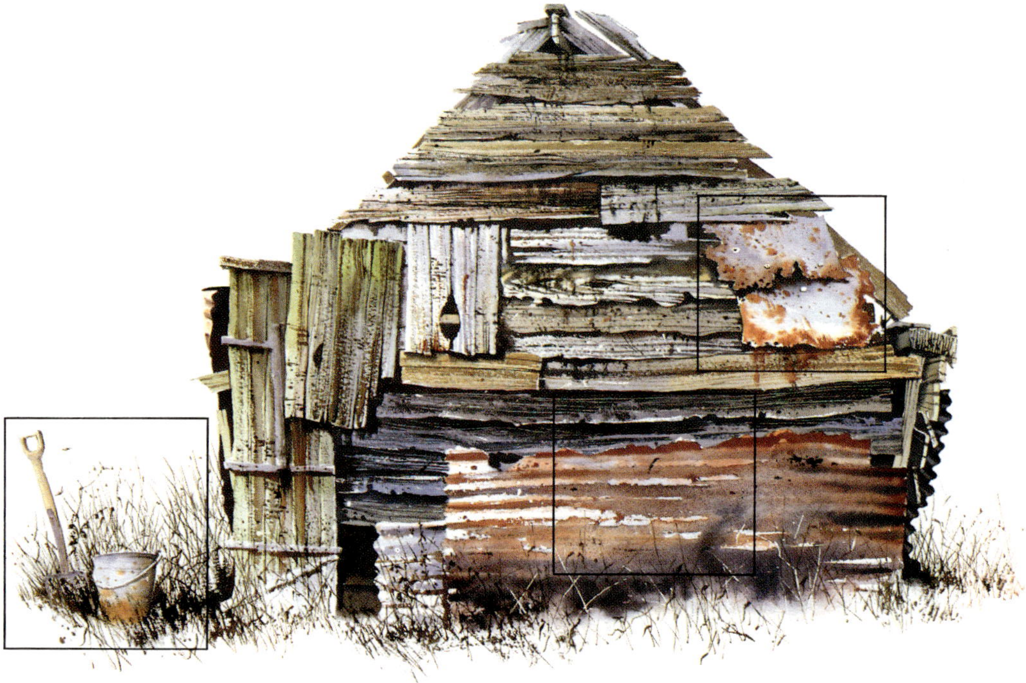

Before painting the bucket, whose soft colors echo the shed's, and the pitchfork, which anchors the shed to the left, I used masking fluid to cover the area. Then I painted in the delicate blades of grass with quick, light strokes. Before removing the fluid from the bucket and the pitchfork, I masked in the bucket's handle. To a fairly wet blue-gray wash on the bucket, I let a weak mixture of Burnt Sienna and Cadmium Orange indicate the subtle effects of rust. The spade's handle is a mixture of Naples Yellow, Cobalt Blue, and Burnt Sienna.

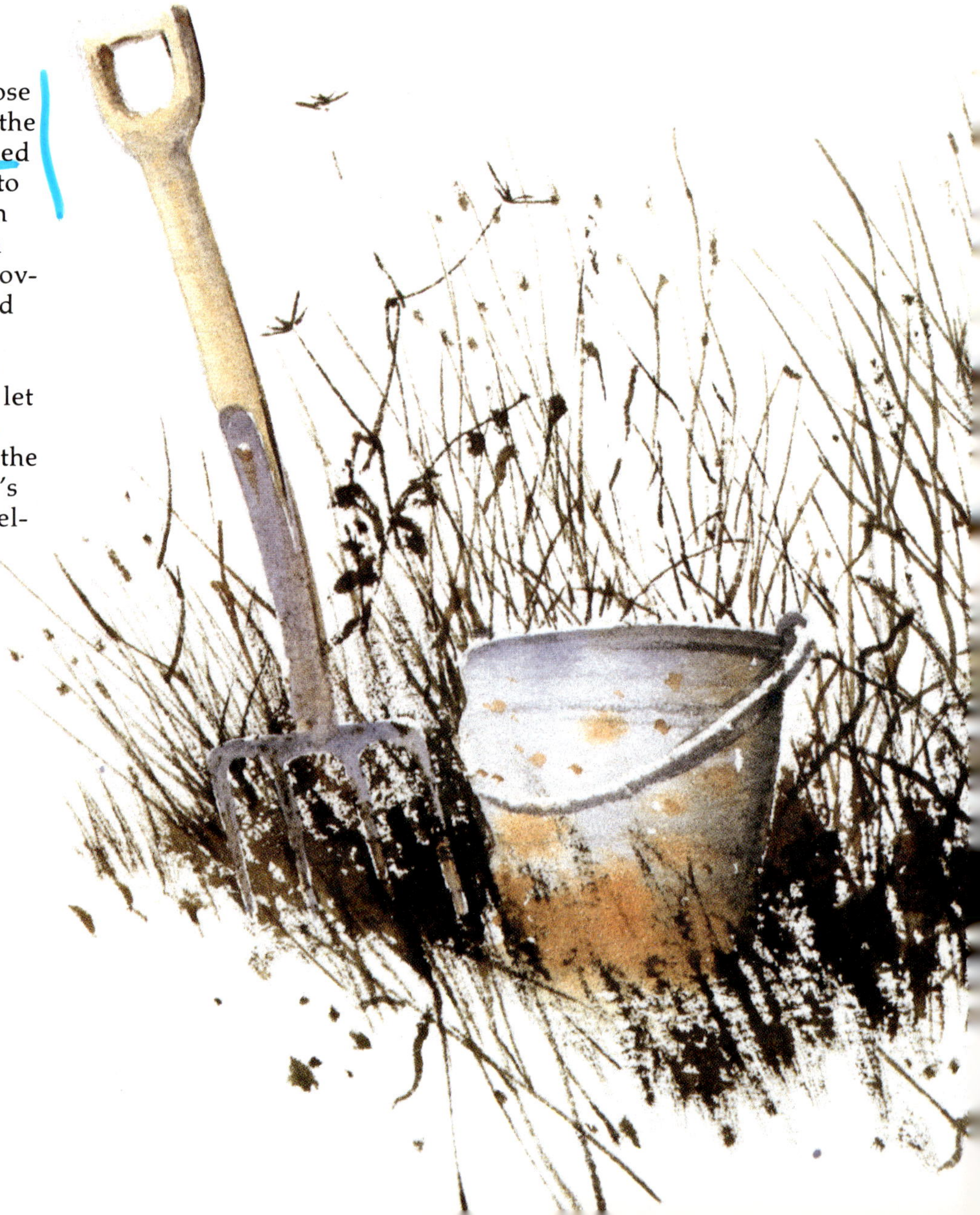

To capture the effect of rust acting on iron I have used two techniques: first I dampened the surface with either clear water or a light wash of Cobalt Blue. While the surface was still wet I dabbed it with a fine brush of Burnt Sienna, varying this with Indian Red, Cadmium Orange, and even Alizarin Carmine in moderation. As these colors disperse softly onto the paper they stain the surface much as the rust does.

Then, when the paper has dried, I scrubbed these same colors, with an almost dry brush, into the paper, working them around and scraping the brush downward to imitate the spreading effect of the rust. Smudging the paint with your finger tip is another way to make the rust appear to run. The iron ridges are indicated with quick drybrush strokes that leave just enough paint on the paper to make the ridge obvious. Highlights are produced by rewetting small areas and dabbing the paint away with a paper towel.

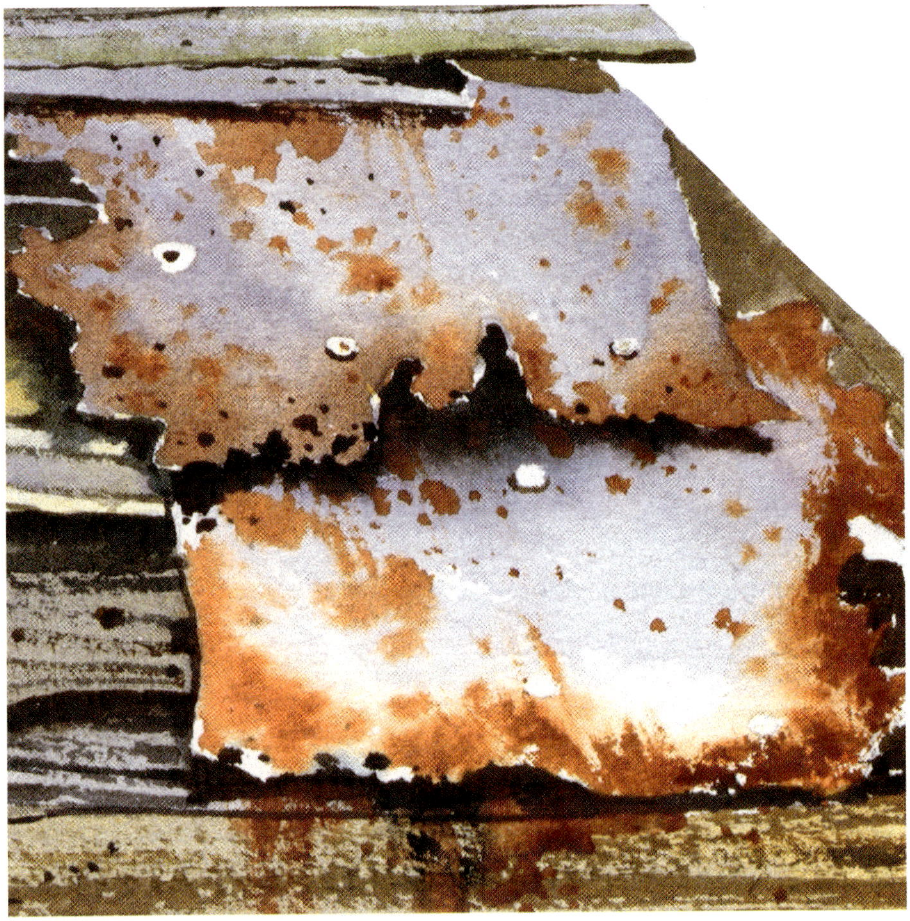

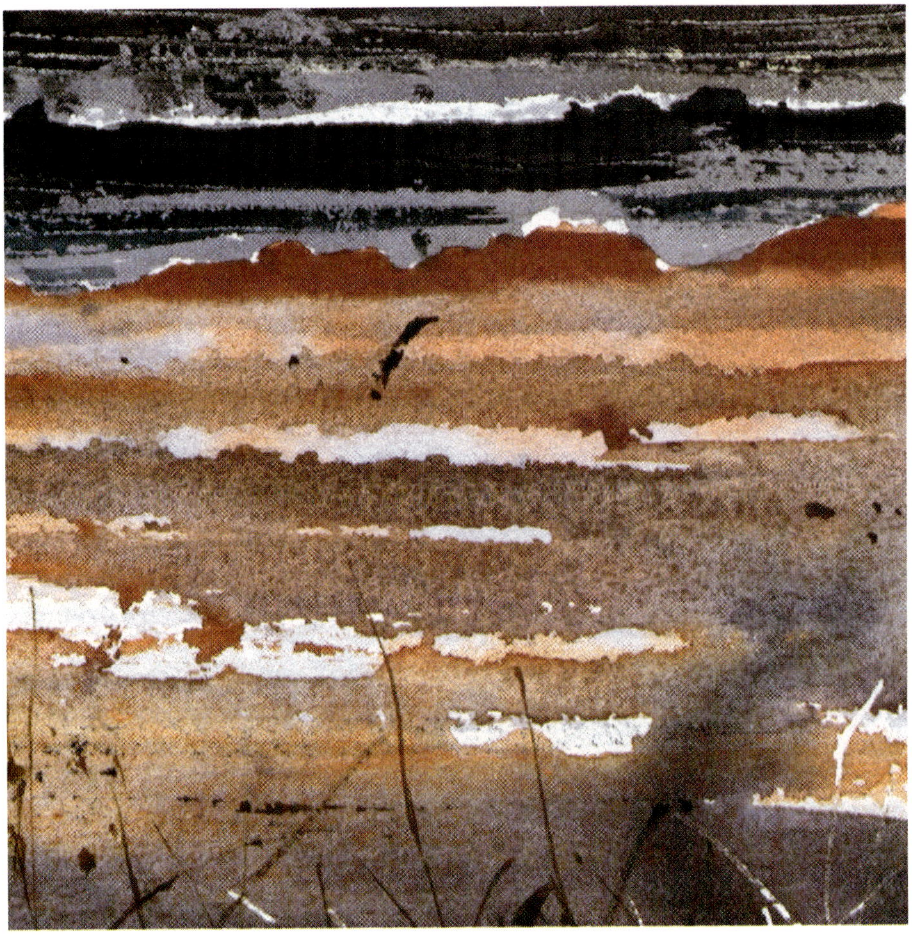

Notice how a small detail from an interesting surface can seem like an abstract painting when isolated. Onto a weak mixture of Cobalt Blue I have dabbed Indian Red, Cadmium Orange, and Alizarin Carmine, which blend gently into the base. When the paper was dry I created a jagged rusty pattern with an almost-dry, sharp-pointed brush of Cadmium Red and Prussian Blue. This dark interior gives strength to the jagged hard edge through sharp contrast.

SUBTLE SHADES OF COLOR

From this side the shed is an entirely different composition: wide sheets of corrugated iron create simple flat patterns complemented by the wavy motion of tiles above. The rust on this side is also quite different and I needed to study it carefully in order to produce the interesting effects it creates on the iron. Unlike the other side, where the rust has spread through the layers and darkened, here it has formed only on the outermost layer, where the original zinc coating has worn off. In some places it runs, staining the surface below it; elsewhere it creates delicate lacy patterns as it eats away at the iron. The light tones of this rust blend with the warm tones of the roof, creating a harmonious overall pattern.

Instead of ignoring the graffiti I decided to incorporate it into the design, using the letters to give interest to the two flat sheets of iron they're painted on, unifying the two sheets at the same time. The white of the characters emphasizes the subtle colors of the shed and contributes to the overall pattern of lights. I printed the letters with masking fluid, which can be rubbed away once the surrounding area is painted.

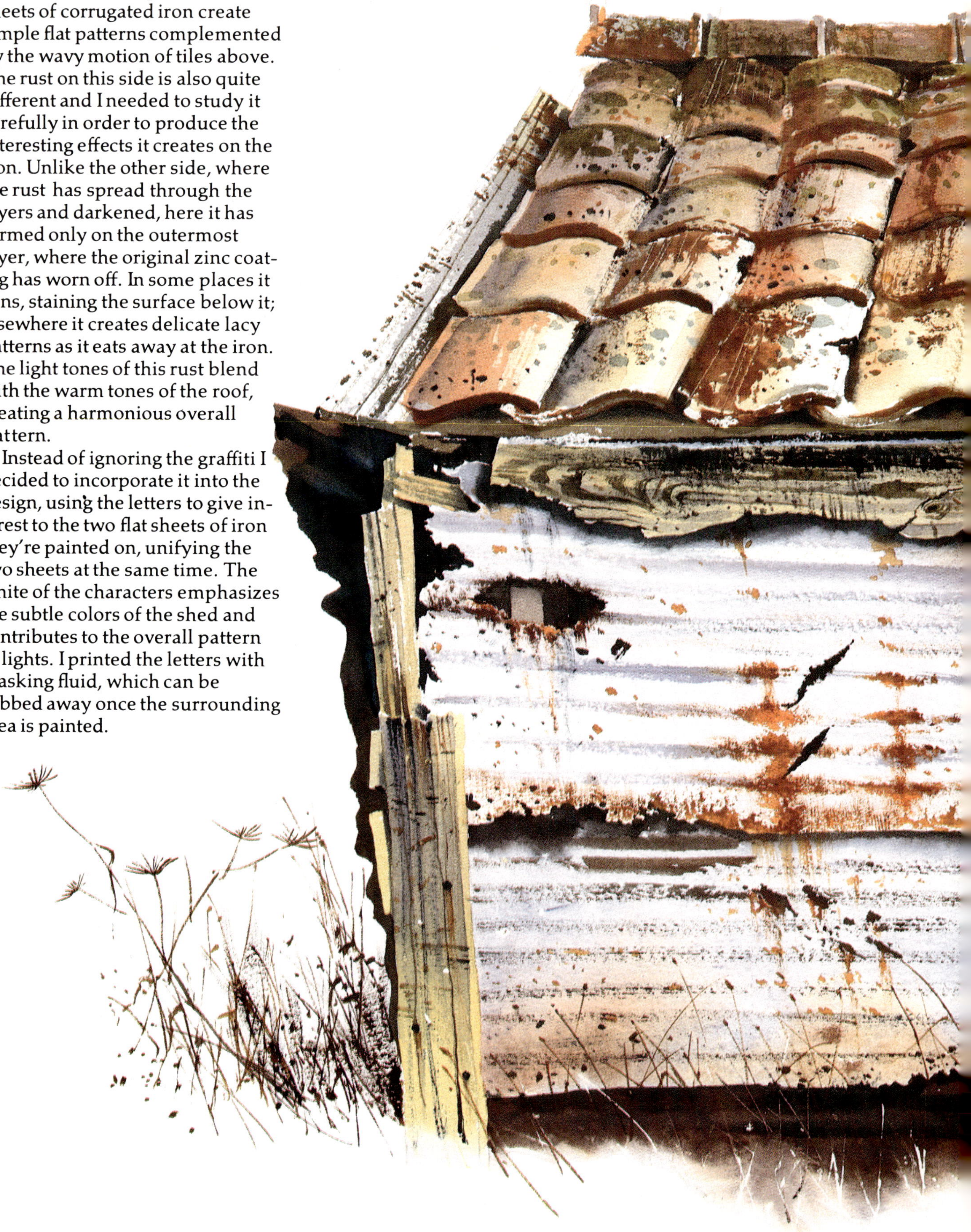

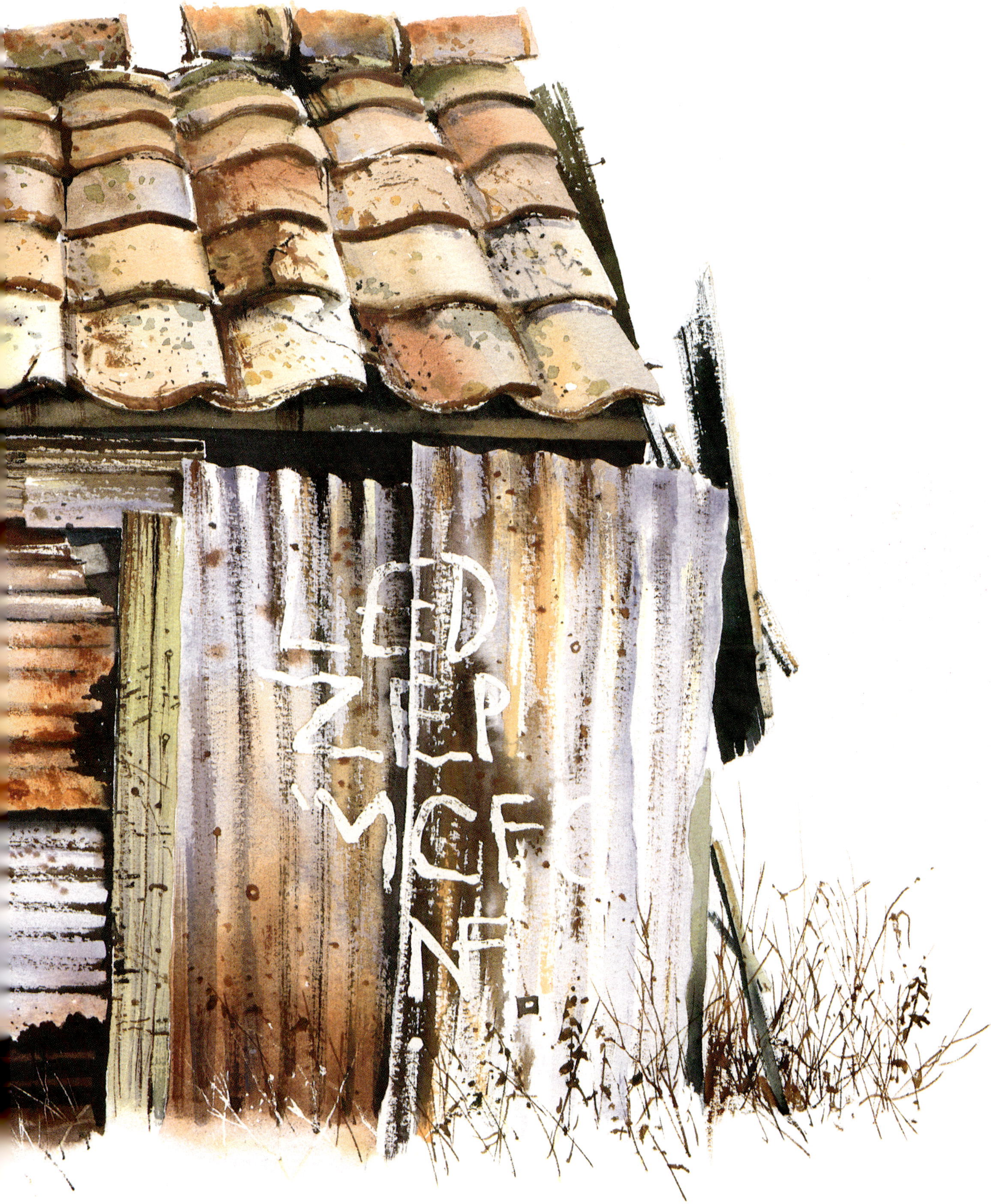

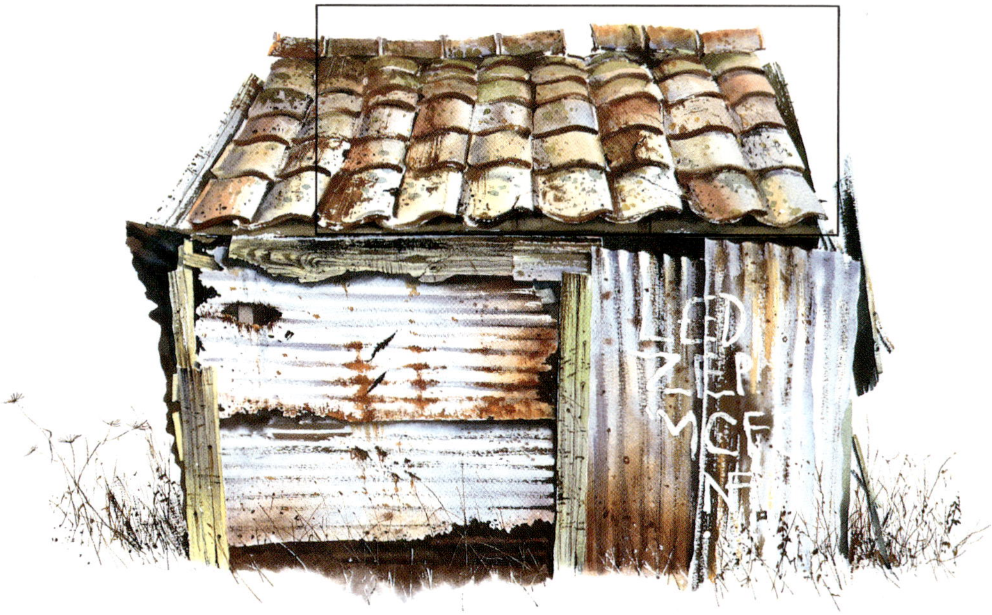

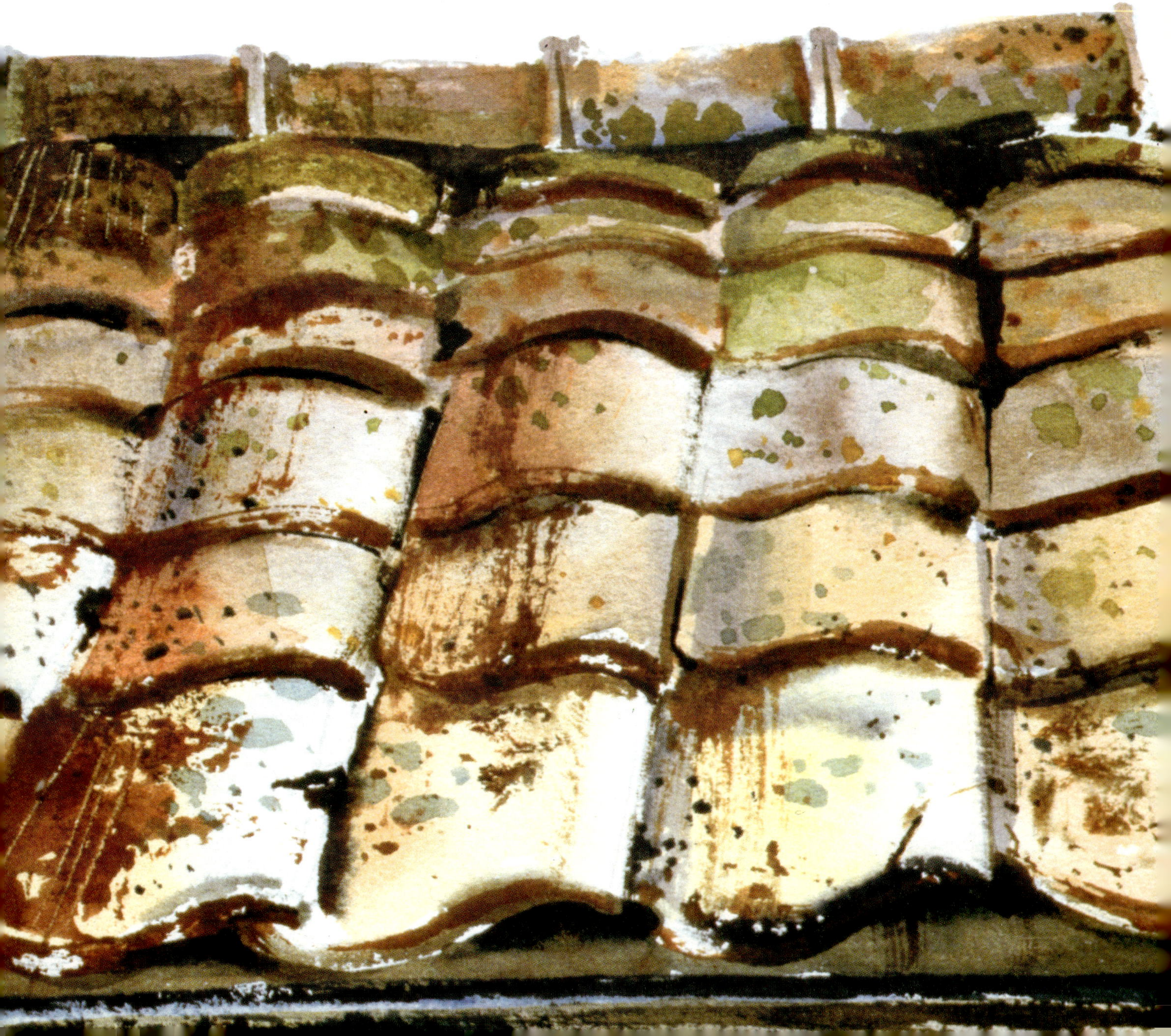

Although the shed was very decrepit, the roof tiles had clung together admirably and so intrigued me that I spent more time painting the tiles than any other part of the picture. (I don't equate the time spent with final result, however, as often laboring over an area will make it look dull and overworked.) The curving verticals and horizontals, separated with thick bands of color, give a harmonious contrast to the flat elements below the roof. The way the tiles are set, one flowing beneath another, creates a more complex pattern of curves than that of tiles merely placed side by side. Carefully examining the basic structure, rather than assuming what it looks like, will often reveal dynamic movement. I emphasized the close interlocking of the tiles with thick bands of color, providing a stability that other elements of the shack do not have.

The tiles were all different colors and I wanted to paint them that way. Some were very yellow, others bright pink, and so it was necessary to treat them individually to capture this soft color scheme. I probably used every color on my palette to produce these tiles, but the main ones were Alizarin Carmine for the rosy tiles; and Cadmium Orange, Yellow Ochre, and Burnt Sienna for the yellow tiles. Alizarin Carmine, having a strong blue tone, creates a refreshingly cool red among the warmer yellows. For the bits of mold I used Sap Green and Burnt Sienna.

Texture was produced by adding a series of thin washes and then dabbing away the colors with a paper towel to get the overall even tone I wanted. The light is coming from the right so Cobalt Blue is used on the left side of many of the tiles to give them form. For the rougher textures I used a dry brush, to create an interesting contrast to the smooth feeling the tiles convey.

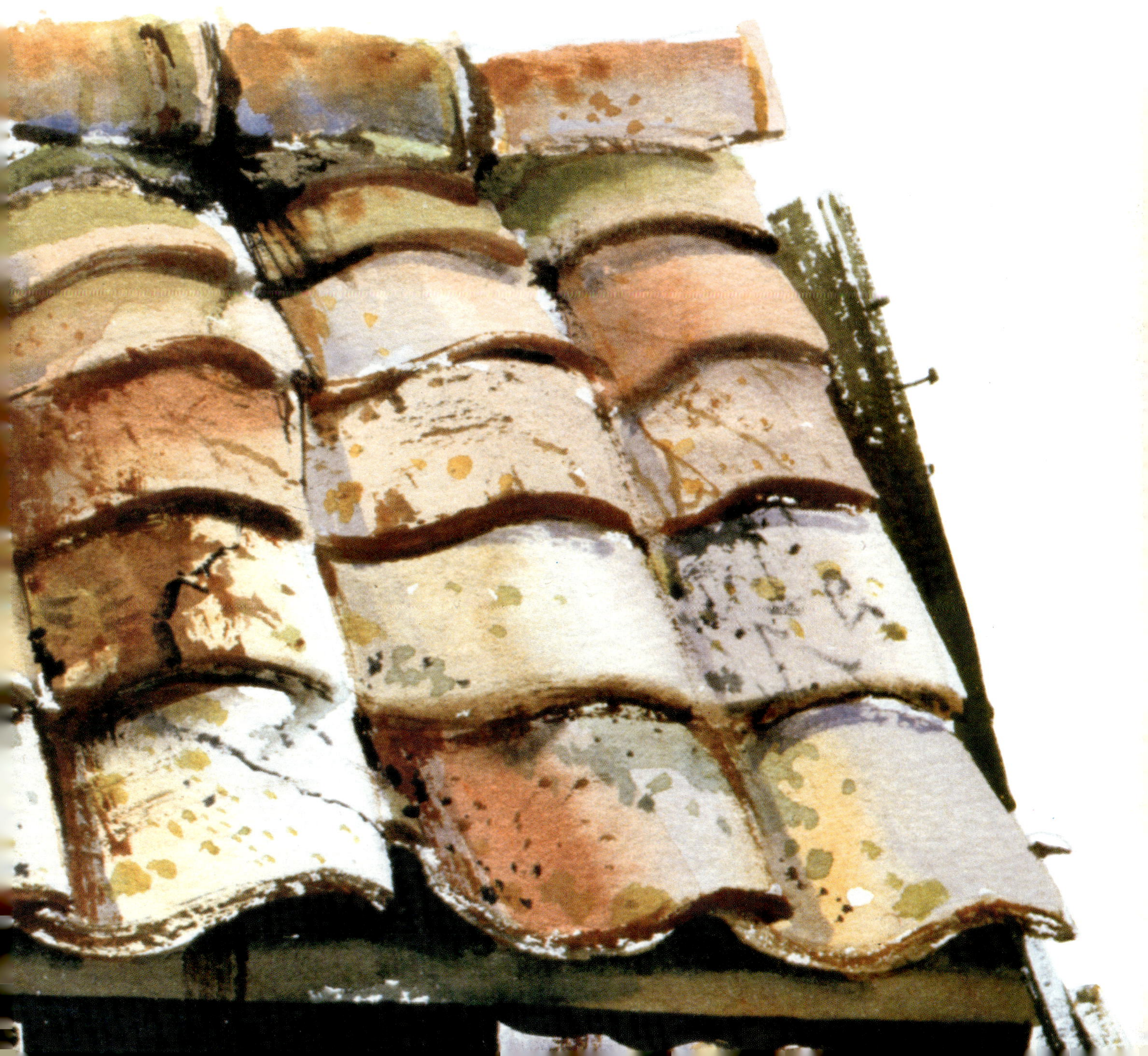

Above the corrugated iron, a curved strip of wood provides a harmonious transition between the light horizontals of the iron and the curving tiles of the roof. This strip also corresponds in shape somewhat to the dark open area at the bottom. Its swirling grain, picked out with the tip of a fine brush, repeats some of the patterns in the metal sheeting, while adding the contrast of a new texture.

To provide a contrast in the painting, I decided to give this area of rust an entirely different treatment, by concentrating on the activity in the shadows behind the rusted-away iron.

As in the above detail, I laid in the palest of washes on the sheet of iron, using a touch of Cadmium Red and Prussian Blue blended together. Mixing up a far richer pool of these two colors, with slightly more red than blue, I put in the lacy edges of the rusty sheet with a fine brush and carried this color down into the grasses, blending it off with water there. While this paint was still just a little damp, I wiped out three horizontal stripes to give lighter bands of value within this dark mass. Allowing the paint to dry, I used a razor blade to cut in some white blades of grass, continuing their form with streaks of the dark mixture across the sheet of iron—very simple, but very effective.

On this sheet of iron the rust has eaten away at the surface and created a coarse texture, created by the variety of brown colors. When tackling a richly textured surface such as this, make a mental list of the order in which to apply the paint. In this way you have absolute control over the buildup of the texture.

I began here by laying in a very pale wash of Burnt Sienna, working from right to left away from the flaky edge. I made this application into the wet paper so that it blended perfectly into the unrusted part of the iron sheet. When this was dry, I put in the thin stripes that create the ridges along the sheet of metal with Cobalt Blue, taking care to make each one as uneven as possible.

Now for the heaviest rust. I loaded a brush with rich Burnt Sienna and used a coarse, scratchy drybrush action to embellish the effect. Notice that these areas of paint are extremely broken up—it is the texture of the pattern of the rust as much as the rich color that portrays its character.

Finally, I made an opaque mixture for the shadow at the right edge of the sheet with Cadmium Red and Prussian Blue. To create the lacy edge, I applied this color with a fine brush, obliterating the Burnt Sienna drybrush and wash in parts.

METAL AND MACHINES

SMOOTH COLOR CHANGES
This tractor, disappearing bit by bit into the marshy ground, shouldn't make such a happy painting. But somehow, in the afternoon sunlight, its warm colors, in harmony with house and background, seem quite comfortably resigned to their condition. Here is nature triumphing over machinery, a favorite theme of mine.

The wheel hub is a mixture of rusts, washes blended together to form the curved shape and shaded areas. The rust color creeps across the paper in the same way that rust runs down the surface of the old tractor. The rough texture of rust patches was added using a dry brush rubbed and dragged across the paper to simulate rust's eaten away quality. Scuffed tire marks were produced in the same way, by actually scuffing or scratching a razor blade across the paper. I have made the paint look faded by dabbing away at a wet wash with a tissue. The surfaces can look stunningly realistic compared with the labored efforts required in other mediums to produce comparable effects.

I used Sap Green in this painting to capture the strong green of mold and because it harmonizes so well with the natural earth tones. The bright green pigment was introduced into a clear water wash, the colors softly blending together on the paper, leaving no hard edges. The nuts and bolts were painted in with a fine brush after removing the masking fluid. I also used the masking fluid on the metal rims to keep a sharp, firm line when I washed in the background.

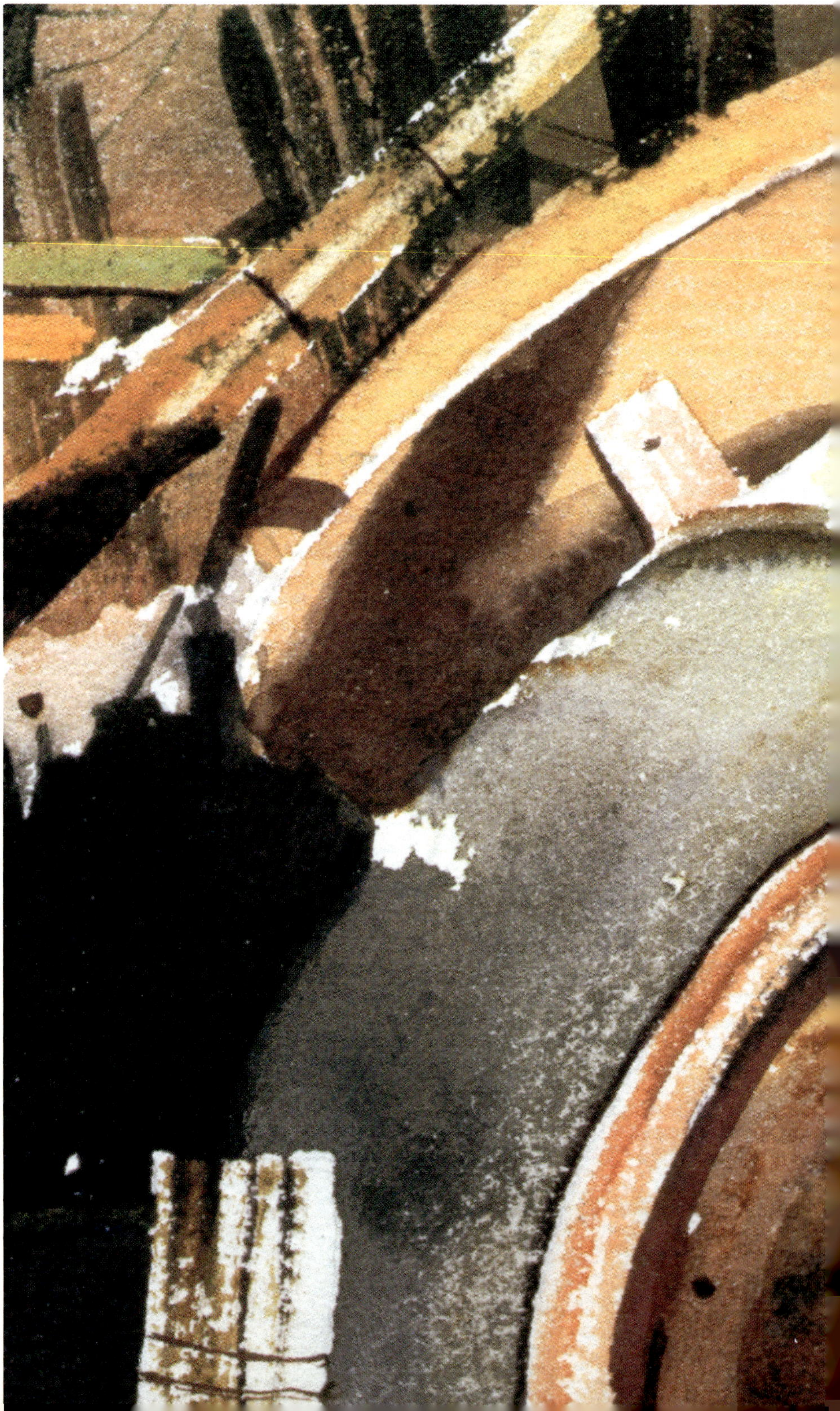

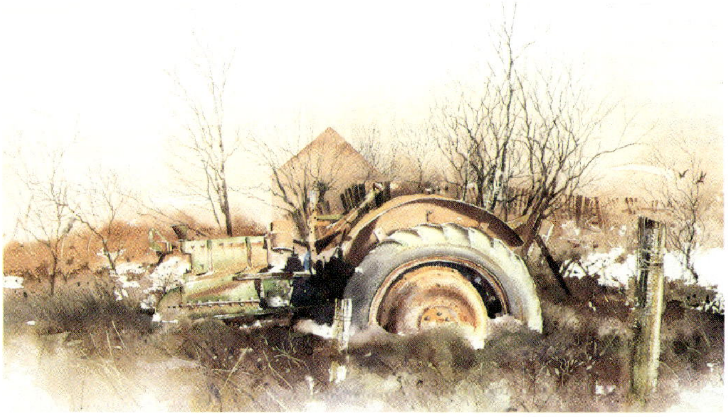

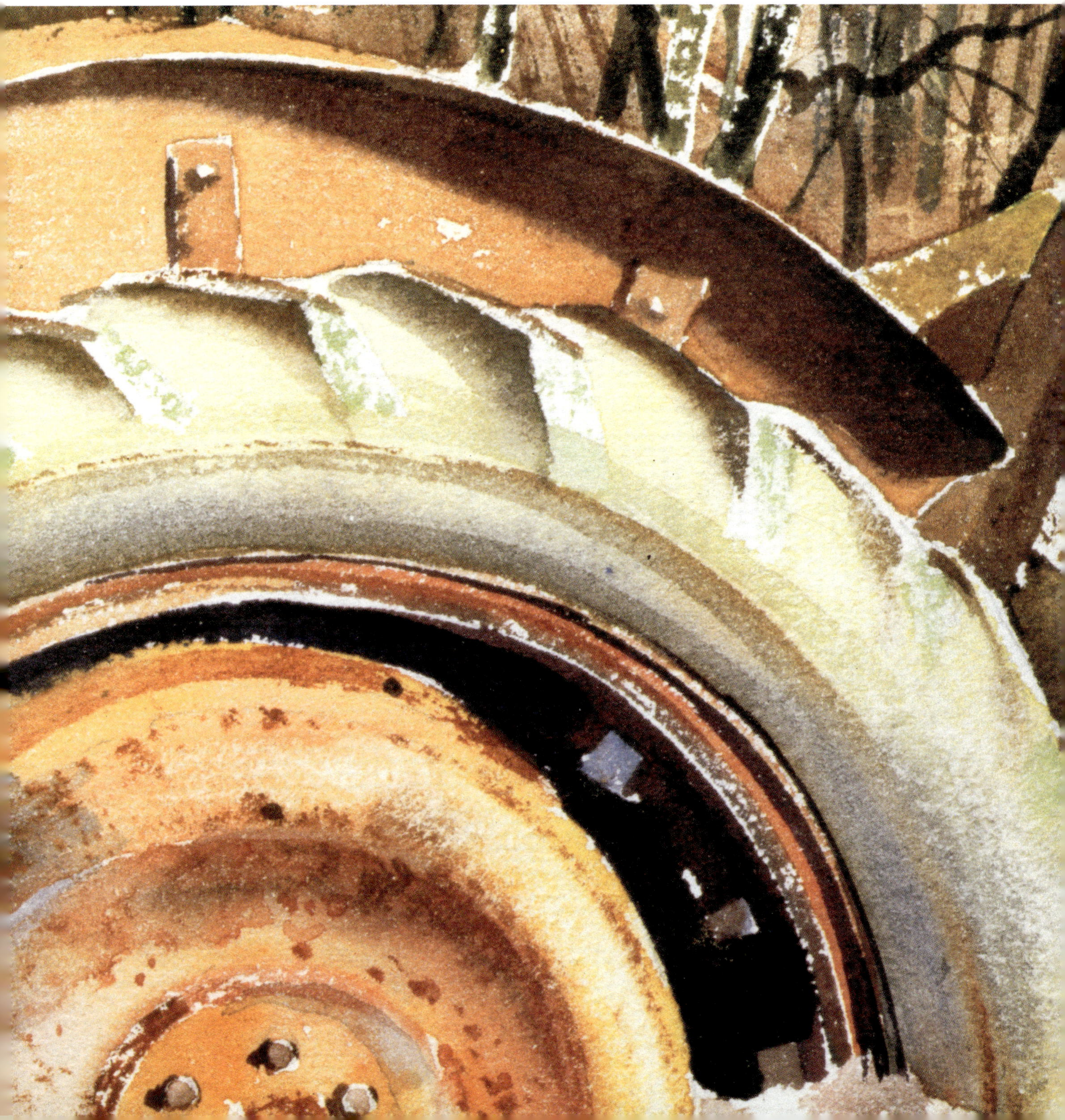

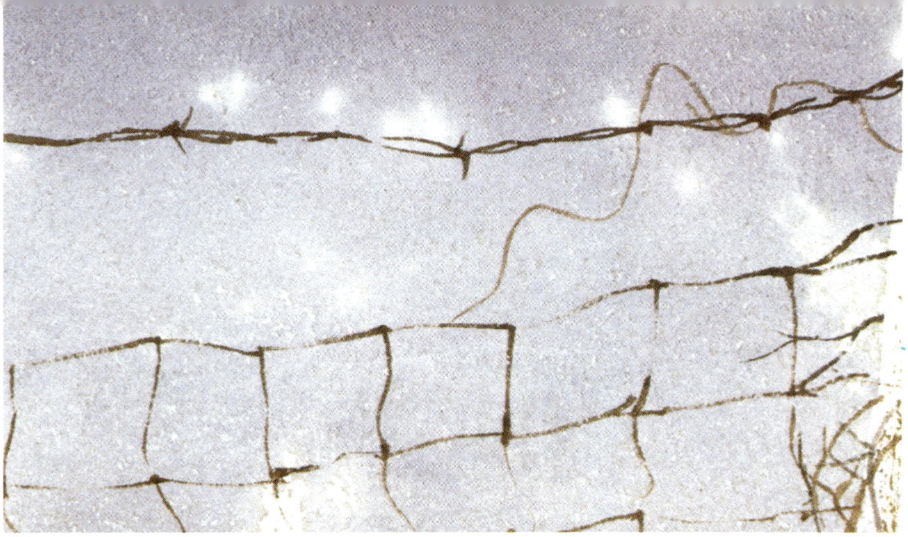

Against the soft blue wash of the sky (Cobalt and Ultramarine Blues), I painted the barb wire with a fine-tipped dry brush. Just a few "barbs" were necessary to make the wire look realistic and also more interesting than merely a wavy line across the paper.

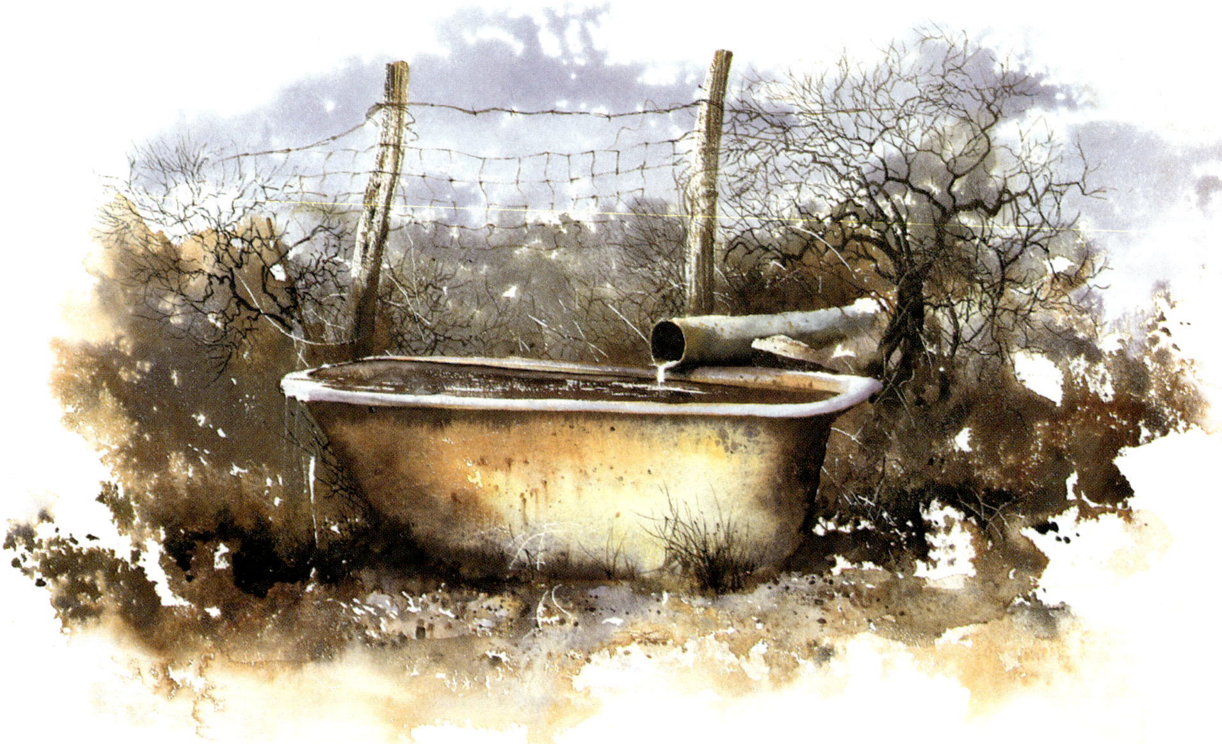

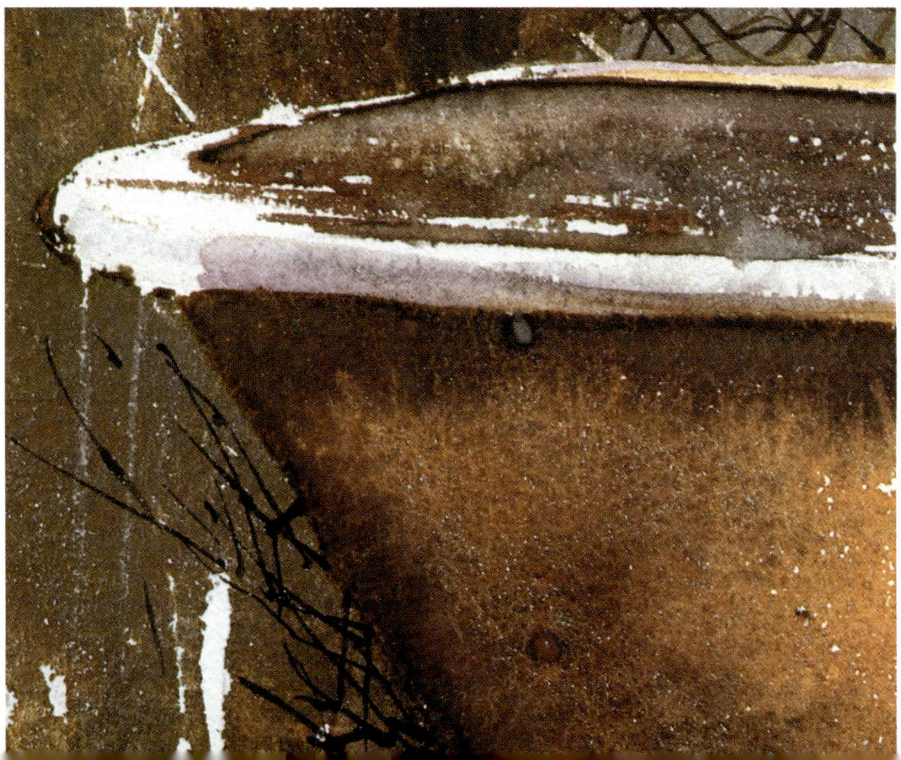

All around the edge of the tub, I used masking fluid to keep the rim hard and clear against the indistinct shrubbery beyond. This was especially useful in showing the water overflowing the rim onto the ground.

I selected my colors carefully to capture the texture of the tub's surface. First I applied Cadmium Orange to the tub's side and then dropped the other colors in, allowing them to flow and blend together on the paper. The other colors I used here were Burnt Sienna, Sap Green, Indigo, Ultramarine Blue, and Alizarin Carmine. When the wash was dry, I used drybrush to obtain more detail and texture.

The pipe's opening edge and the water that flows from it were masked out first. Then a weak Cobalt Blue wash was applied to the top side of the pipe, followed by a wash of Indigo for the underside. When the wash was dry I dotted the pipe with Burnt Sienna to create a rusting effect.

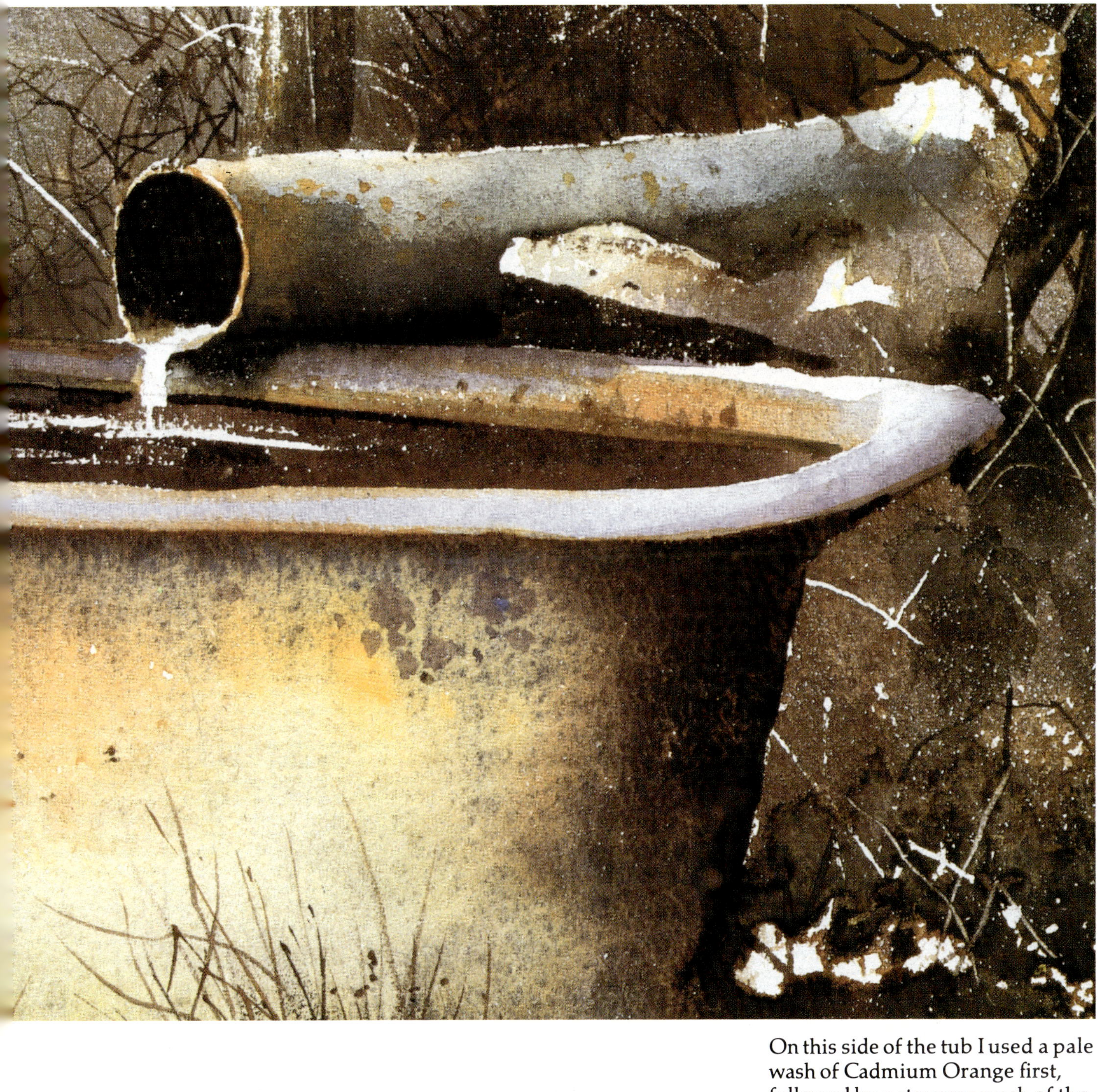

On this side of the tub I used a pale wash of Cadmium Orange first, followed by a stronger wash of the same, and then dots of Ultramarine Blue when dry. Touches of Alizarin Carmine added specks of rust over the Cadmium Orange.

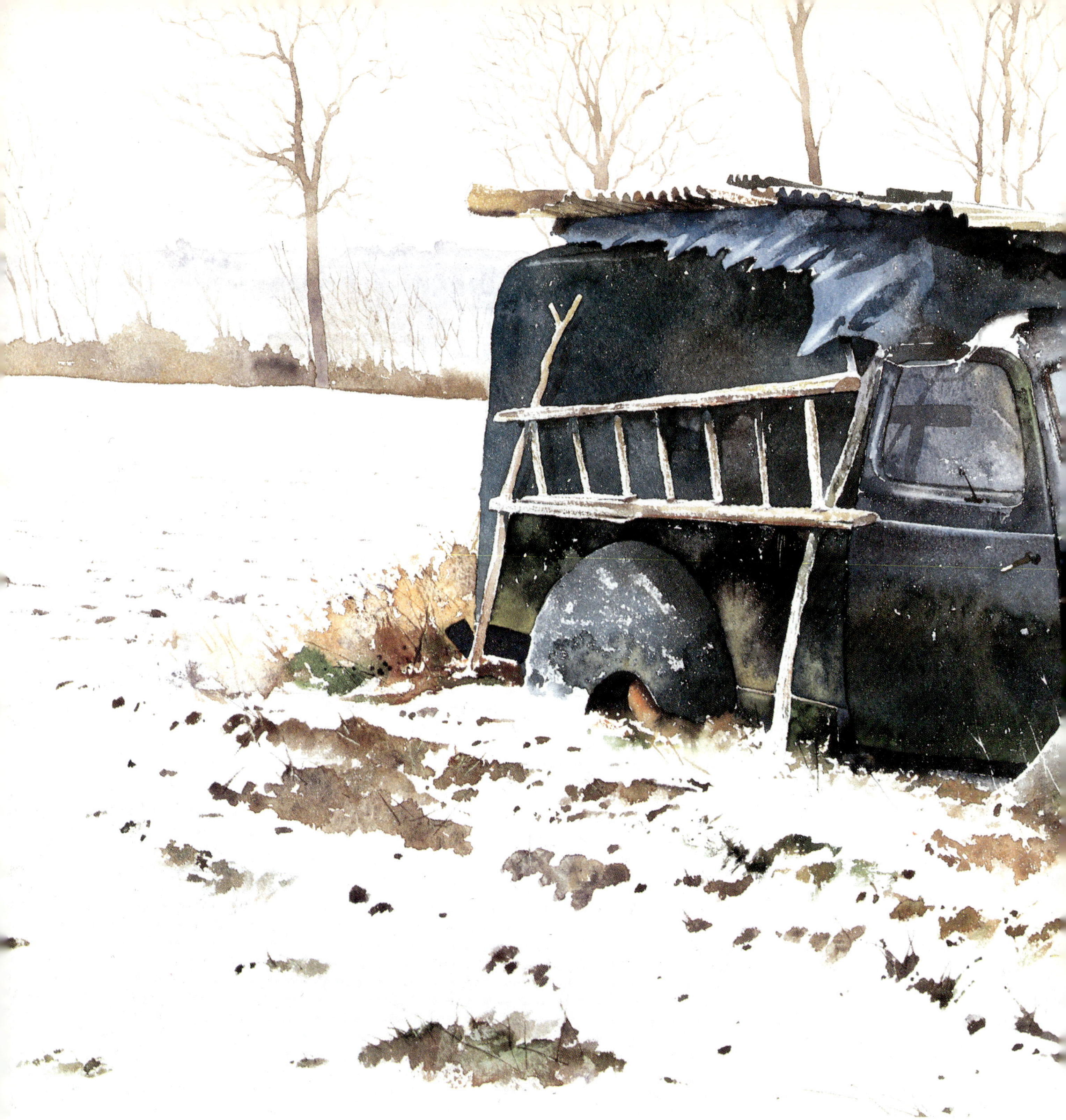

FADED PAINT ON METAL

I came across this old van while driving through a remote part of the country. What a great painting subject! It had all the elements that interest me most as a watercolor painter. It seemed as if it was home for a tramp or a den for some kids, for someone had fixed the roof to keep out the rain.

The scene was bleak and isolated in the melting snow that had fallen a few days before, making the van appear stark against the tall, leafless trees. The vehicle was in an advanced state of dilapidation, and a whole range of naturally evolving colors seemed to be spreading over the original dark blue paint, as if to absorb the man-made van back into the earth. I trudged around the field and examined the van's paintwork closely. I took some reference photos for work later: it was too cold to draw or paint on the spot.

Back in my studio, I planned a painting of the van. I decided to play down the background to make the van a central, dark, looming object. Once I had fixed the composition in my mind, I concentrated on how to render the

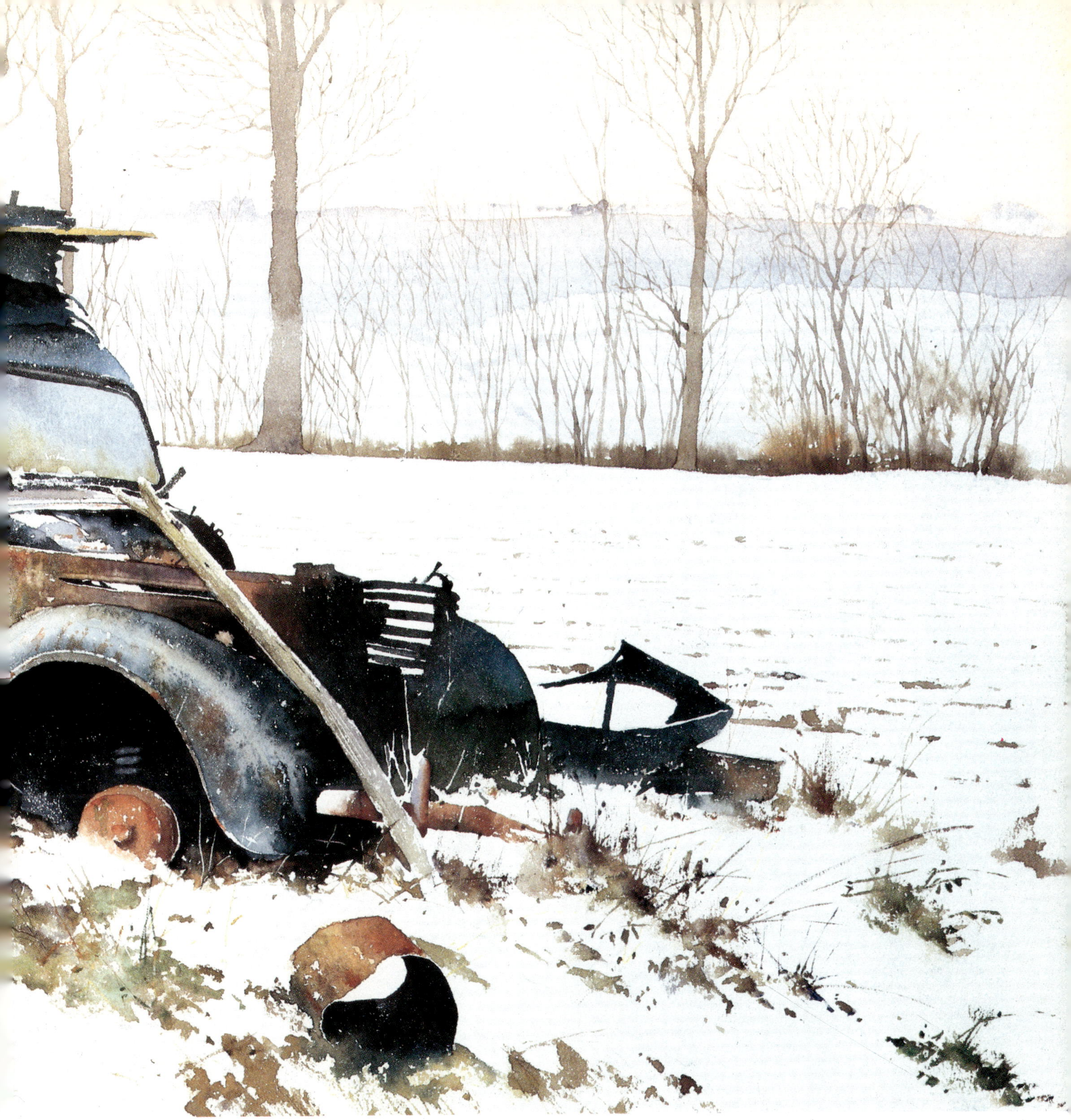

character of the color changes in the paintwork. The easiest way to emphasize a subject in a painting is to exaggerate the size, shape, or color: in this case, there was no way I could make the component parts of the van larger, so the emphasis had to be in the color and texture. First, color: I made the rust a little more red than in reality; I made the near-front fender a little more bleached by the sun; I pushed the dark blue into a dark green along the lower edge of the side; and I darkened the reflection in the windows with pale washes of Prussian Blue. The textural variations were more subtle. I did not use bold, wide drybrush strokes that would have given a very rough speckled surface; instead, I concentrated on overlaying broken, pale washes, lifting out color or dispersing it with ox gall, and allowing small white pockmarks to appear undisturbed on the paper's surface.

I used seven related colors to minimize strong contrasts and enhance the effect of subtle changes. The distant trees, fields, and sky were all stated in pale color, giving that cold, damp feel to the scene.

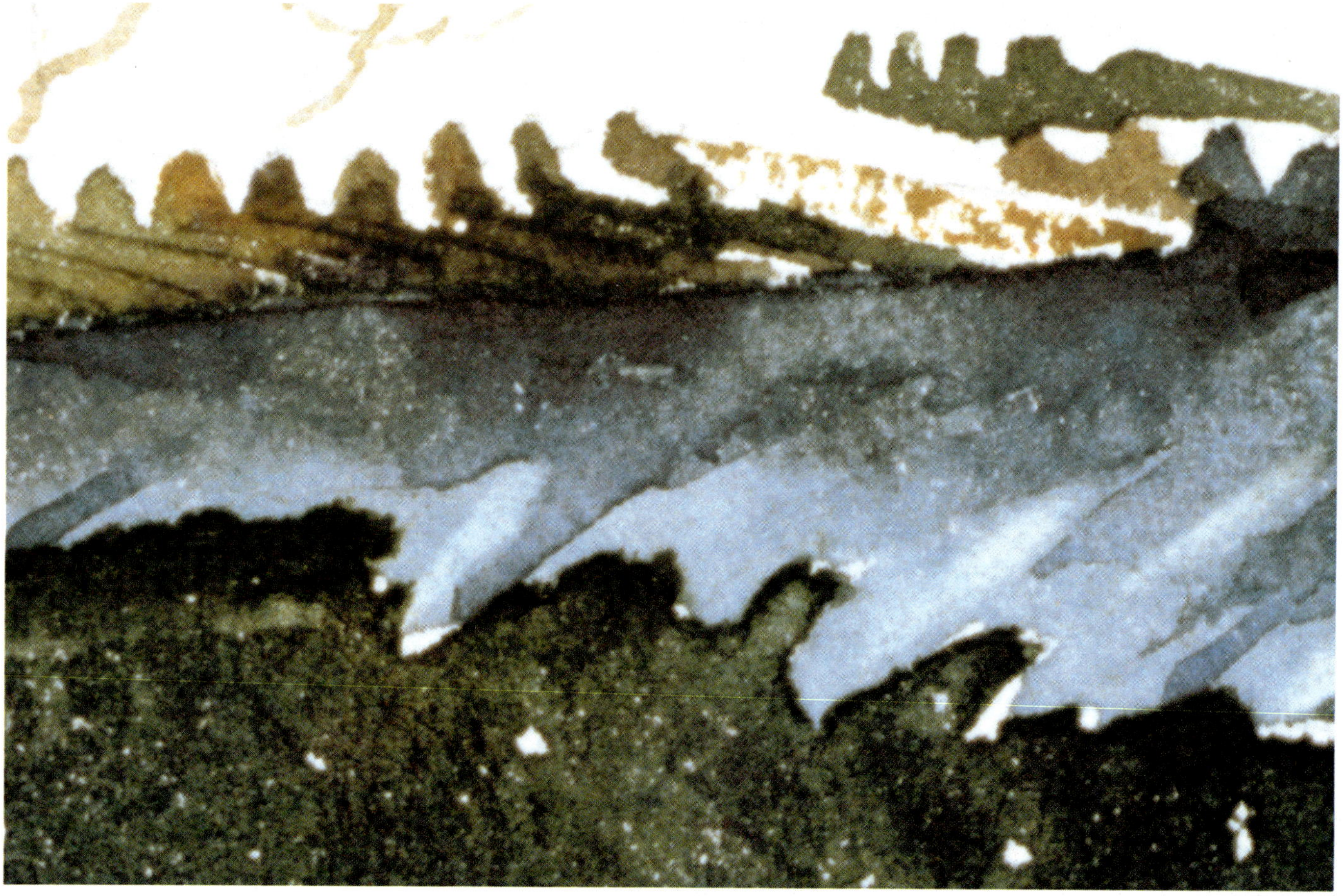

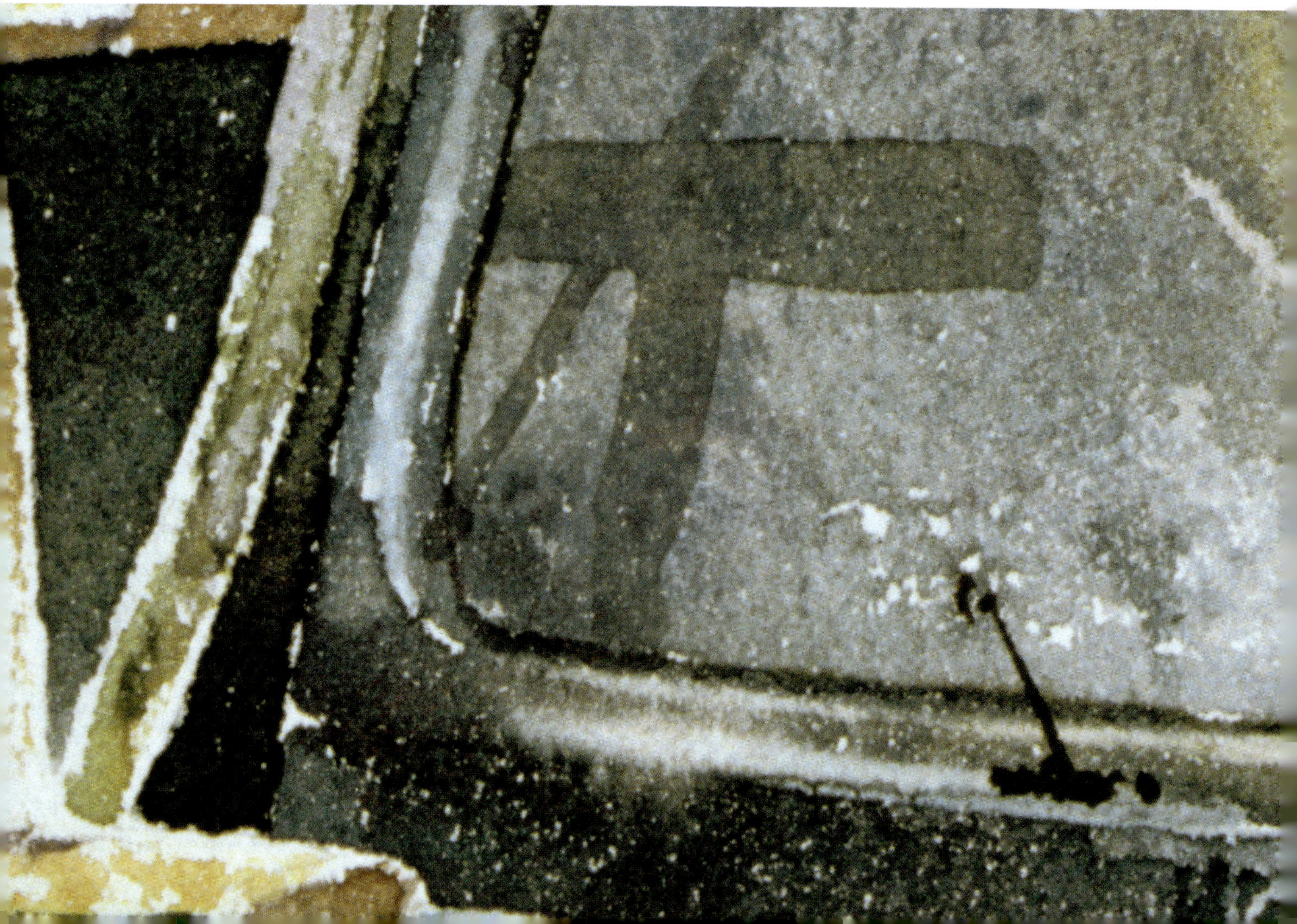

I painted the van panel by panel, starting on the side with the ladder, by loading two brushes with the same dilution of Prussian Blue, so that I could paint in an entire panel without any risk of the color changing or drying out and creating an unwanted hard edge.

In this detail, I laid in the pale wash of the tarpaulin, butting it up to the dark blue wash of the side of the van, after it had dried. This created a hard edge, which I exaggerated by making the tarpaulin edge very ragged. Next, I painted in the underside of the sheet of corrugated iron and streaked in a drybrush stroke to simulate its speckled edge. When this was dry, I deepened the shadows underneath the corrugated iron with a second wash of Prussian Blue, all the while varying the intensity of the color, and lifted out some small streaks to create the gaps between shadows on the tarpaulin.

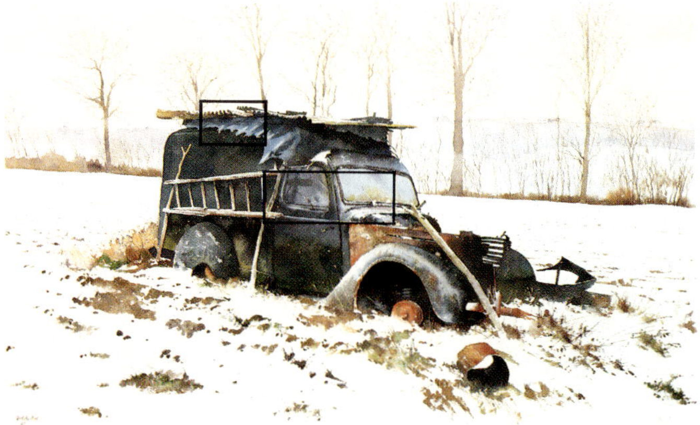

The key to the successful rendering of the glass and steel in this detail is in the edges and highlights. By working from panel to panel and allowing the paint to dry, I created those fine, dark hard edges where the door frame meets the glass and in the shadow where the front edge of the door meets the frame of the windshield. I made the side window darker than the windshield and added a dark shadow of the ladder, then concentrated on creating the modeling along the bottom of the side window, by lifting out very fine highlight edges. Notice the fine pinprick holes in the surface of the main wash that are the natural effect of pigment laid on a lightly pitted paper surface.

Along the top edge surface of the hood, I used the surface of the white paper and some brisk drybrush. The windshield was a thin wash of Prussian Blue, with a touch of a dirty yellow added and laid in over a masked-out wiper.

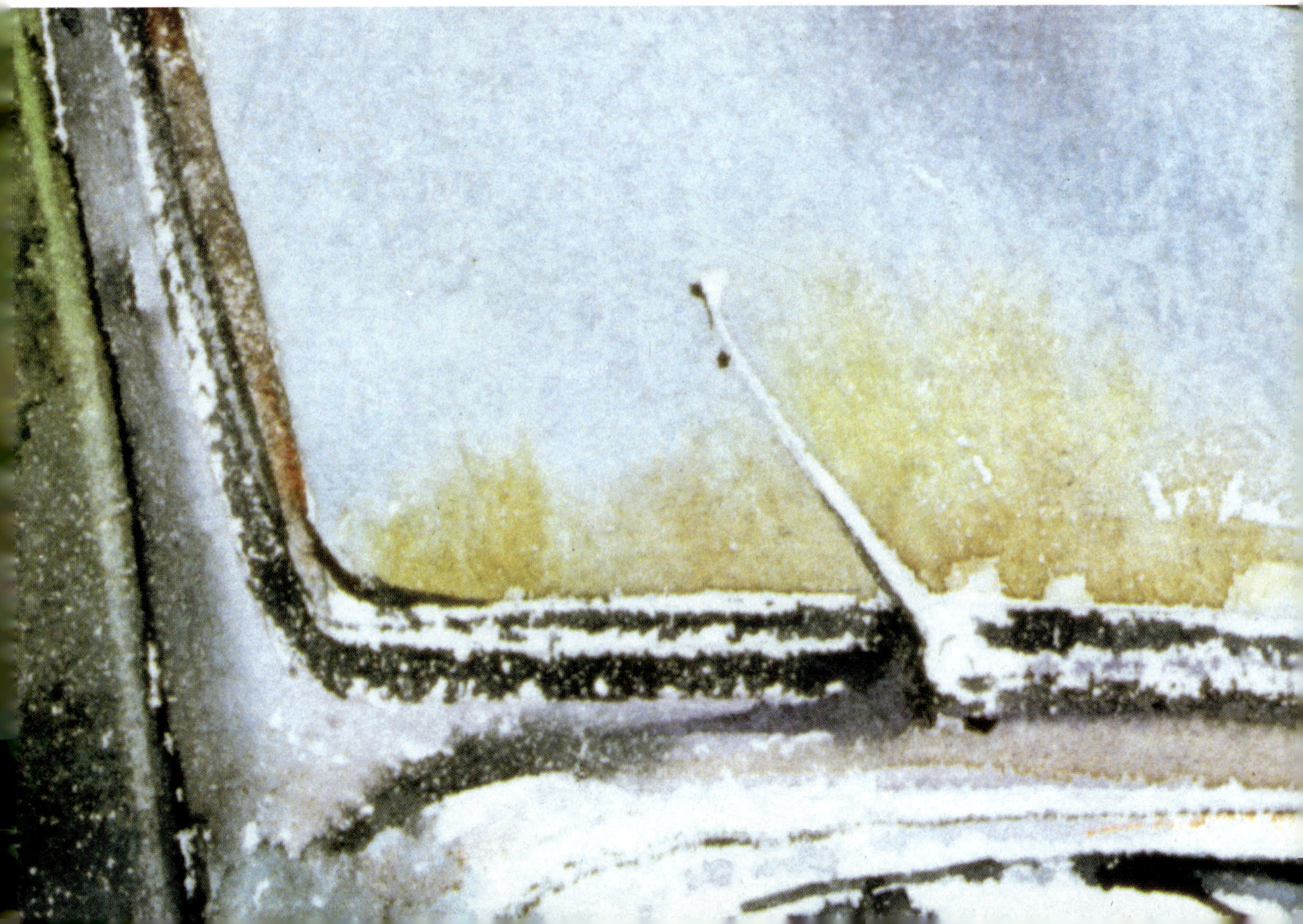

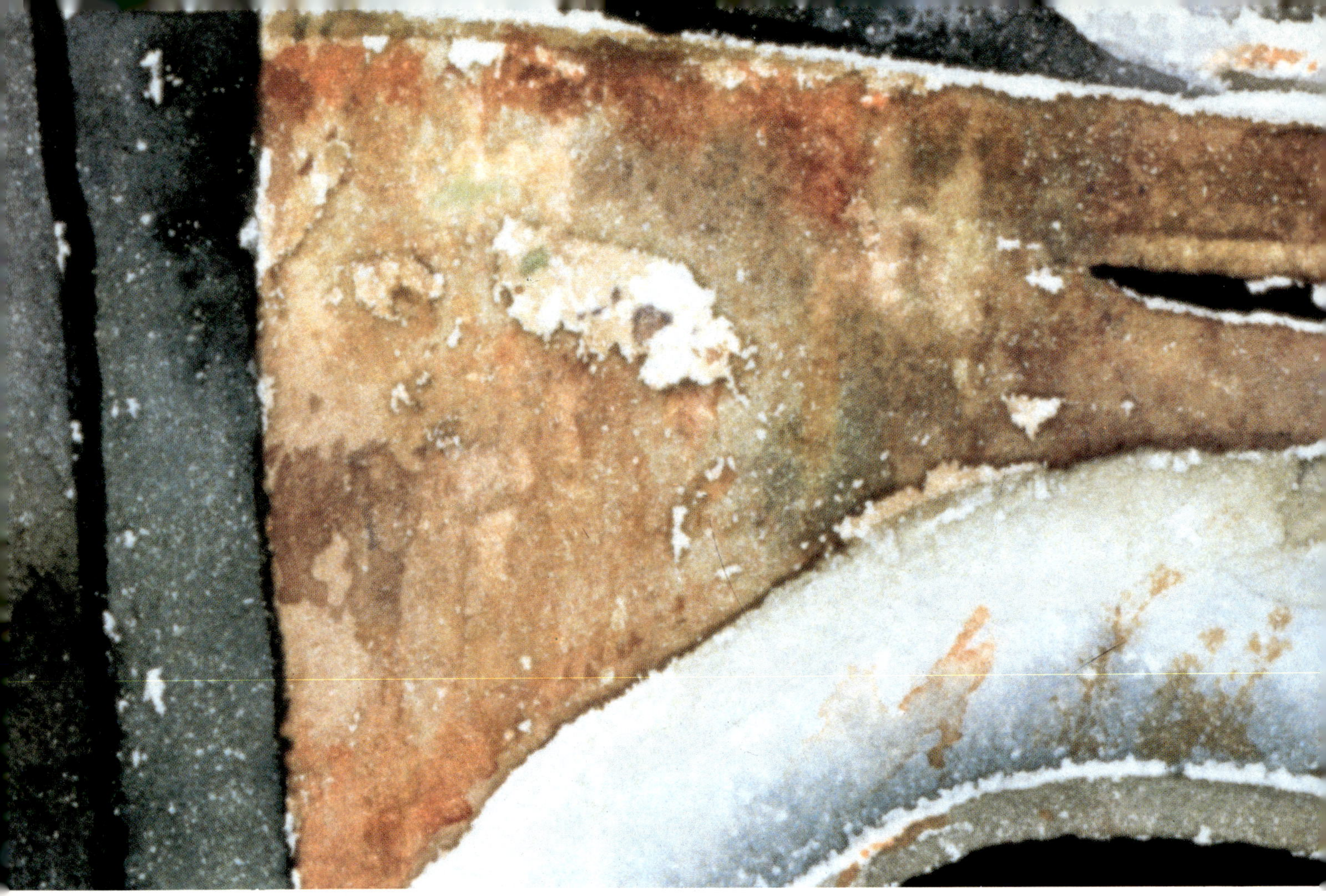

I think that the front fender and the rusty engine panel are the focal area of the whole painting: I certainly concentrated on a rich and varied texture in both these areas. The rusty engine panel was built up with a pair of thin washes of Cadmium Orange, streaked, blotched, and interfered with by introducing Prussian Blue in varying densities. The graphic qualities of the watercolor pigment do most of the work, and it is worth noting that I did not push the color about on the paper, once it was there.

I washed in the front fender with a brushload of Prussian Blue, then while the paint was still wet I swept in one stroke of a brush tipped with ox gall. Instant drama—the pigment fled away from the line of ox gall, leaving a nice, soft-edged highlight around the fender. When this was nearly dry, I touched in a little Cadmium Orange to suggest some patches of rust.

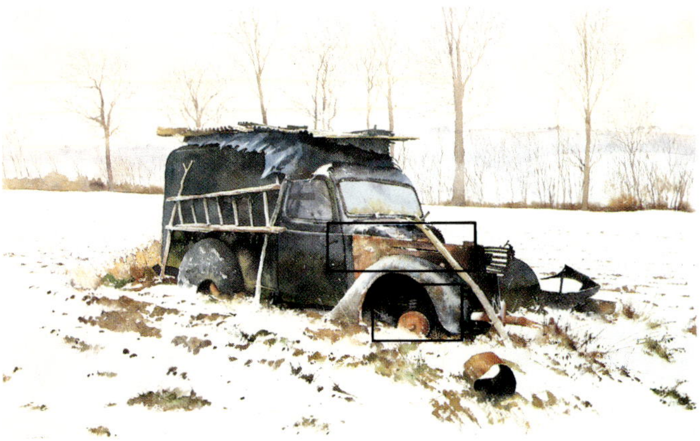

The outside of the fender was rendered as described in the caption on the left. The inside of the wheel arch provides a contrast to all the other washed-out and dappled areas of paint and rust, because it has pure deep color. An even rich wash of Prussian Blue went in first, and I smudged out three small vent holes when it was nearly dry. I painted the brake drum with Cadmium Orange, keeping surface texture to a minimum, and dropped in a shadow under the axle stump in the center of the drum with a touch of Prussian Blue. These two colors also became the dead grass peeping out from under the melting snow: there was no need to change color, because it is the tonal value of the grass in the shadow of the fender that is most important.

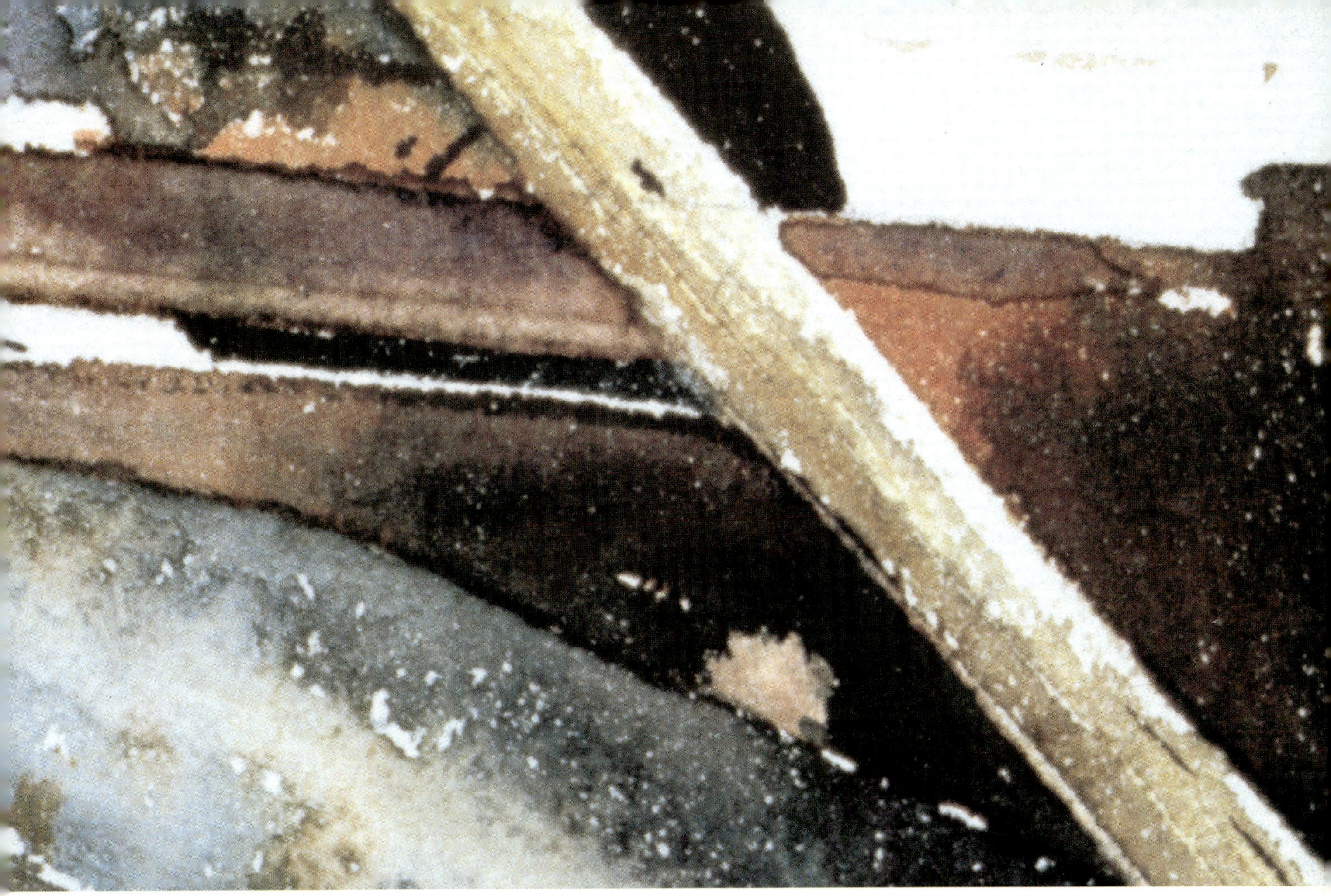

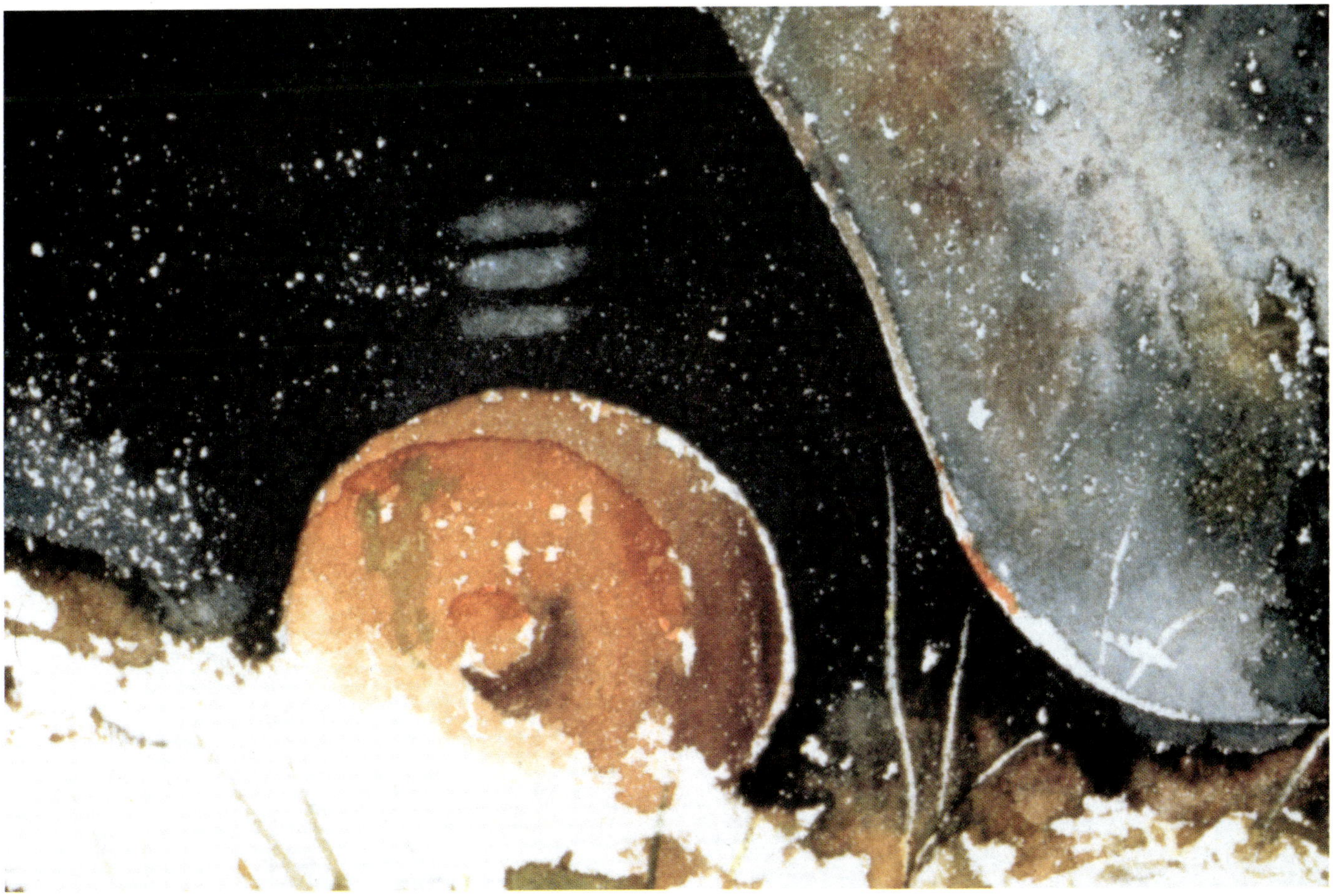

OLD MACHINERY REFLECTED IN WATER

I used to visit a nearby farm that stocked one of the largest collections of traction engines in the country. I spent a lot of time painting the engines, many of which were rusting and in need of repair.

The dramatic reflections here are the result of the frequent floods in the flat East Anglia countryside, which have provided me with much good painting material. Usually the floodwaters are quite still and reflect images like a mirror.

Traction engines are far too prized to be found in a setting like this now, though when I was young I can remember seeing the rusting hulks standing in the corners of a field. For this scene I have relied on memory and a few photos I took before these engines were all auctioned off.

It's very easy when painting such a bold subject to allow the picture to become heavy, especially in the treatment of the traction engine. And so here I have paid particular attention to keeping the colors light and subtle, using darker colors only where they are really needed, as in the foreground grass and the shadows on the traction engine.

To paint reflections with any sense of reality it is important to understand what reflections are. This is not as simple as it might appear. Areas of reflection here are cut out by the grass banks, and totally new views are given of the objects being painted, as shown by the view of the underside of the engine. While all of this may sound obvious, getting it down on paper can be quite a task. I achieved this effect by turning the painting around continually and looking at it upside down, which helps me to see errors in perception before they get out of hand.

As usual, textures are an important consideration: the dark grass has been scraped repeatedly with the corner of a razor blade; and rust patches on the engine have been painted in with Burnt Sienna, as have patches of dirt on the wheels.

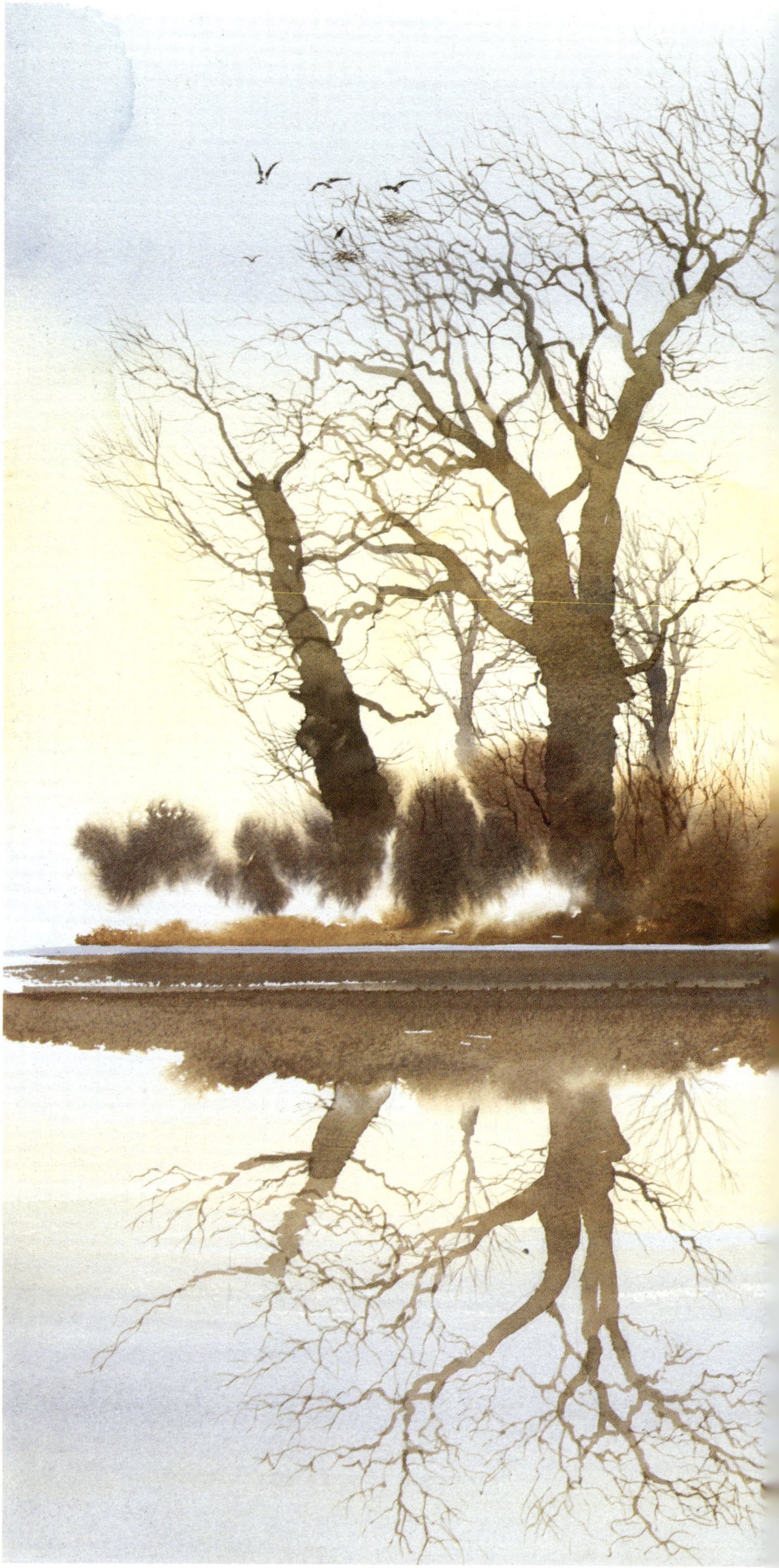

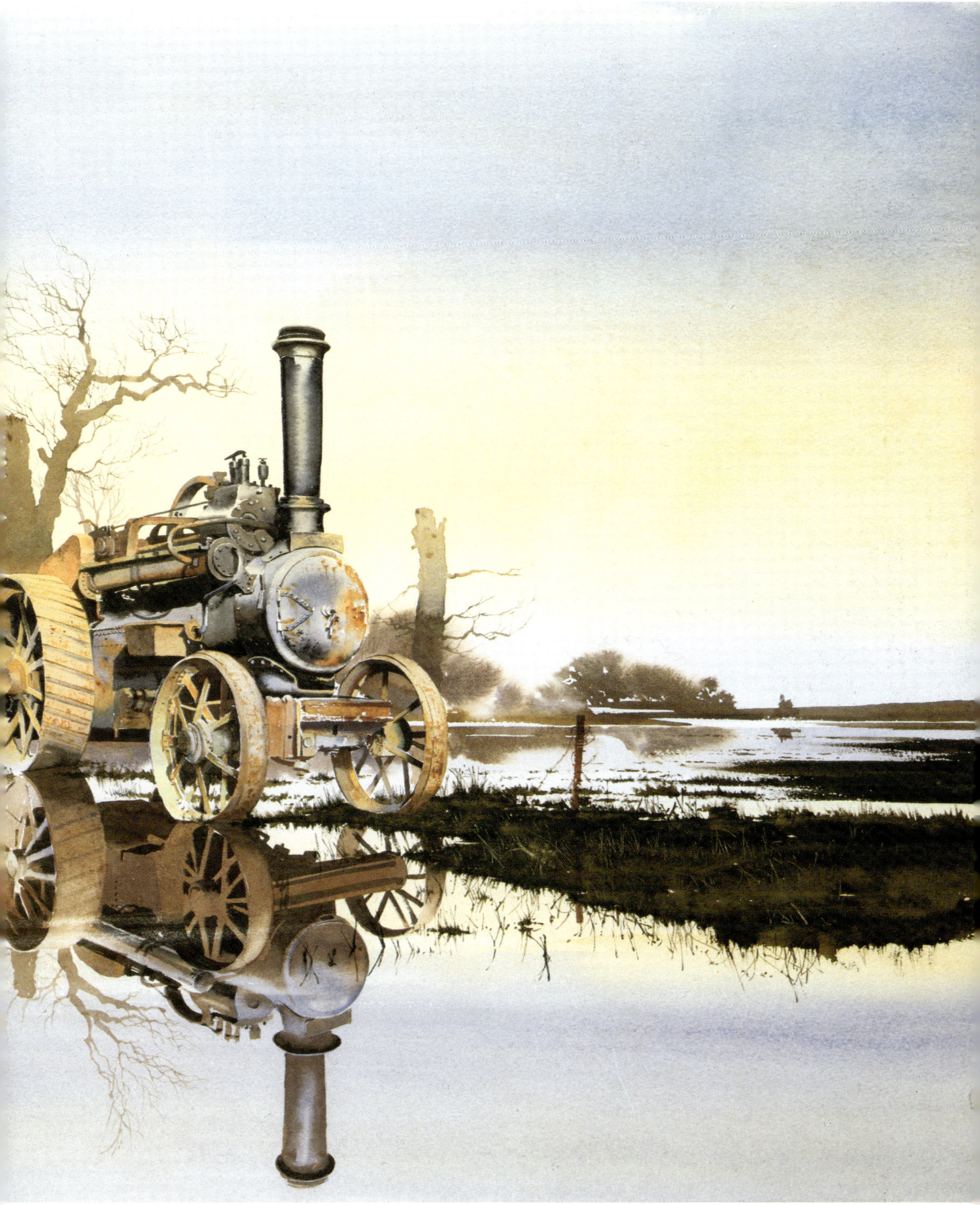

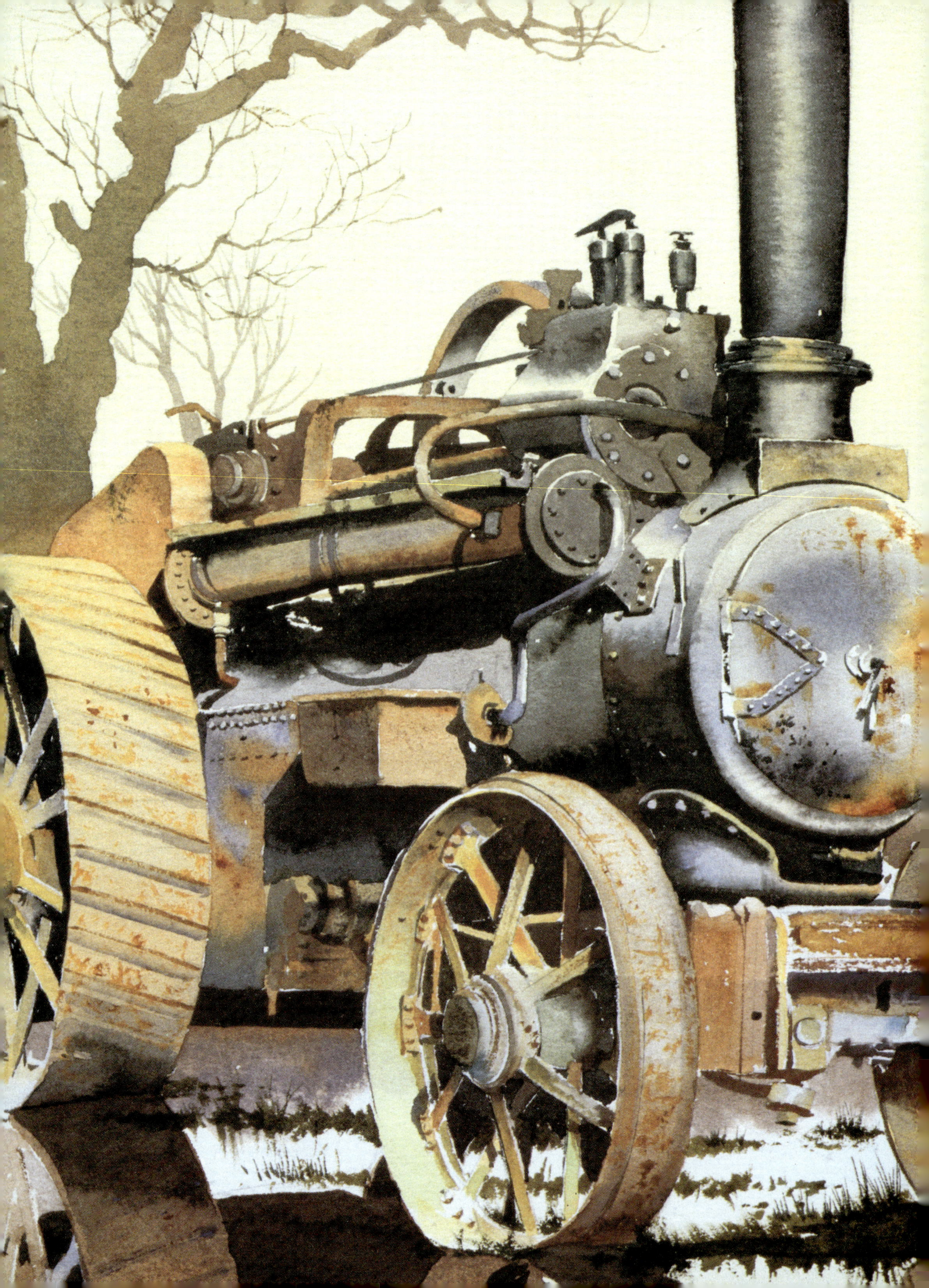

Because this traction engine is a fairly complicated bit of machinery, I made a light pencil sketch on the paper before painting. Edges were blocked out with masking fluid before the smooth background wash was laid in. A thin dry brush was used for the detail and the shadows. I allowed the tree trunk to the right of the engine to reflect the image of the stack, much as the water itself does below.

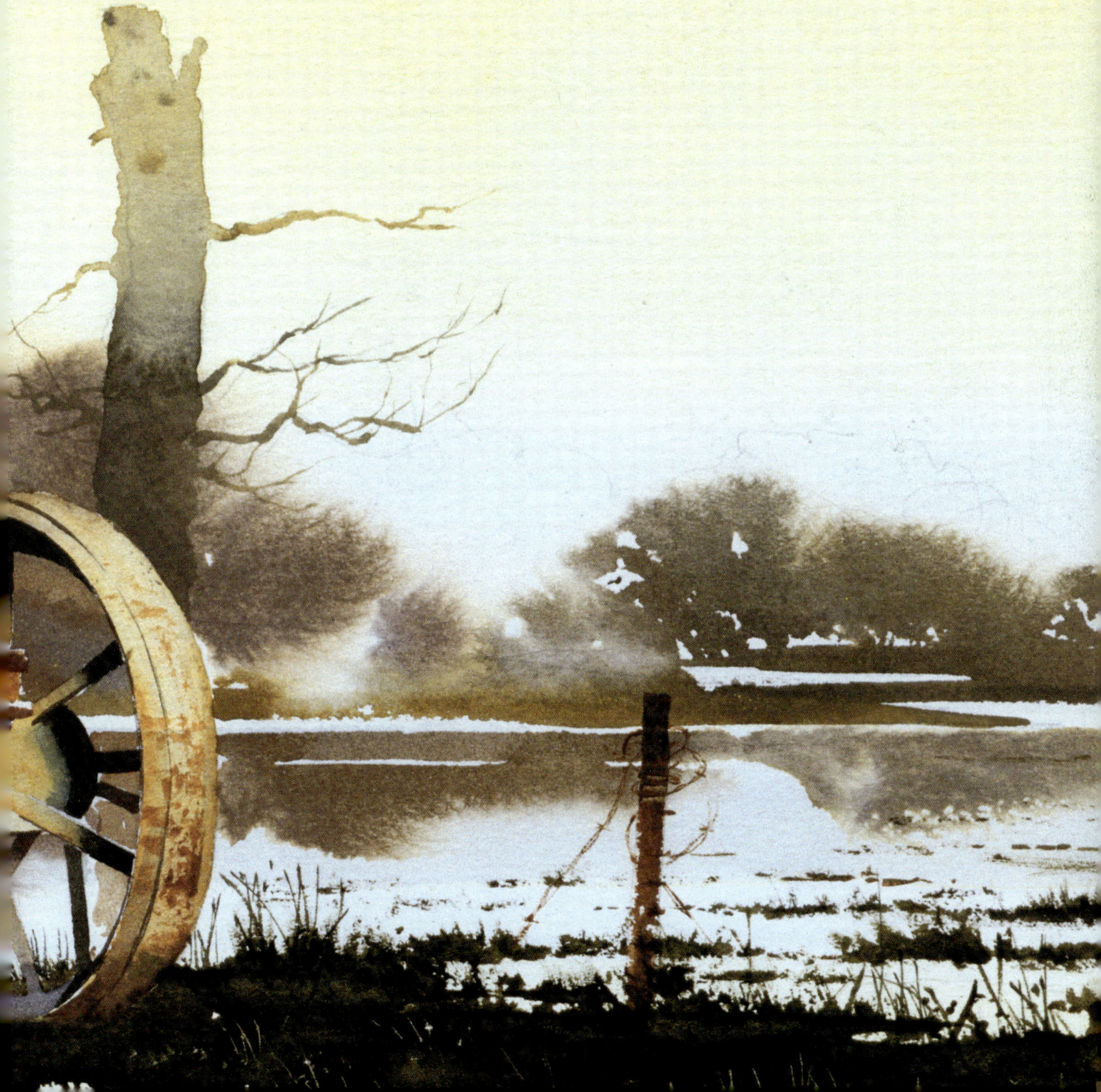

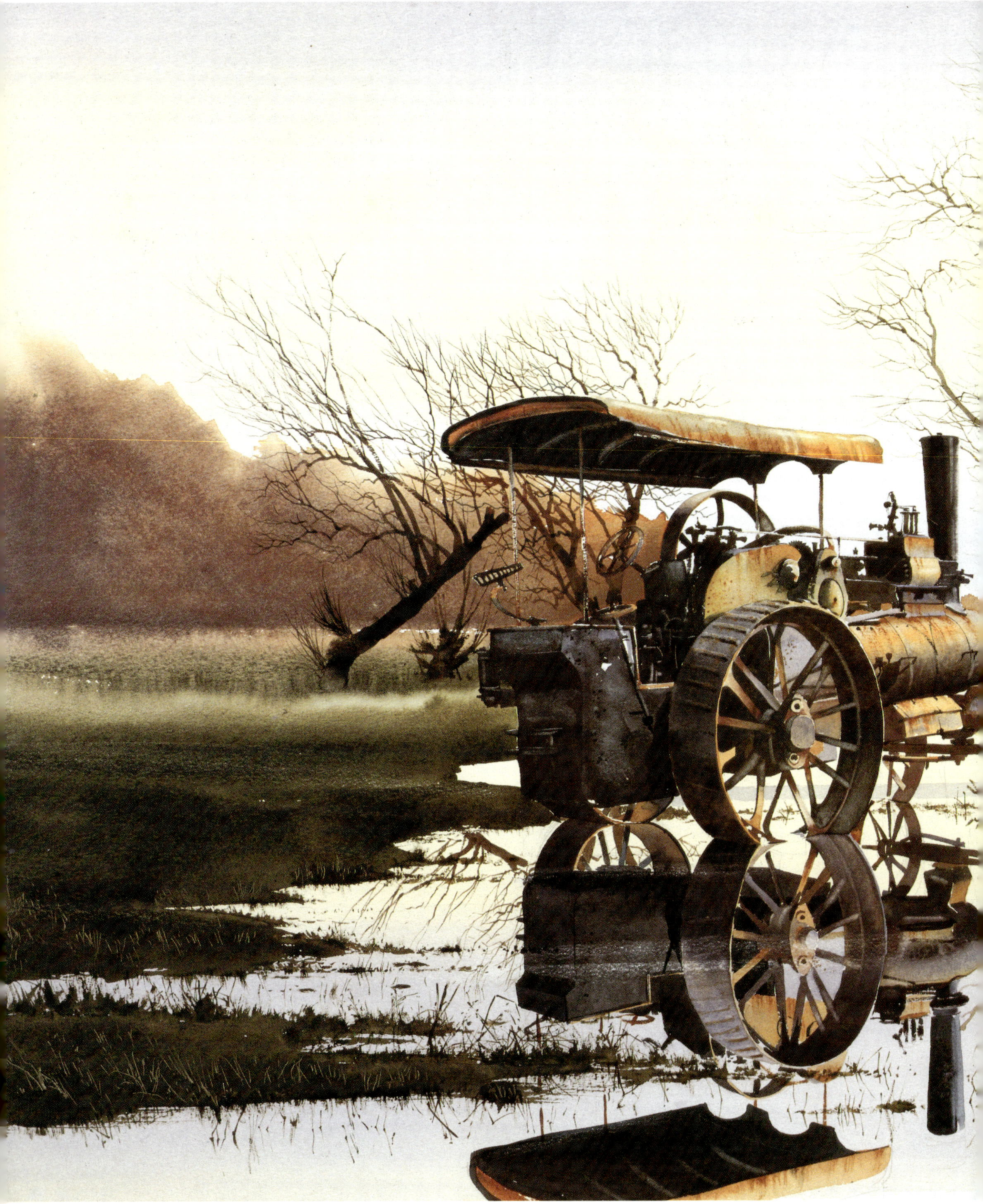

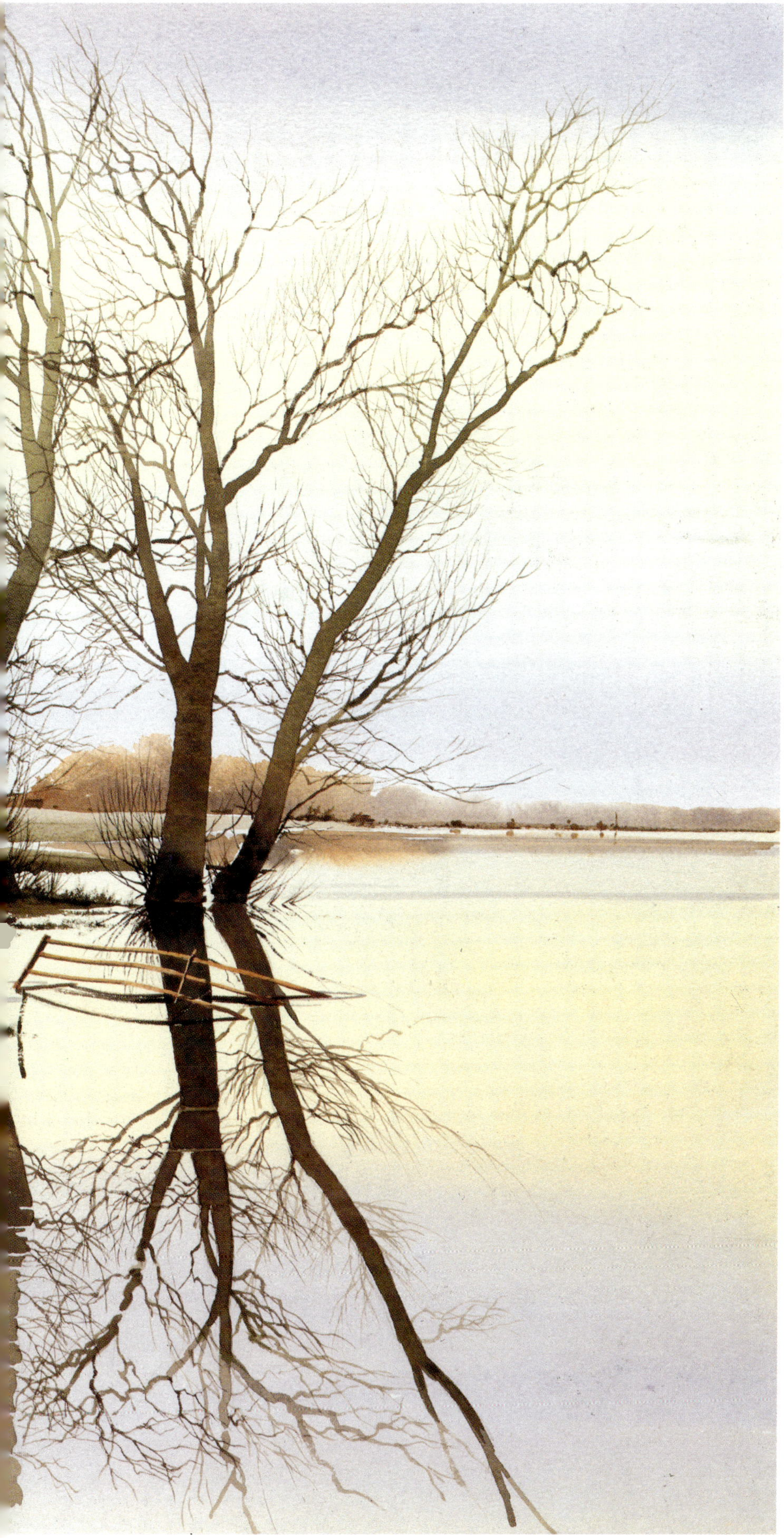

SUBTLE VARIATIONS IN RUST COLORS

As I mentioned earlier, flooding is quite common in my area of the country. In winter I have only to look through my window at home to see the meadows covered with water. It gives the landscape a new character. Views that were mundane before take on new dimensions when trees and bushes, patches of grass, and whatever else is about are mirrored in the flooded field, which is sometimes broken and disturbed by gusts of wind.

I prefer to paint winter scenes with the rust colors of the stark landscape. In summer the green foliage dominates, obliterating much of the structure that intrigues me. Trees in winter are subjects to paint on their own, with their twisted, angular shapes breaking up the landscape. Elms and willows dominate, the elms tall and angular, the willows with their slender upstretched branches. They lend themselves to the artist's brush and can be painted with an almost rhythmic motion. Practice is needed to create the skills that enable you to differentiate with a few strokes between the various kinds of trees. Branches don't just happen; they always have a pattern to their construction, however tangled they seem to be. They always must give the feeling of growing out of the tree, not being attached to the bark from the outside.

For most of the trunks and branches I used a bamboo brush; its uniquely malleable quality lends itself to the angular bends, twists, and turns of a tree's structure. For the fine twigs I used a size 1 or 2 sable brush, enabling me to produce lines of a hair's thickness.

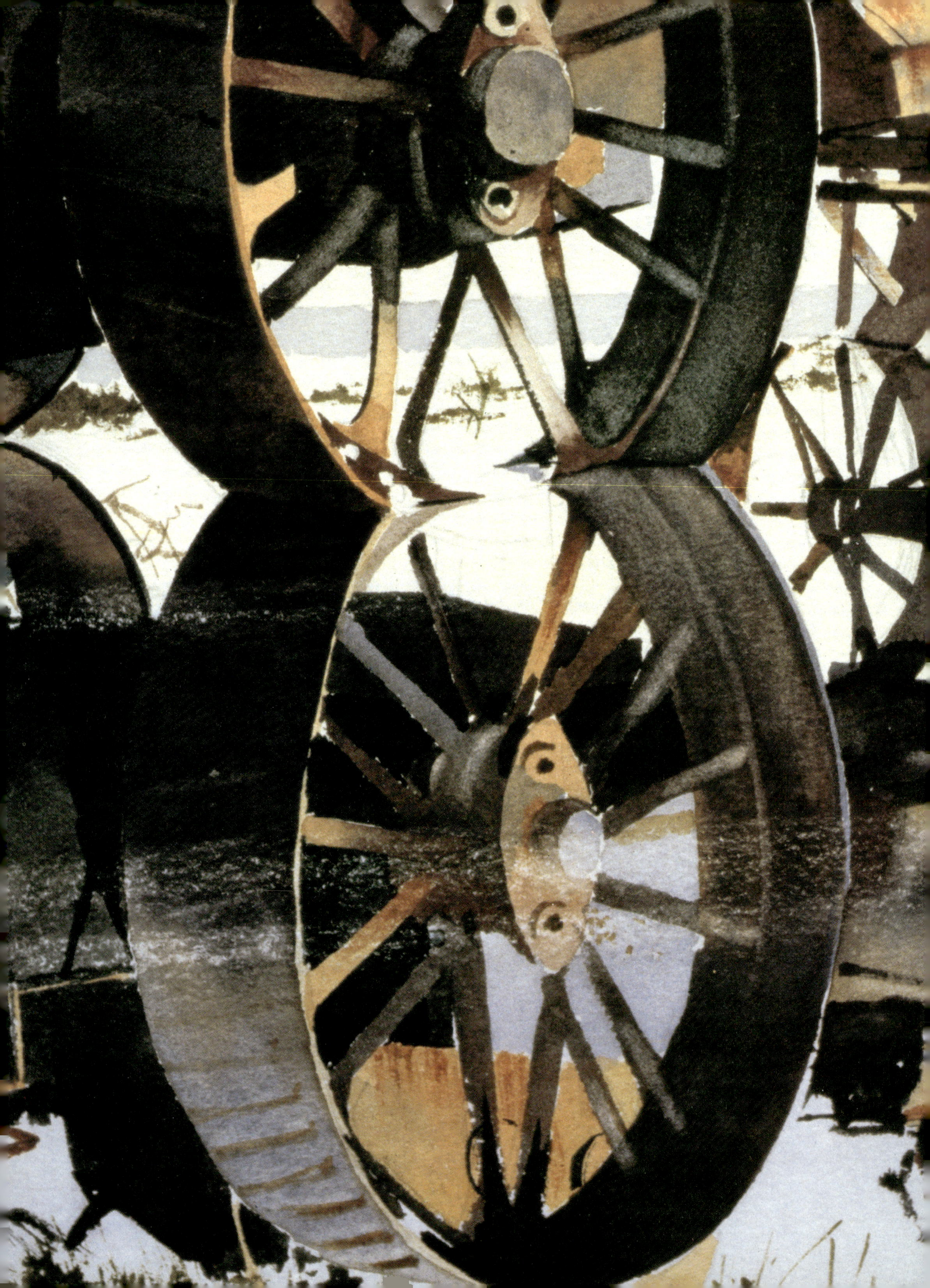

These wheels are almost identical, given the clearness of sky and water at the moment. The image has remained sharp against the background with the use of masking fluid, which keeps the intricate outline clear of paint. The wheel's reflection is slightly bluer than the wheel itself, and I removed part of the paint with a brush run horizontally across the paper to create the appearance of ripples.

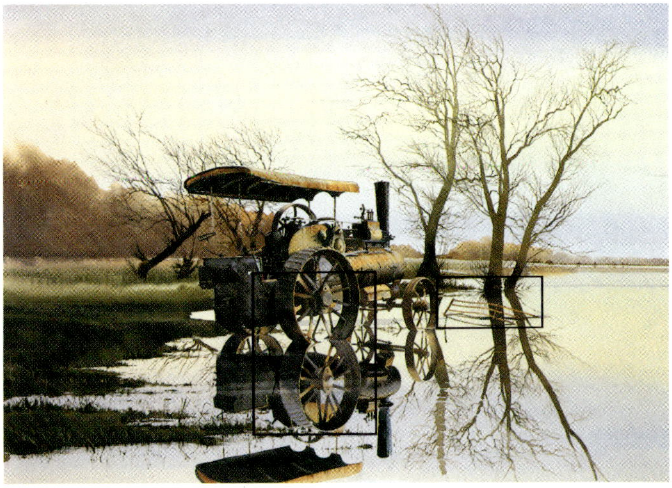

Masking fluid was used for some areas of the fence, then the pale water and dark tree forms were added. When the masking fluid was removed, I painted in the fence with Burnt Sienna and then created its reflection in the water, turning the paper upside down to get the proper perspective.

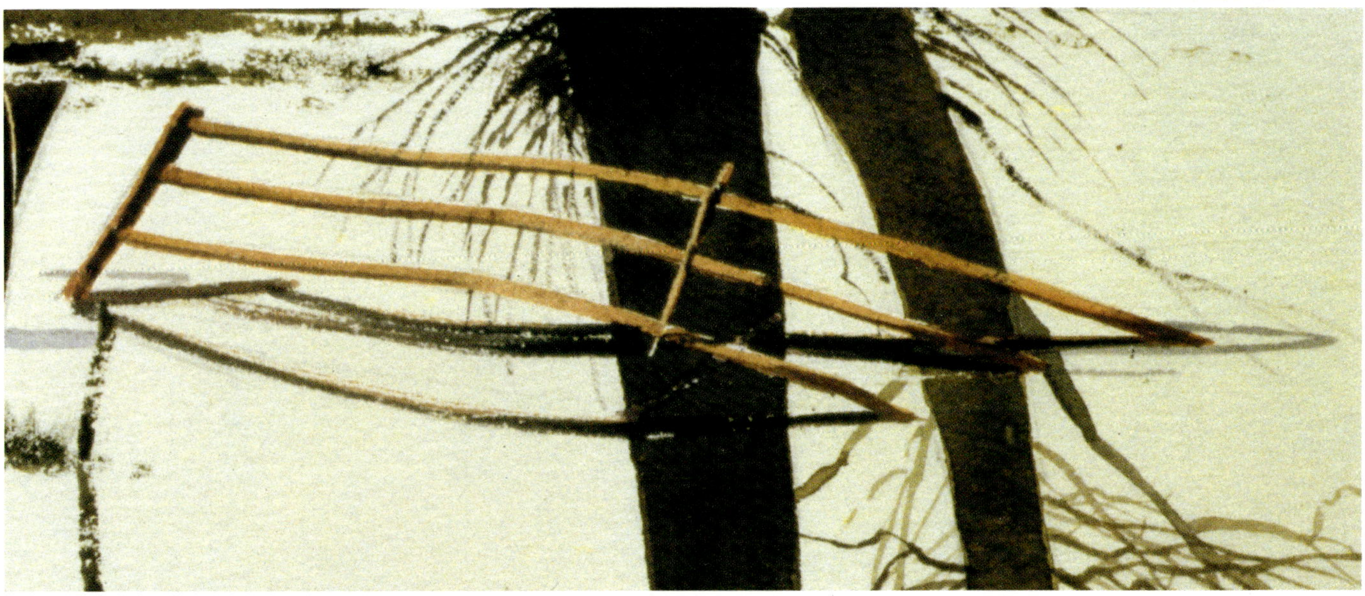

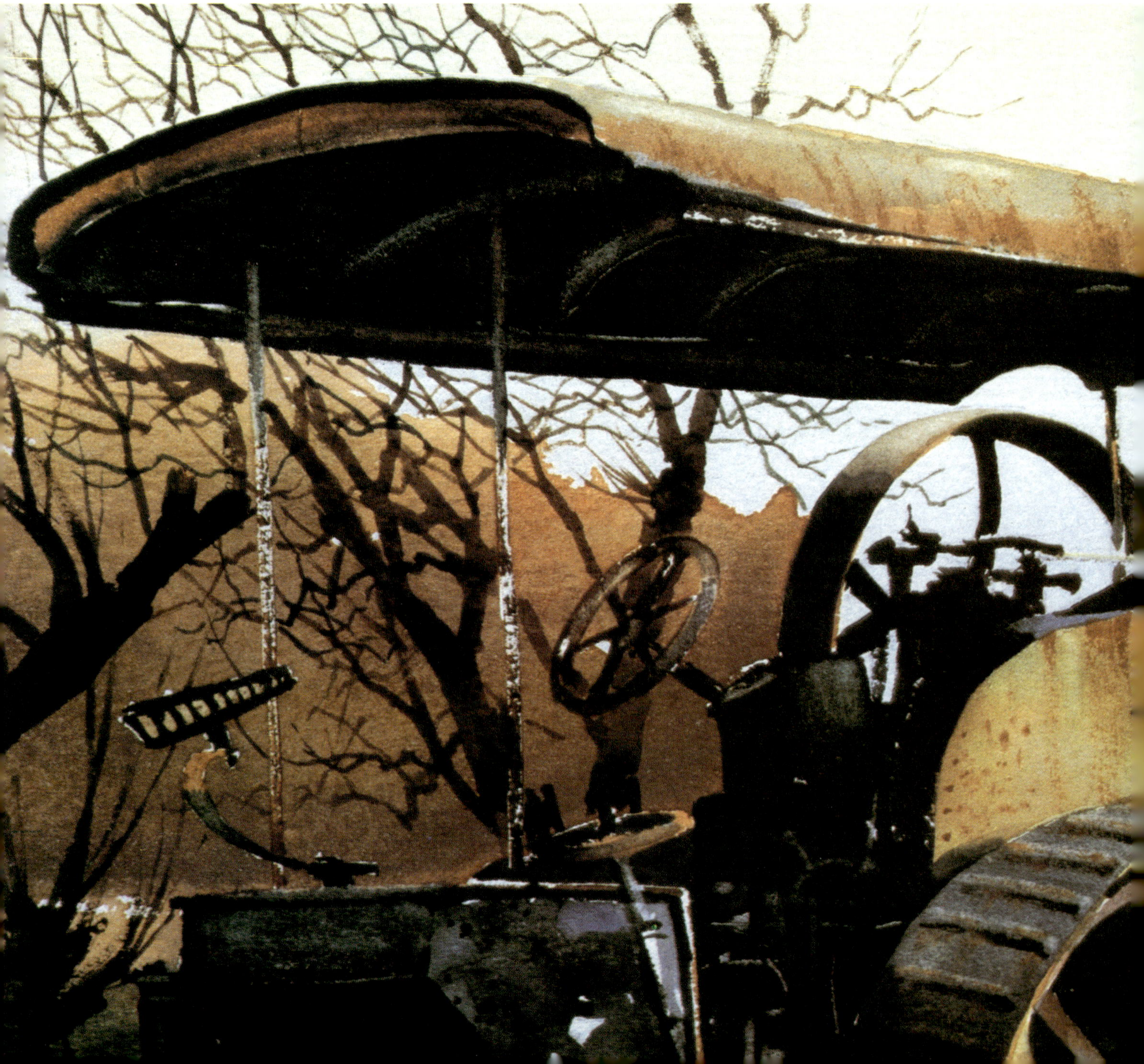

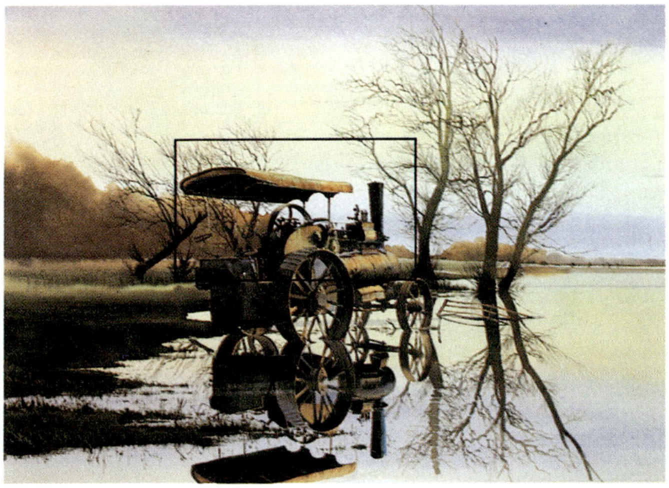

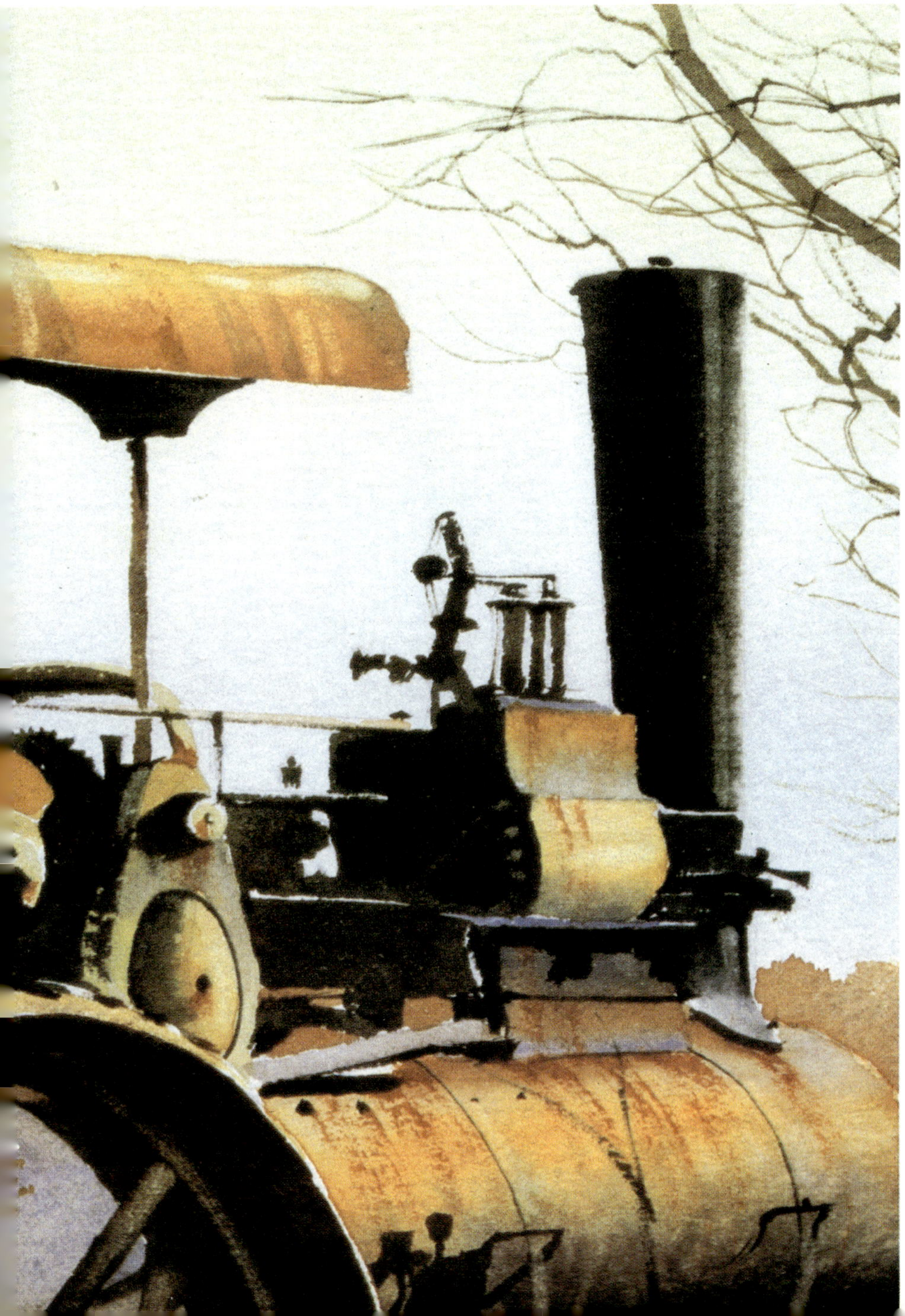

The rusting hulk provides rich colors and textures that are mostly applied by dry brushwork, using the irregularities of the paper to add to the rough texture. I built up the paint on the engine gradually, working on a small section at a time. There is always the danger of muddy colors and overworking, which usually is the result of trying to overpaint mistakes. Where colors have become too heavy or I wished to create a highlight, I gently rubbed the area with a tip of a wet brush and blotted away the excess with a bit of tissue, as shown on the tank here.

Masking fluid has been used for the details such as the steering wheel. Then the Burnt Sienna background was brushed on. Bits of white were left to brighten the area and create a new texture. A very dry brush was used over the wash when dry to create the filigree of tree forms.

WOOD AND VEGETATION

TWISTED TREE TRUNKS AND LARGE LEAVES

Old sheds make interesting subjects for paintings and as I wander through garden allotments, I am always intrigued by the variety and ingenuity of their construction. Frequently they are improvised from bits and pieces of widely differing shapes and textures. Roofs can be a crosshatch of corrugated iron sheeting and doors reused from abandoned houses.

The twisted willow struggling to grow in front of this shed was an added attraction. These sometimes eerie-looking trees are part of my local landscape and are found alongside the ditches and flat fields of the area. The whole scene provided a rich variety of color and texture, from the dilapidated old shed to the shapely rounded cabbages of the foreground.

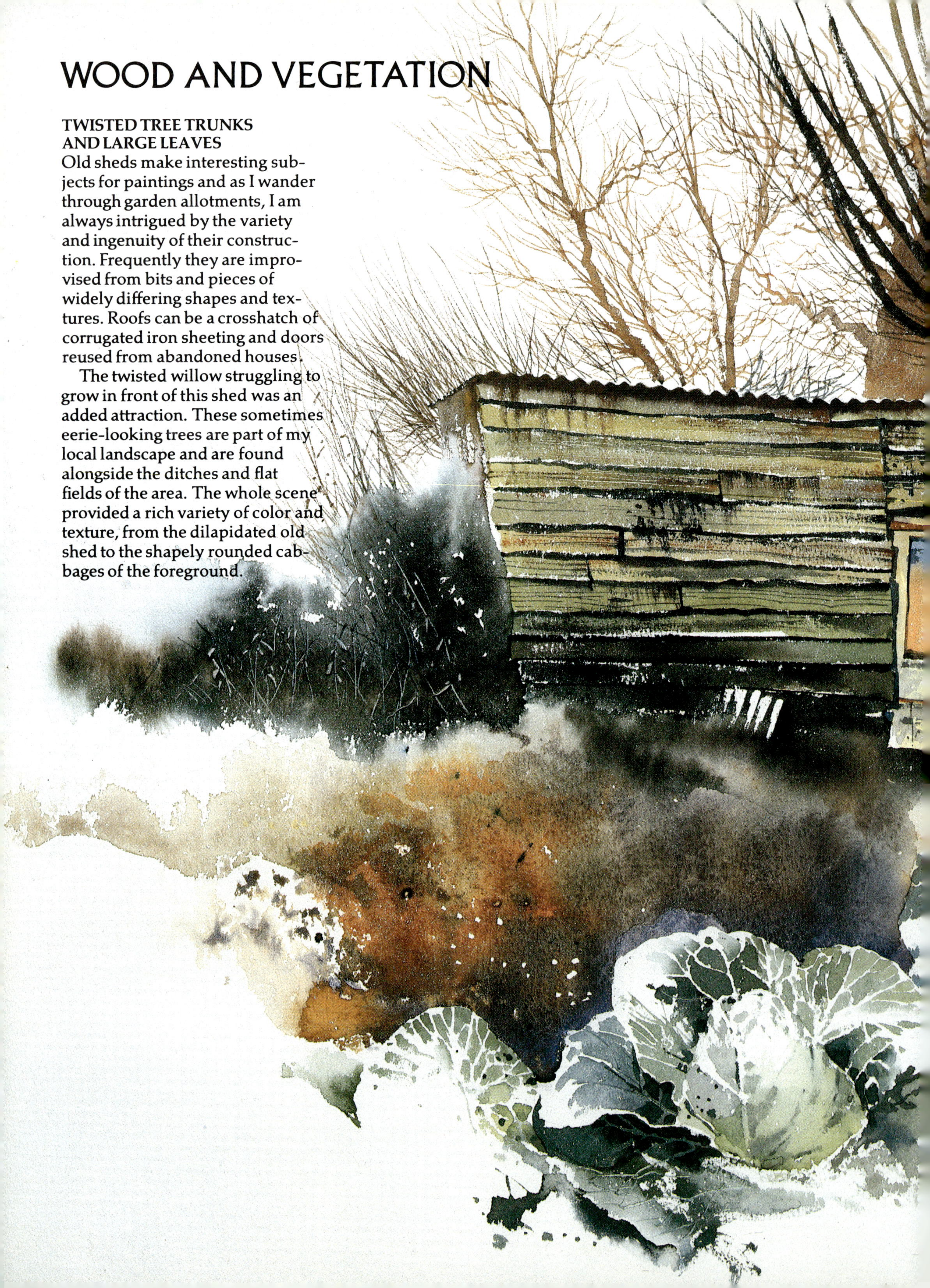

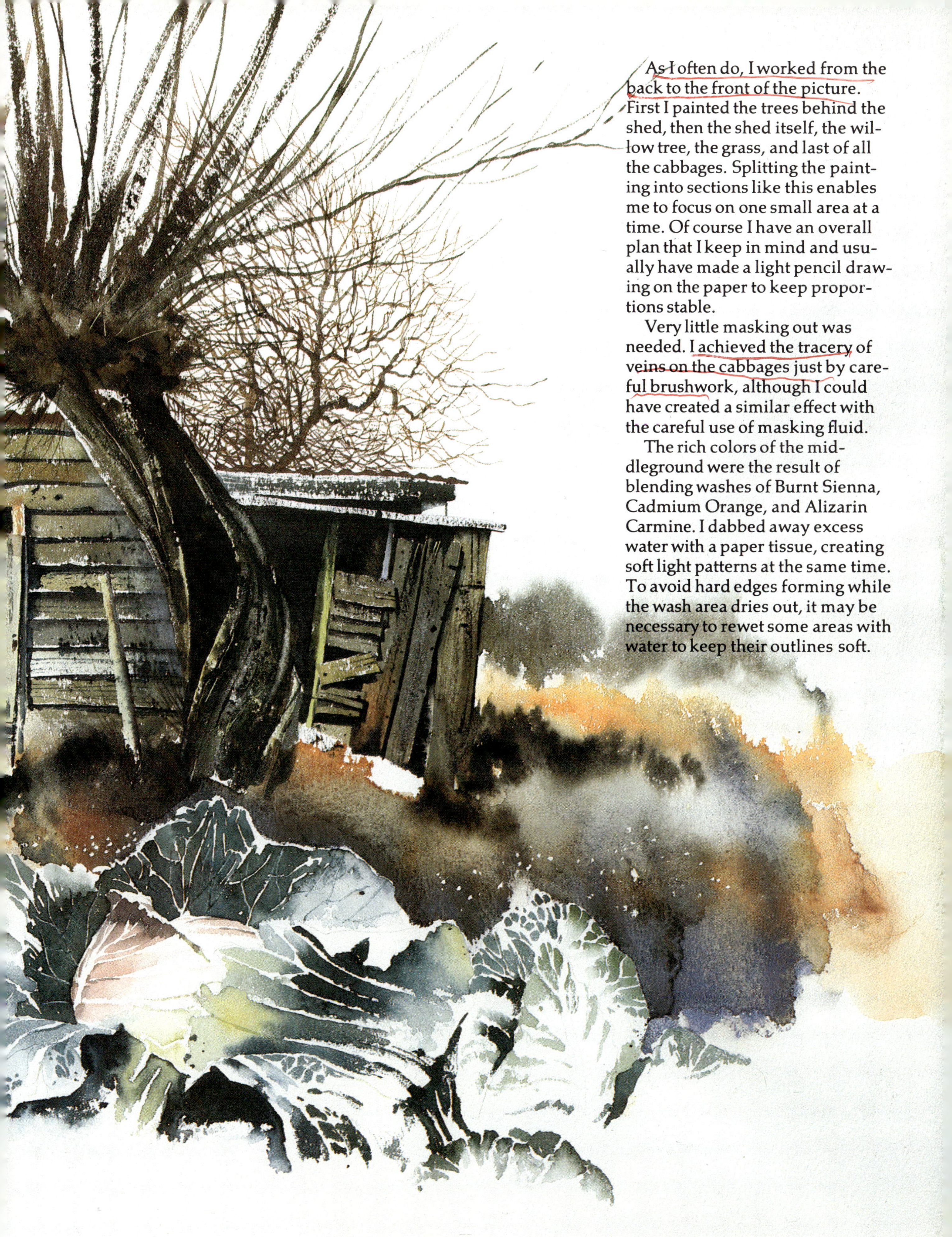

As I often do, I worked from the back to the front of the picture. First I painted the trees behind the shed, then the shed itself, the willow tree, the grass, and last of all the cabbages. Splitting the painting into sections like this enables me to focus on one small area at a time. Of course I have an overall plan that I keep in mind and usually have made a light pencil drawing on the paper to keep proportions stable.

Very little masking out was needed. I achieved the tracery of veins on the cabbages just by careful brushwork, although I could have created a similar effect with the careful use of masking fluid.

The rich colors of the middleground were the result of blending washes of Burnt Sienna, Cadmium Orange, and Alizarin Carmine. I dabbed away excess water with a paper tissue, creating soft light patterns at the same time. To avoid hard edges forming while the wash area dries out, it may be necessary to rewet some areas with water to keep their outlines soft.

Much of this work involved painting the shadows and dark areas underneath the leaves and then adding the ribs on the leaves to create their form. The ribbing in dark shadow at the top center was the negative shape left by a second wash laid into the first while it was still wet. The ribbing on the leaf in the front was made with the wrong end of a brush by dragging it through the almost-dry paint, leaving lighter stripes with dark edges.

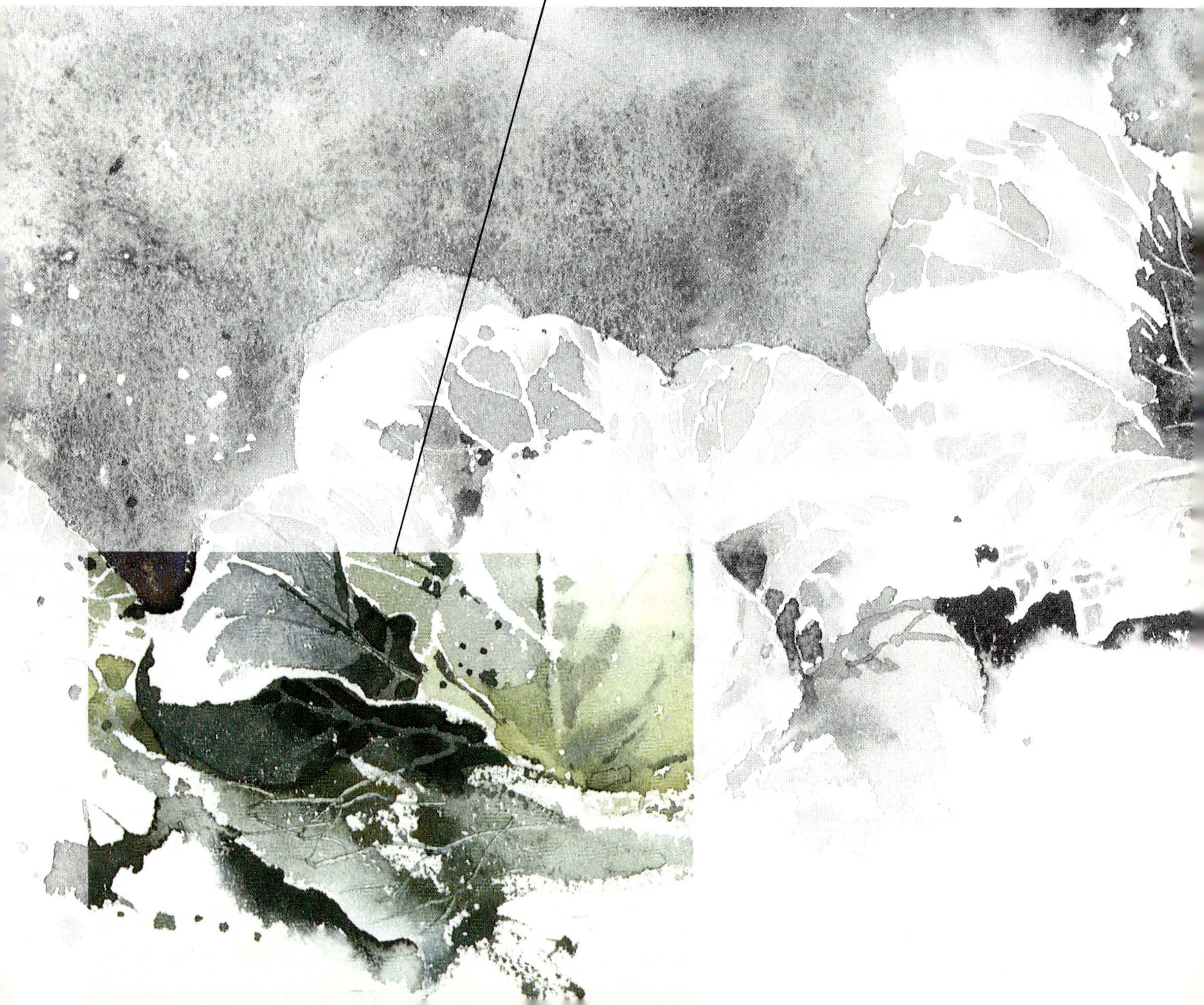

Pale Alizarin Carmine was used to paint the area between the ribs on the heart of this cabbage, and by gently curving these washes around the front of the cabbage, I made it fat and full. I darkened the underside of the top of the leaf and left the top rim completely white.

I almost overworked the ribbing in this leaf: there are so many small islands of green that the overall shape and form of the leaf have become lost, and it really doesn't look like a cabbage leaf anymore. Be warned—it is always better to understate a subject like this.

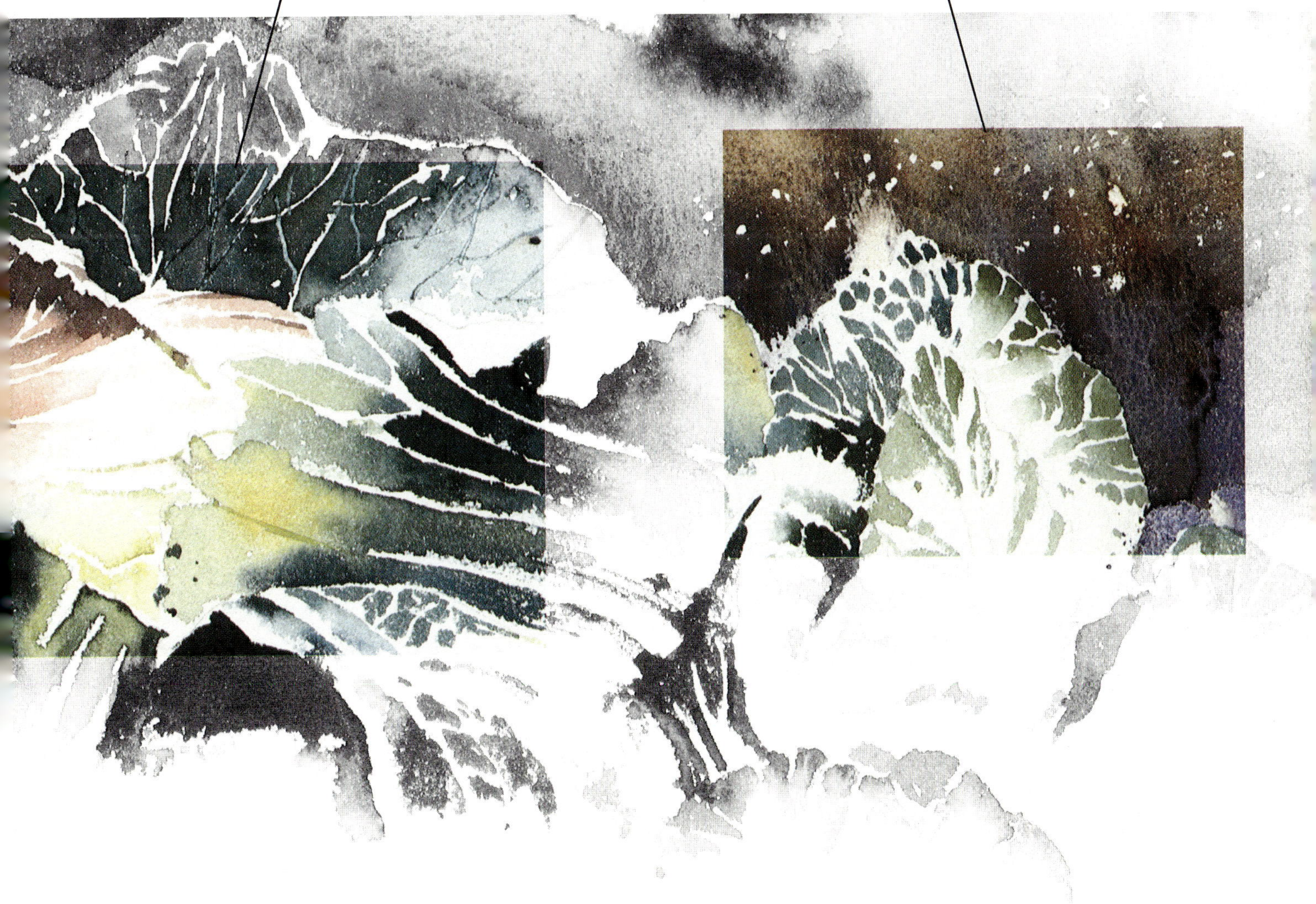

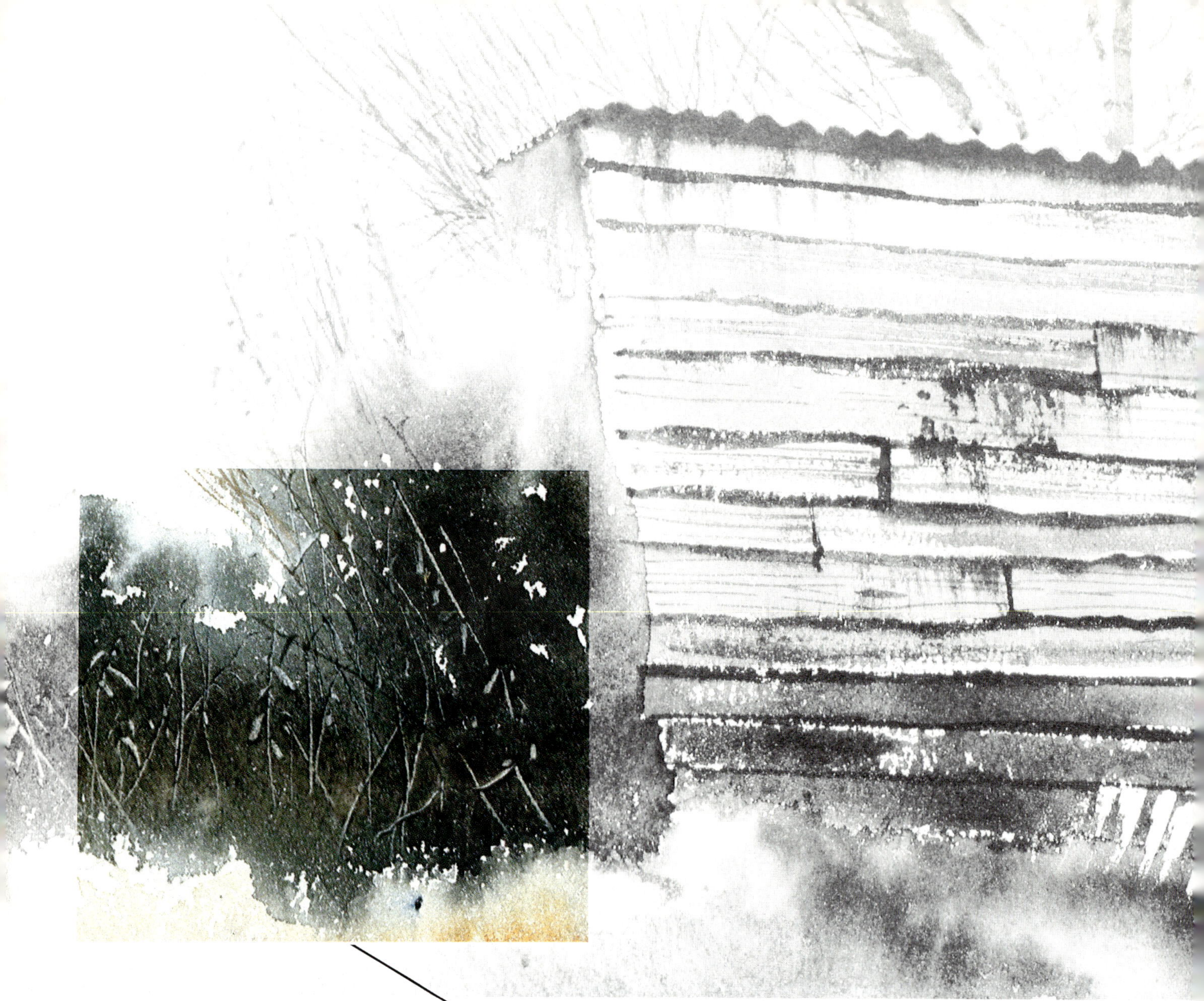

This was an area of low interest in the painting, so it needed only a modicum of activity. I kept the color cool and scratched in a few tall weed stems and leaves while the paint was damp.

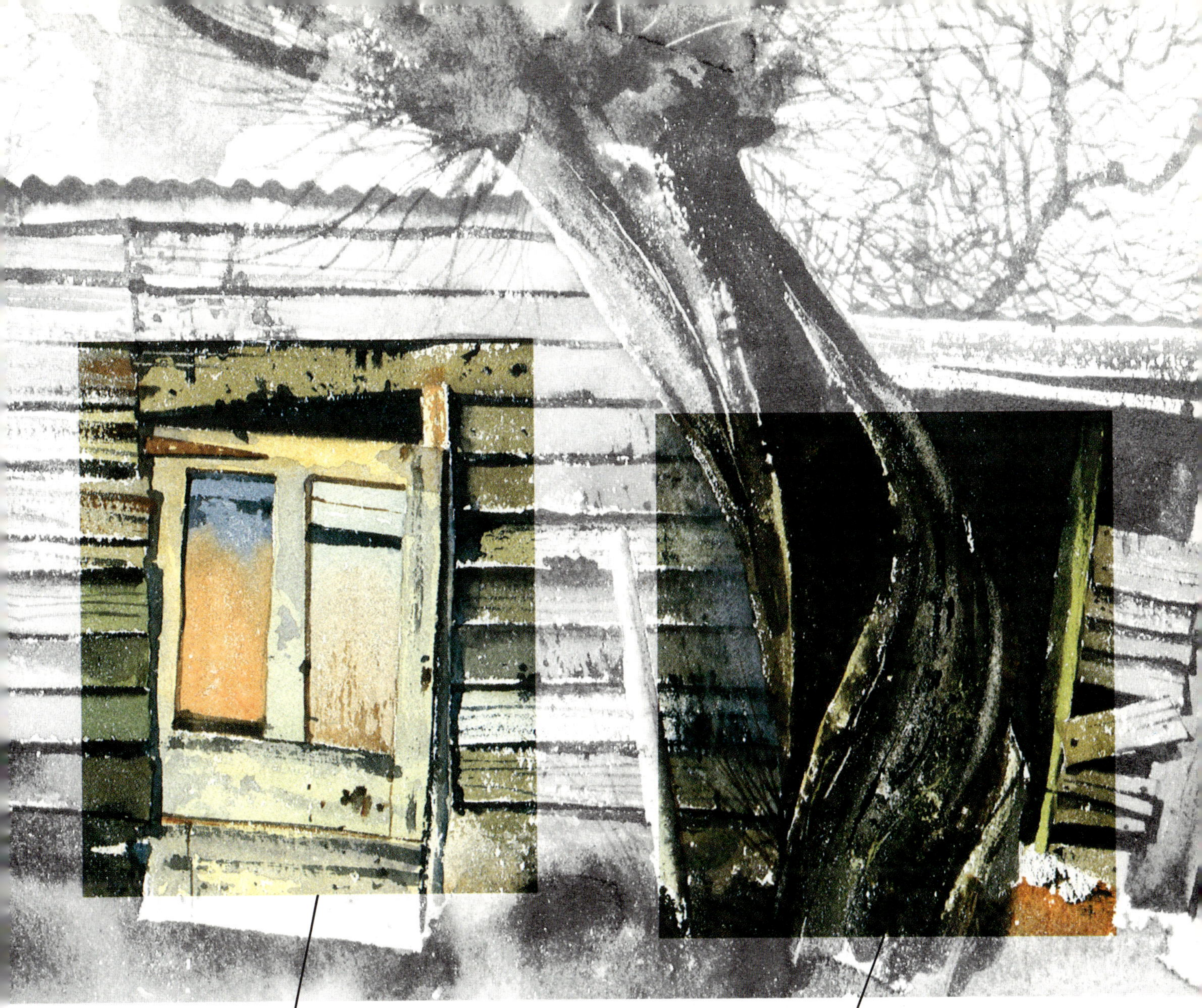

The ill-fitting shed door was so patched that I took complete license to paint it my way. I used thin, veil-like washes for all of it apart from the two panels, and laid these indiscriminately over one another, taking care to let each wash form a hard edge. I painted each door panel with a different color and texture and finally used darker shades of some of these colors to cast shadows at the edges of the woodwork and at the front and back of the door.

I used a rich mixture of Prussian Blue and Burnt Sienna to make the dark, hollow center of the willow tree, and then concentrated on the twisting trunk with the same colors, laid over a wash underneath. I enhanced the texture of bark by lifting out some lighter stripes with a tissue and by grazing the surface with a razor blade when it was dry. Finally some very thin dark lines went down the line of the trunk to emphasize the twist.

WITHERED FLOWERS AND DRYING LEAVES

What I wanted to do most in this painting was to capture the overall feeling without getting too involved in detail. To enable me to work quickly, I first painted out the flowers and one or two of the leaves with masking fluid.

The natural patterns of the flowers seemed to compose the painting for me, their diagonal movement giving energy to the composition and an interesting variety of directional lines.

Even in an uncomplicated study such as this, I found that each daisy was quite different from the others, varying from the overblown and ragged mature flower to the dried-up flower heads, which were rapidly going to seed. Each flower, at each stage, has its own points of interest.

I treated the tangle of leaves in the background vigorously, using dark colors: deep cool greens that enhance and project the white flowers.

This is a technique that I use quite often. High contrast serves to enliven what could be quite a dull picture. Leaving some of the masked areas white against the Cobalt and Ultramarine Blues gave added sparkle.

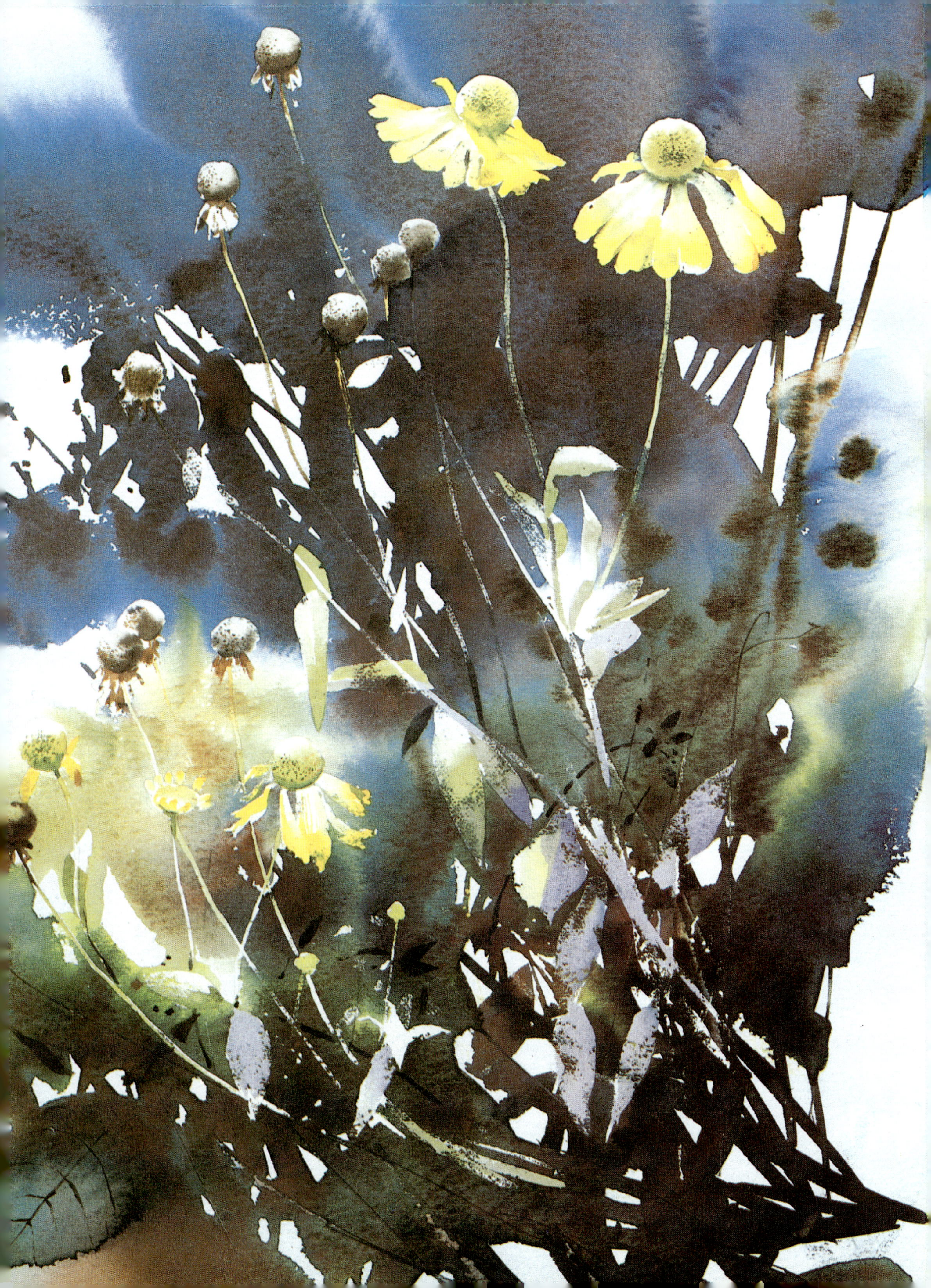

These withered flower heads were each treated slightly differently, using more or less highlight as a means of varying the round centers of the flowers. The brown and torn petals were enlivened with a touch of Cadmium Orange and Burnt Sienna, contrasting against both very dark and very light backgrounds.

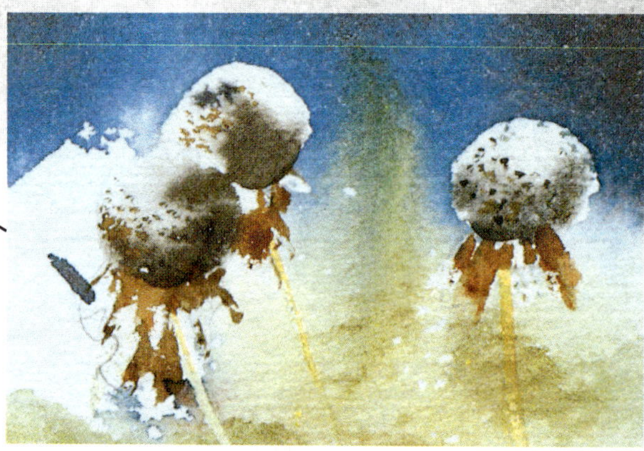

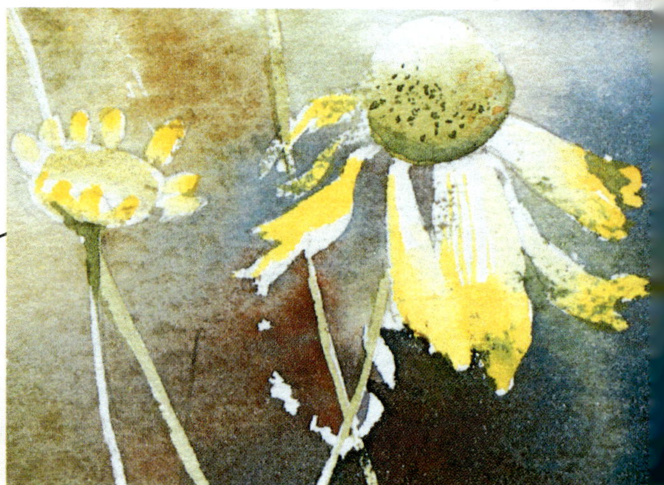

Lemon Yellow against Indigo and Cobalt Blue was toned down slightly here by adding a bit of Sap Green to the flower's center. Breaking up the edges with color gave a realistic, ragged look to the petal tips.

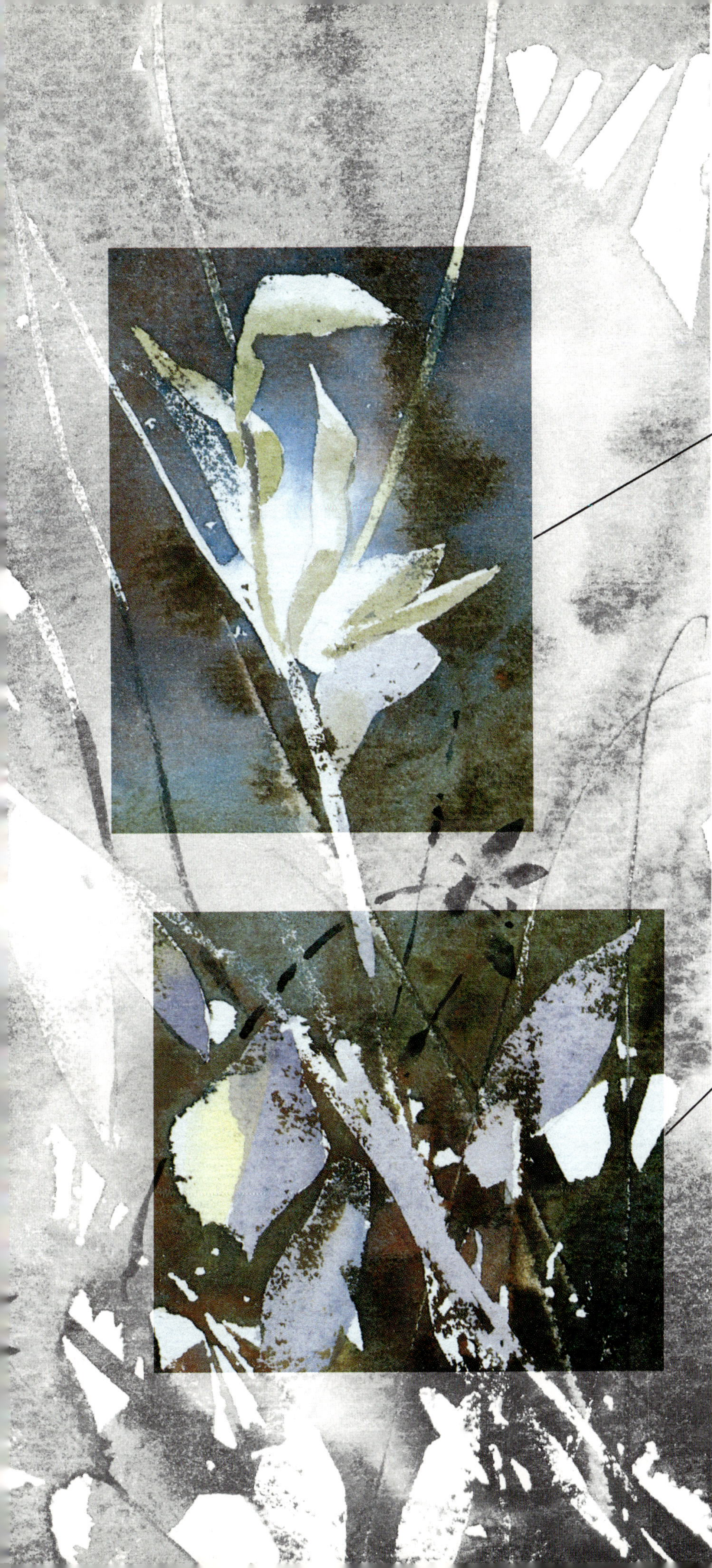

Pale Sap Green against a dark blue background, with touches of Cadmium Orange dropped into the blues when wet, were strengthened by keeping the area immediately behind the leaves light so that the forms could be drawn in clearly and gracefully.

This area of high contrast was achieved by early use of masking fluid, then a progression of washes added here and there on the leaves. Cadmium Orange and Sap Green in bold strokes against the white enlivens this area of tangled leaves.

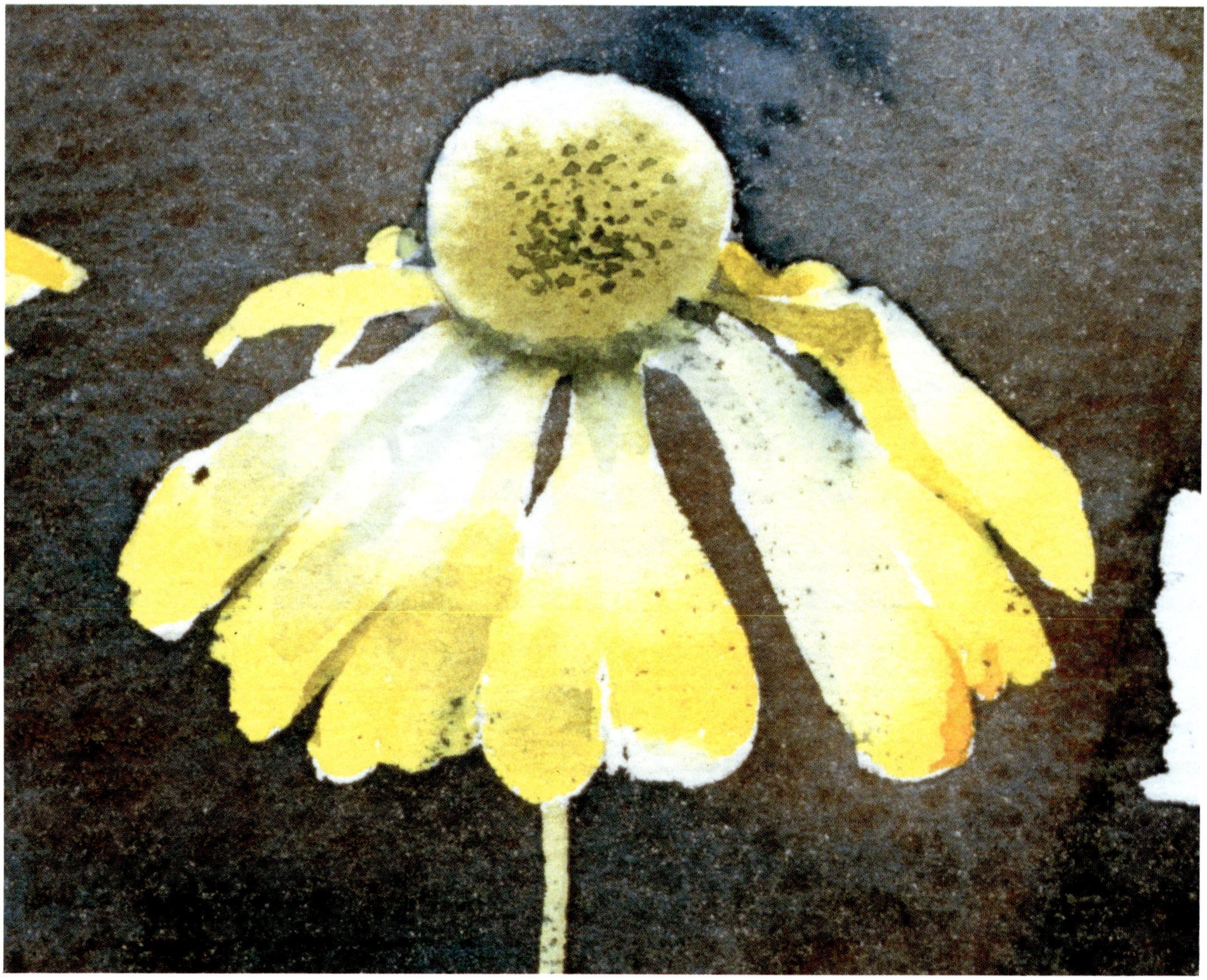

This, the largest and most vivid flower, has careful though quick detailing at the center and an important contrasting shadow beneath it.

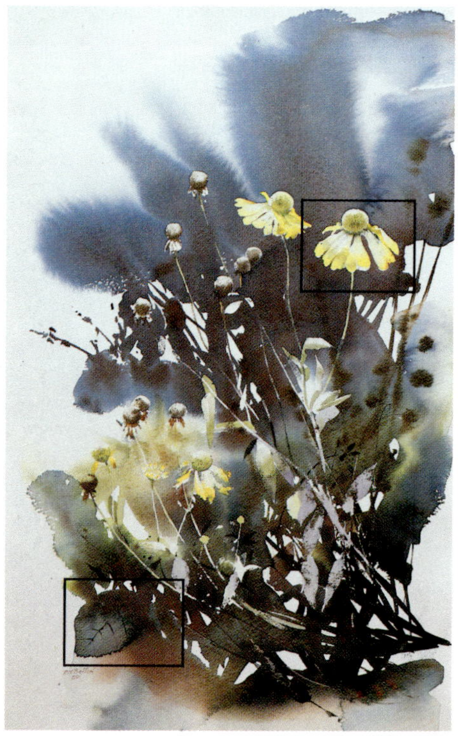

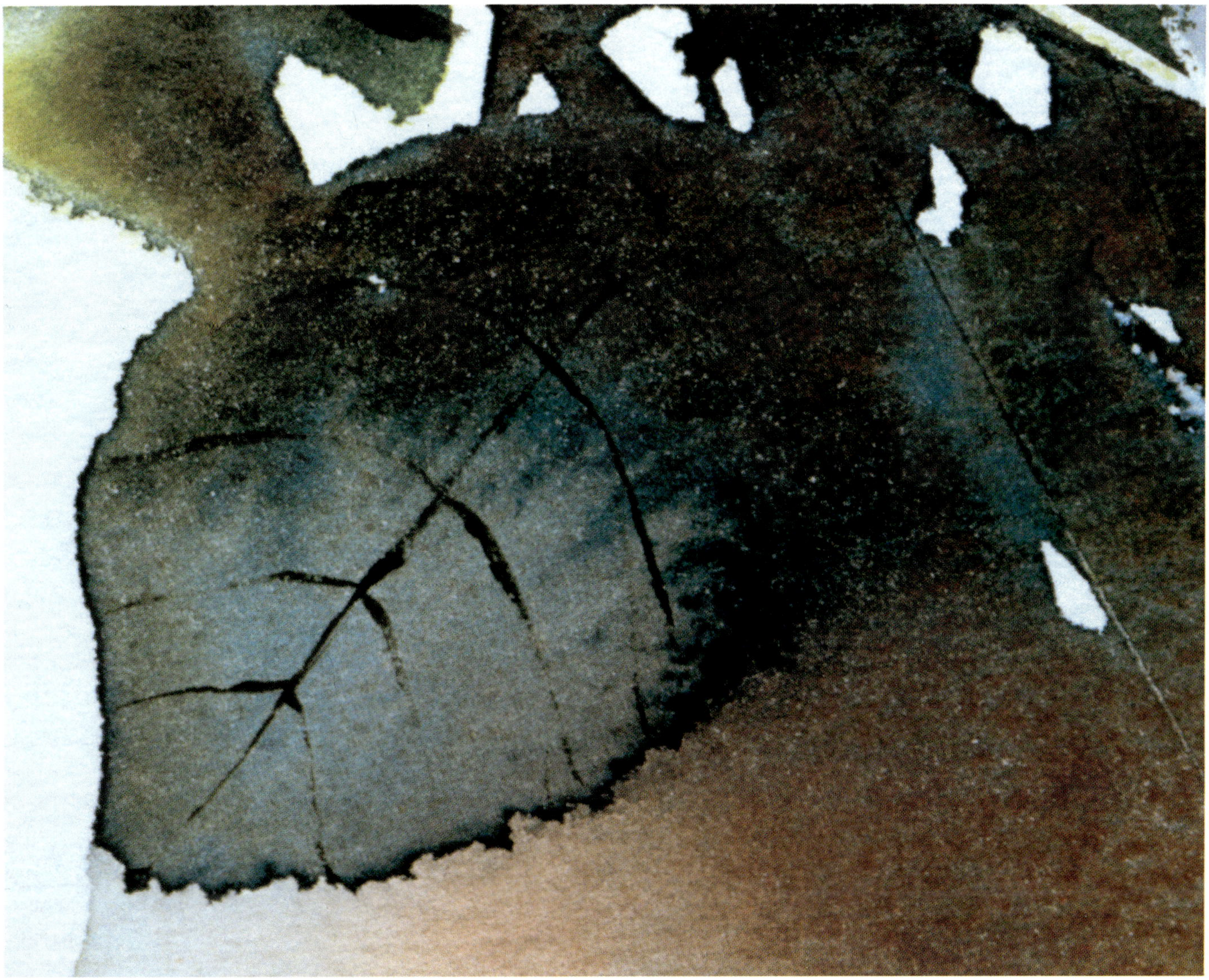

Ultramarine Blue, Indigo, and Sap Green make up a richly colored leaf, its edges darkened for emphasis. Cadmium Orange and Lemon Yellow have been allowed to run into the leaf, dramatizing its shape and delicate tracery of lines.

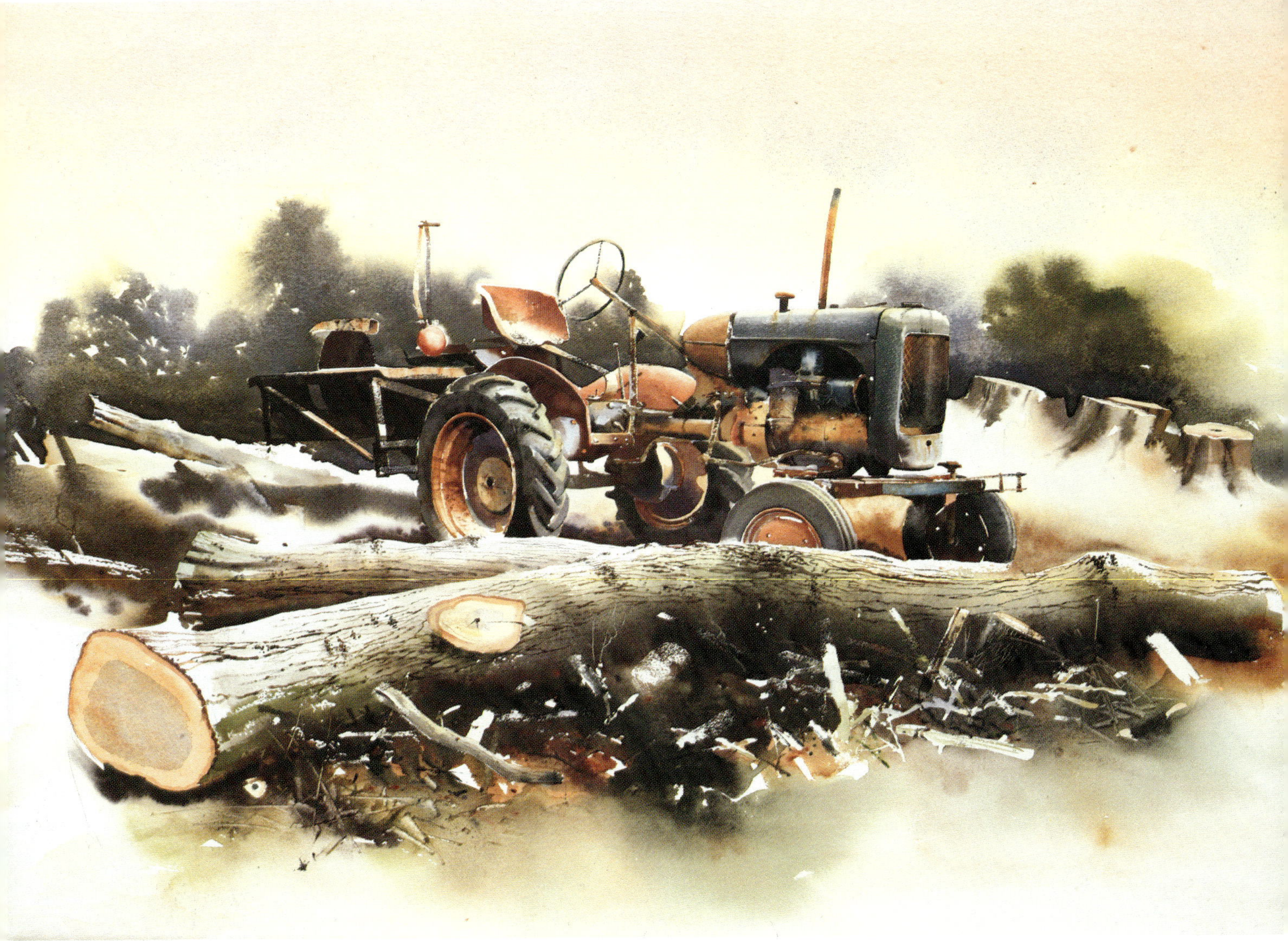

FELLED TREES, WINTER BRANCHES AND TWIGS

The bold contrast of machinery and wood is the essence of this painting, done when the local elms were being cut down because of Dutch elm disease. The round wheels and round, sawed-off tree bottom and knot complement each other, as do the warm and cool colors.

Masking fluid plays an important role in this painting. The tractor and the wood chippings in the foreground were masked out first, allowing me to splash paint around loosely to form the background and logs, and yet still retain the detailed outline of tractor and chips.

Keeping a balance between loose brushwork and tightly controlled, detailed painting is the thing. If too much attention is paid to detail and not enough to the overall painting, the picture may become stilted and disjointed, and so it is necessary to be selective. In this case I have focused on the tractor and the trunk in the foreground. All else has been allowed to fall back into the picture in a haze of soft shapes.

As is often the case with watercolor, the unimportant parts of the painting end up looking more effective because they were painted spontaneously and not overworked. I made no attempt to define the bark on these tree stumps, but simply let the washed-on color wander vaguely of its own accord, which resulted in these muscular-looking stumps. I had masked out the top of each stump and completed each one with a very pale wash, as used for the tree rings in the foreground.

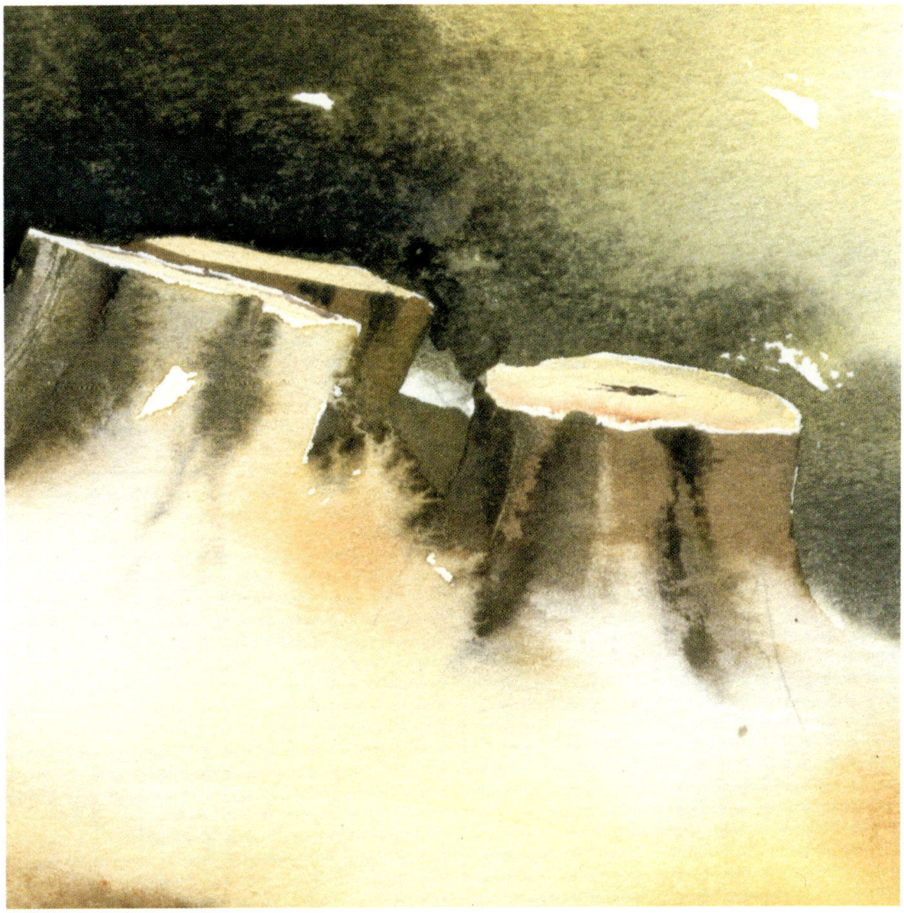

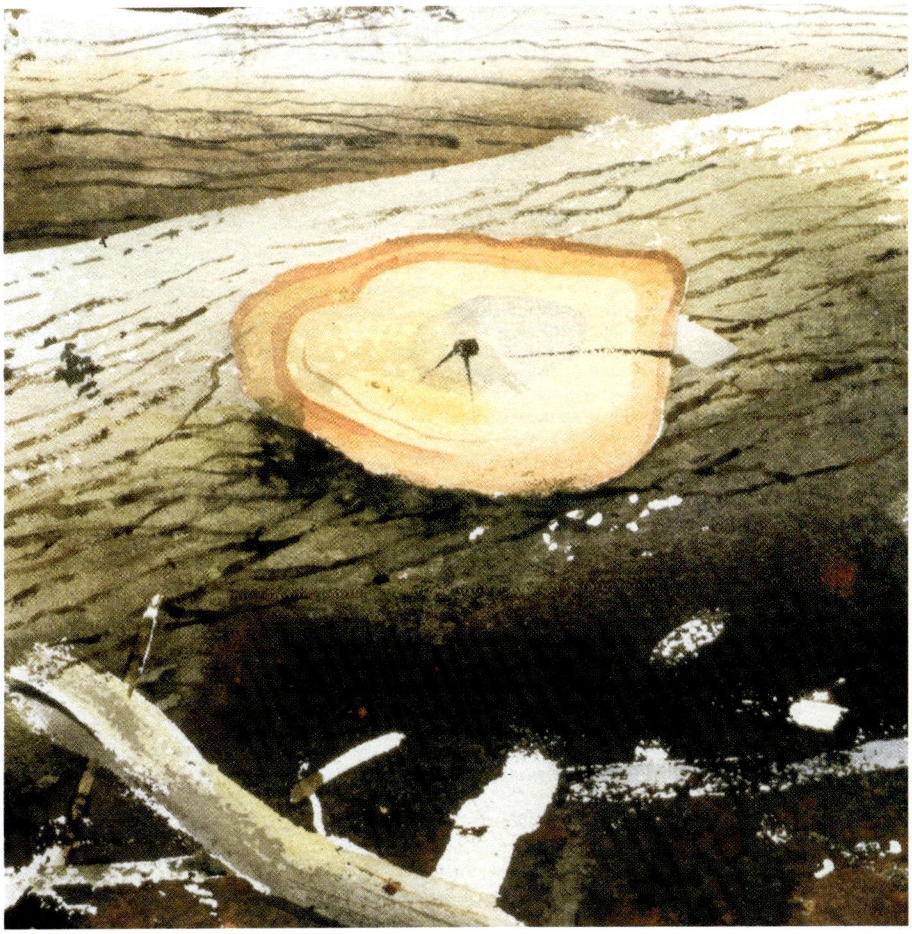

Painting the bark on the tree trunk in the foreground presents problems. To try to paint in all the cracks and bumps in the bark will most likely lead to an overworked muddle. So again selectivity is necessary, catching the effect of bark by picking out the essential features. The salmon pink of raw cut wood and the irregular pattern of cracks in the bark are painted over a loose base color of Sap Green, Burnt Sienna, and Ultramarine Blue.

Most of the work was done with bamboo brushes, but the finer details were touched in with size 2 sable. I used successive thin washes to give the effect of rings where the branch had been sawn off, and added a tiny dark dot and dashes to simulate early weathering.

WINTER TREES

Unlike many watercolorists, I think this is just the medium for tackling machinery. Watercolor doesn't need to be a wishy-washy medium, suited only to misty landscapes. Once you come to terms with its strengths and limitations and overcome your guilt over using such heretical helpers as masking fluid, pen and ink, razor blades, and anything else that helps create the look you want, you'll find it has just the subtlety that machinery requires. Machinery looks waxy new for a very short time. In the out-of-doors the shiny metallic look gives way to weathering.

Here I found all the wonderful intricacies of a tractor combined with a witchy tree, broken earth, dead grass, old cottage, and a desolate gray-blue wintry atmosphere. This is essentially a cool painting, but the tractor wheel and appendages, the warm darks of the earth, and the yellowish cast to the sky provide warm relief.

It's surprising how few colors are needed in a painting. The whole scene except for the tractor was built up from two colors: Burnt Sienna and Ultramarine Blue. This combination gives me oranges, ranging down through brown to blue, which is all I need for these winter colors. For the tractor I added Cadmium Orange for rust spots, Sap Green for tractor-tire mold, and Cerulean Blue mixed with Burnt Sienna for the paintwork. The license plate number had been crudely dabbed in with a brush of thick white paint. To mimic this effect, I painted out the numbers with masking fluid, leaving a clear white impression when it was later rubbed away. A spot of Cadmium Orange gave the look of rust staining.

In the foreground I scratched the corner of a razor blade gently through damp paint, which rendered delicate grass stems against a dark background—giving more life to the background and adding new texture.

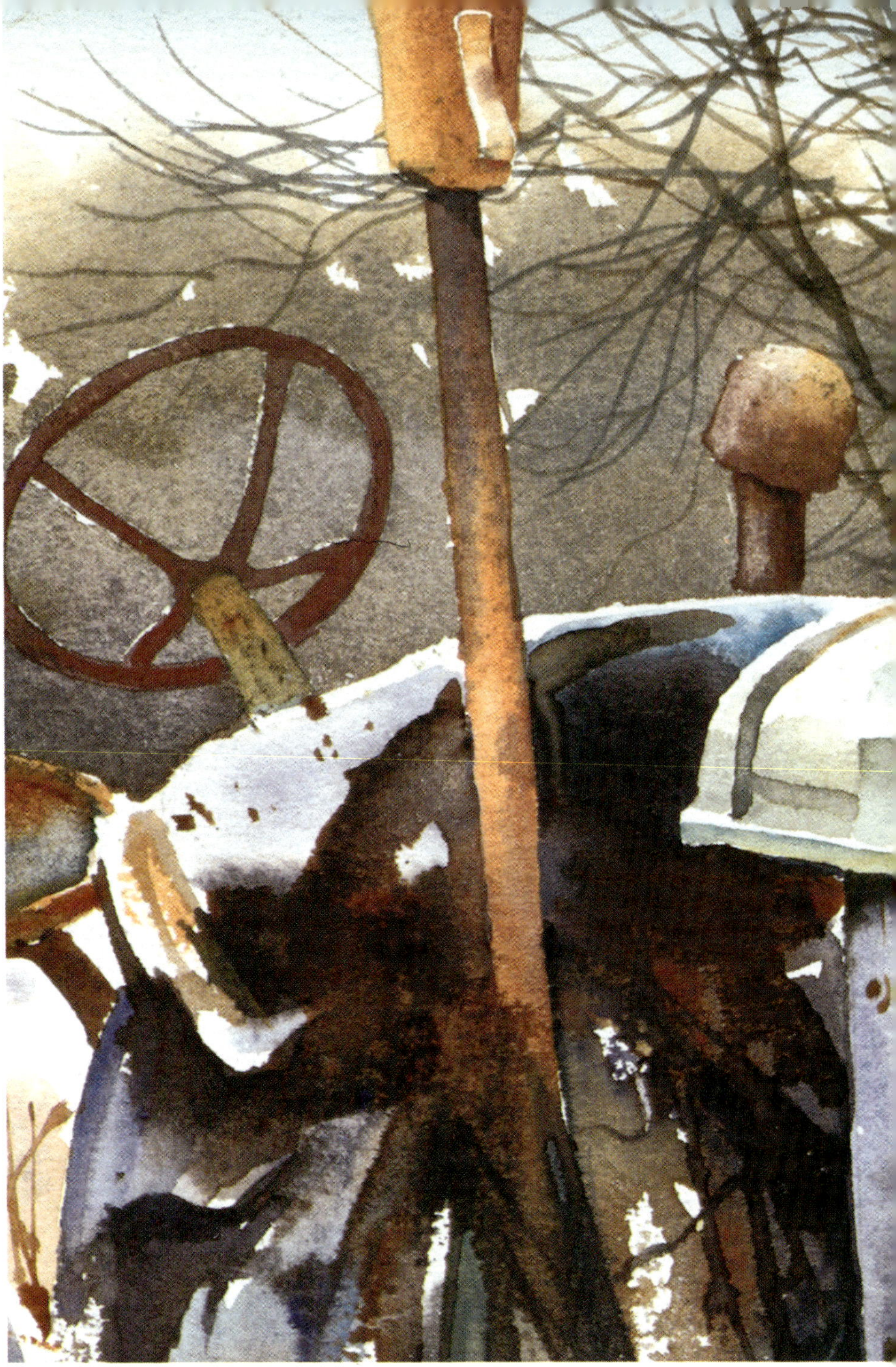

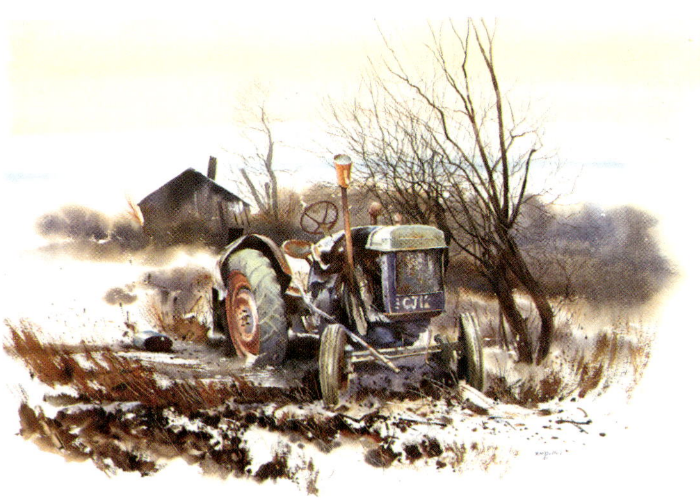

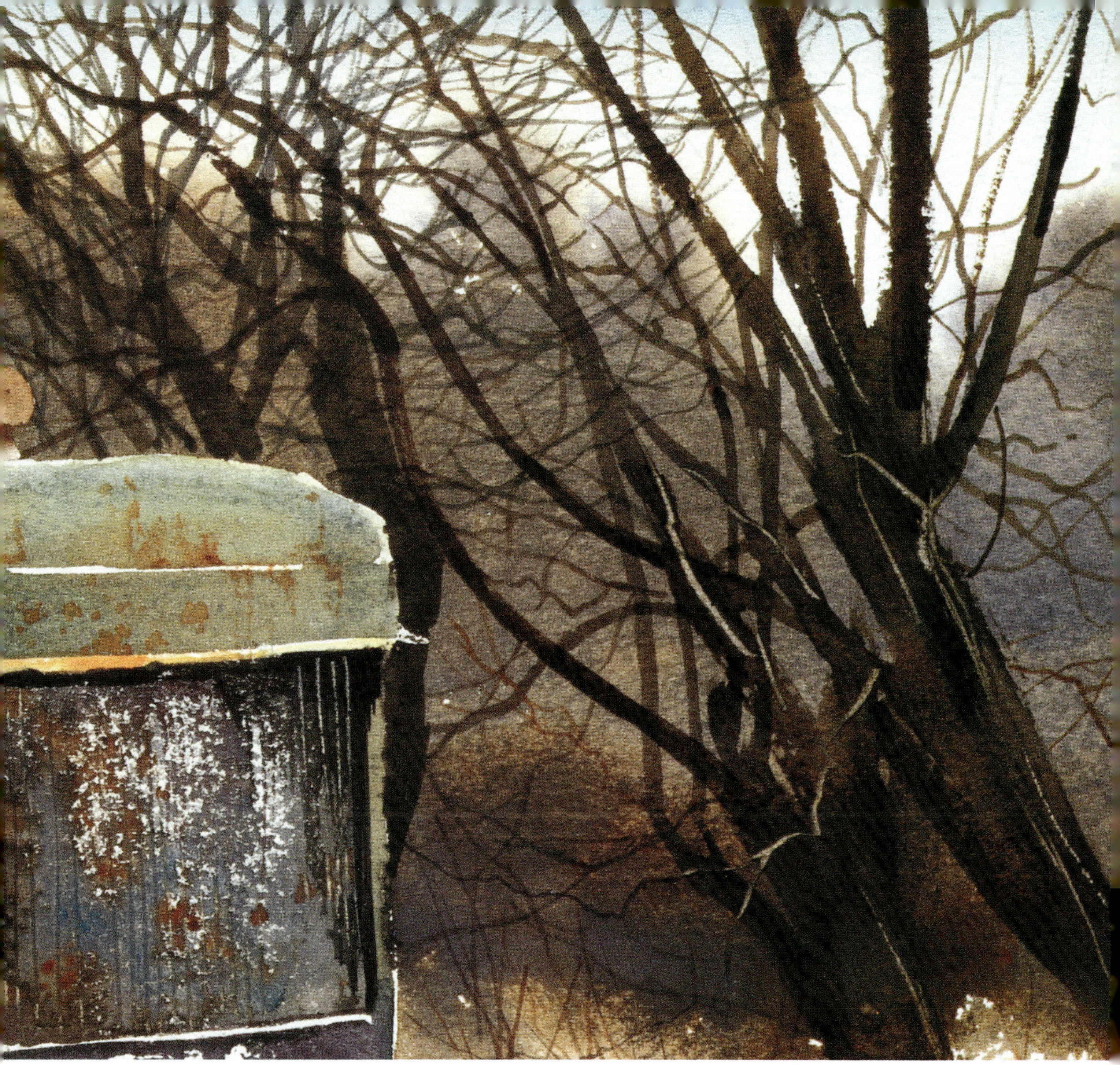

I introduced light and pattern into the dark, heavy mass of this tractor radiator. To open up that wide area, I used a little candle wax, which caused the paint to speckle, and razor blades for the straight lines. I made some razor marks before painting over with Cerulean Blue and Burnt Sienna. These are seen as darker than the surface blue. The white ones were picked out after the paint was applied and still damp.

The long, delicate tree branches were painted with a dry, long-haired sable brush using Burnt Sienna and Ultramarine Blue. The delicate pattern of branches next to the rusting tractor gives a formal and emotional contrast. The filigree effect of the background branches provides further contrast with the massive form. I used warm and cool colors both on the machine and in the moody wood.

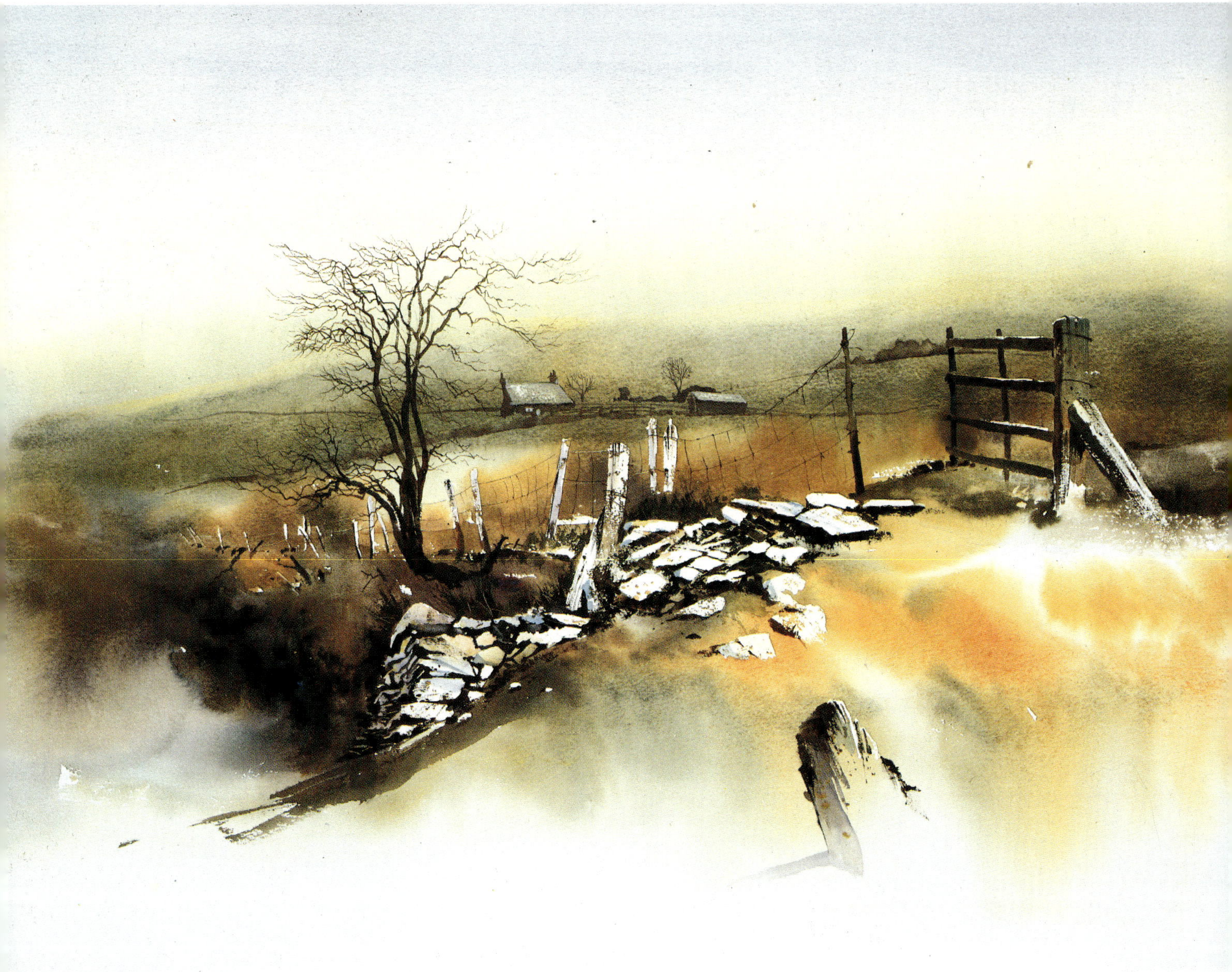

LOOSE STONES

It is often said of watercolor painting that what you leave out is as important as what you put in, for the attraction of watercolor lies in its spontaneity—the sparkle of white paper, those unexpected effects such as the jagged drying edges.

This hillside scene typifies this idea. I have carefully kept the painting uncomplicated, letting colors flow together, as in the horizon merging into the sky.

Detail is kept in the foreground, developing the stones, trees, and posts. The stones almost shine out from the painting, leaving the white of the paper to work for me. In contrast, the tree is almost black, silhouetted against the background. Care has been taken to render the cracks and shadows among the stones. Using a small dry brush, I have twisted, turned, and scraped it around to capture the texture.

I made considerable use of masking fluid to keep paint off the white highlight areas, such as the stones and the wooden fencing. It allows me to paint freely and in an uninhibited style. Candle wax can sometimes be used for highlights. It causes the paint to speckle in an attractive fashion, but it is not as durable and versatile as masking fluid and cannot be removed from the paper for overpainting.

The black and white pattern against a Cadmium Orange, Burnt Sienna, and Ultramarine Blue wash is the secret of this detail; also the web effect of branches contrasting with the plain fence posts. Masking fluid, of course, kept the posts and rails white while I applied the wash.

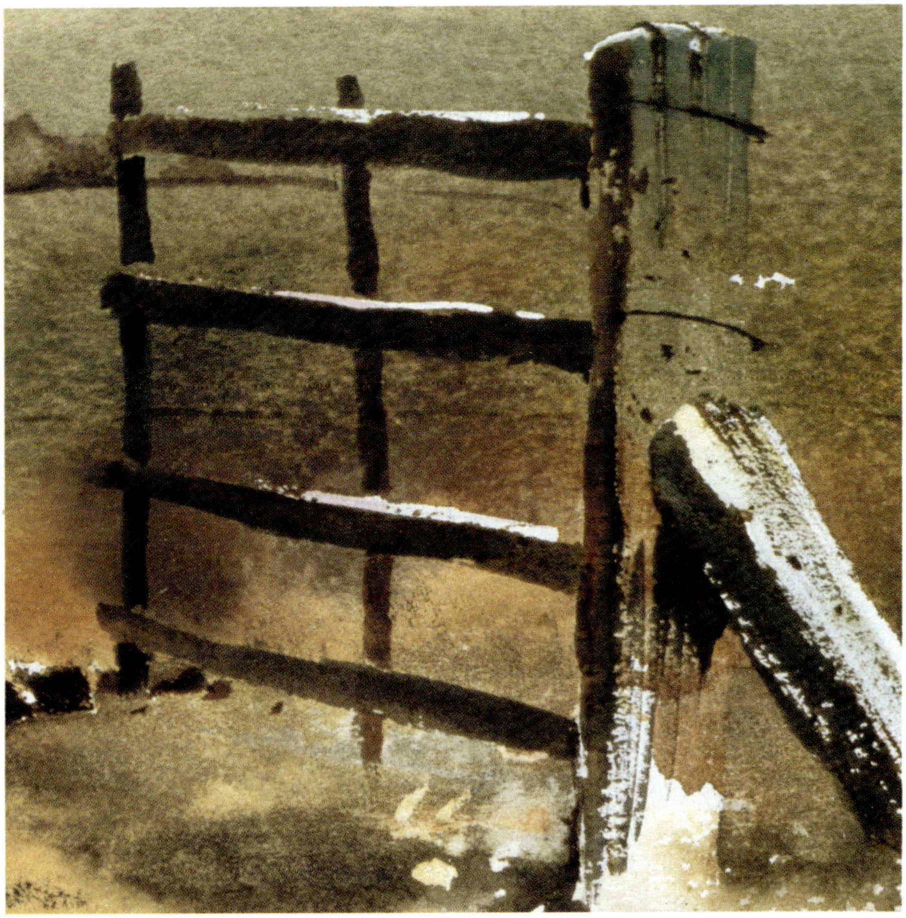

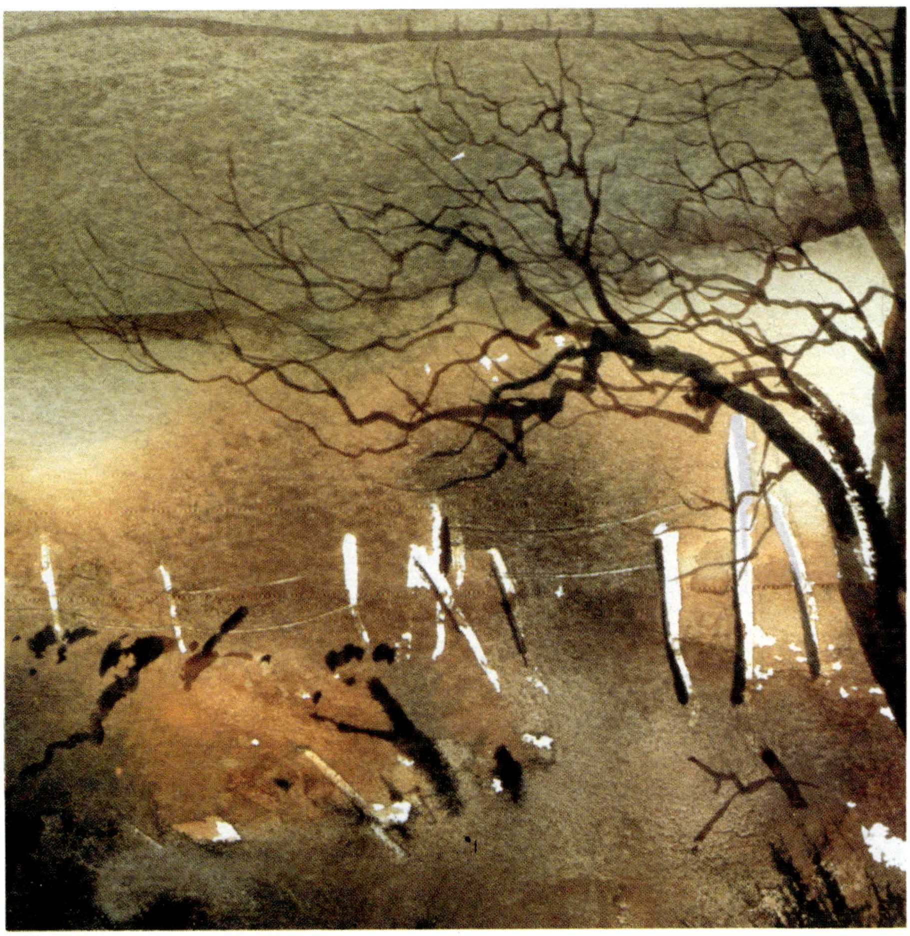

This fence against the dark background has a lively look to it because of the bright highlights. I brushed the same smoke-colored wash over it after the masking fluid had been removed, breaking the overall form and lending perspective to the fence.

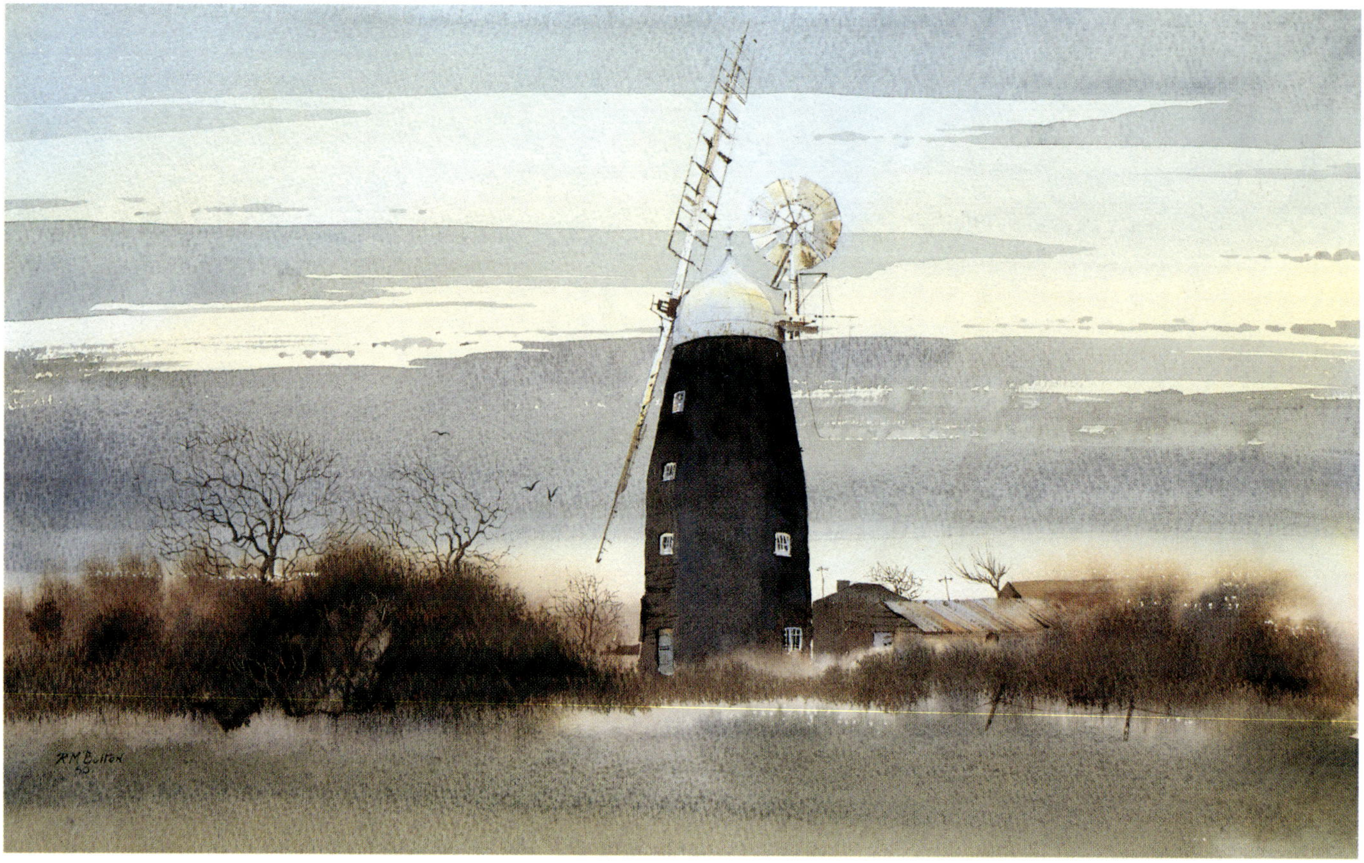

EVENING LIGHT
I came upon this windmill one evening unexpectedly. It seemed to be waiting for Don Quixote, with its spear at the ready. In any case, the lone dark windmill against the sky on a wintry day sent me to my paint box to capture the moment.

At any other time of day, however, it would have had no impact at all, for in reality it stands on an island amid a housing project. It was my artist's imagination and license that transformed an uninspired scene.

Early morning and evening often present the best time to paint. With the sun low on the horizon, unexpected and inspiring effects can be found. Trees produce a complex latticework against the skyline, their twisted and intricate shapes contrasting sharply against man-made structures.

In the half-light, colors take on a decided hue. Sometimes it is the rosy sunset that everyone is familiar with, and at other times the sky is icy blue, verging on green. This winter scene of Soham Windmill typifies the atmosphere of winter sunset here.

I kept the palette very simple. The windmill is mostly Burnt Sienna and Ultramarine Blue. The sky was made from two washes: the first of Winsor Red and Cadmium Orange; the second of Cerulean Blue and Burnt Sienna, producing the pale blue-green sky. All the foreground was painted in mixtures of Burnt Sienna and Cerulean Blue.

I drew in the white cap of the mill and its equipment lightly with pencil first. I let some of the sky reflect on the white top to keep it in harmony with the time of day and general effect. The vanes at left were also drawn in first, with a warm dark accent to emphasize their attachment to the windmill and to provide contrast with the light colors and the blue-greens. After penciling in the wheel on the right, I drew it in carefully with a fine dry brush. I had added the blue wash first and allowed it to dry and left the white area as is. Each panel was treated individually, and so there are light ones and dark, perhaps rusted ones, with a strong central area at the hub of the wheel.

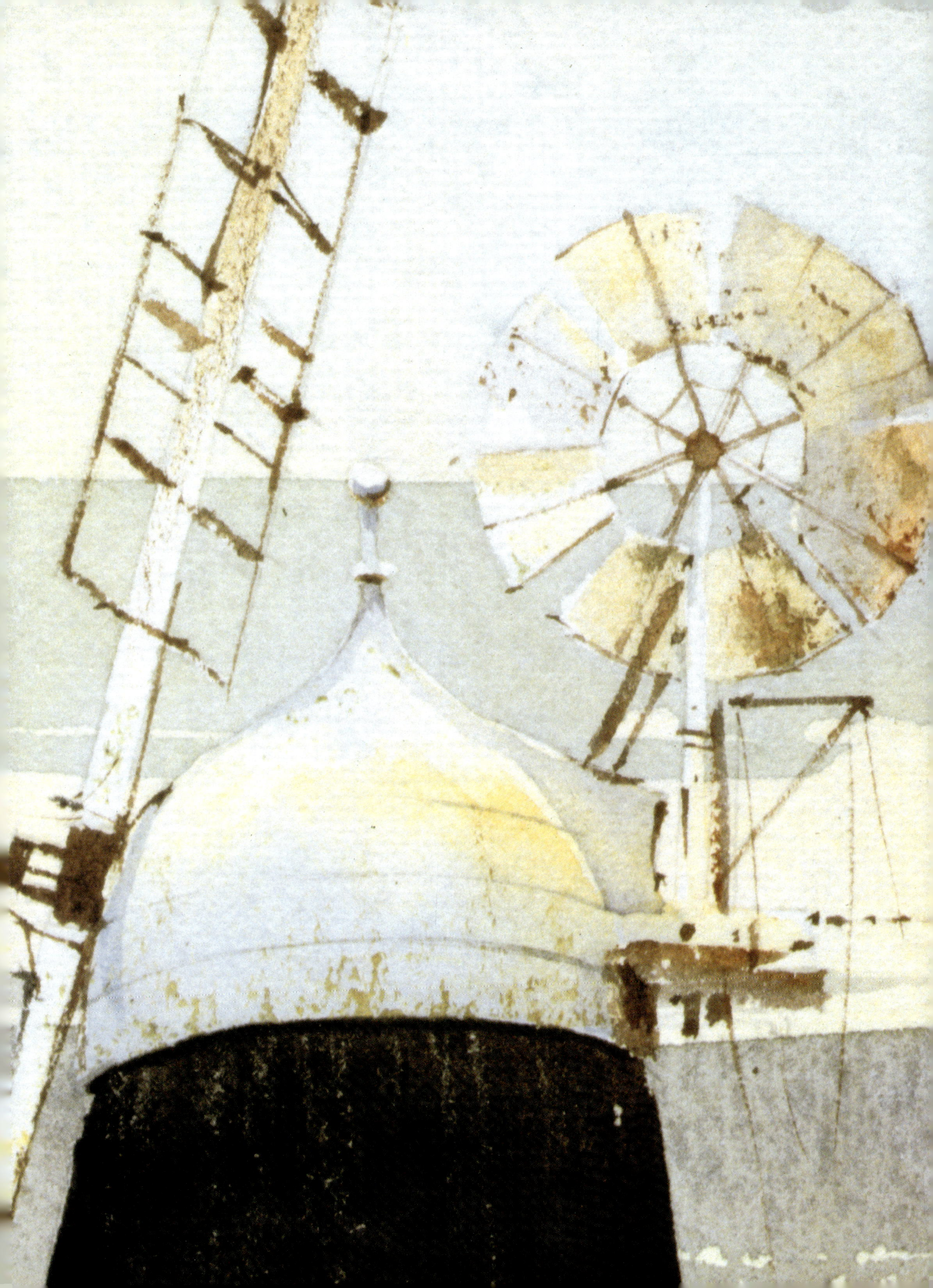

WATER AND BOATS

BEACHED BOAT HULLS, FLOTSAM AND JETSAM

Since detail and texture are the bases for much of my work, I like to paint subjects like this fishing boat in drydock. The scene is packed with interesting textures, such as the rust breaking through the paint on the hull, bits of old rusty metal, driftwood and pebbles, which all add to the feeling of long use and heavy wear from the rough seas. All of this romance tends to vanish in a modern boatyard where fiberglass, plastics, and concrete are the common surfaces.

Dominating the painting is the hull of *RX 35*, with particular attention being given to the wooden side, with its rust patches and other surface weathering. The boat is kept from being overpowering because of the many supports, lines, and deck gear that break the expanse and relate it to its surroundings.

The hull is pock-marked, stained, and weather-beaten. Its deep red coloring was mixed from Indian Red, Bright Red, and Cobalt Blue. Underneath the hull, the shadow is a mixture of Ultramarine Blue and Indigo. I felt this area was not dark enough so I painted some black ink into the wet paint. While all this was still wet I painted in the colors of the sand, which mixed with the paint from the hull's underside, blending together in a natural shadowy way rather than a hard line.

The foreground driftwood was painted in briskly with a medium-sized brush. Detail has been suggested, scratched in with a razor blade or dashed in with a brush rather than allowing the work to become too tight. The lively brushstrokes enhance the painting, contrasting with some of the more worked-over areas.

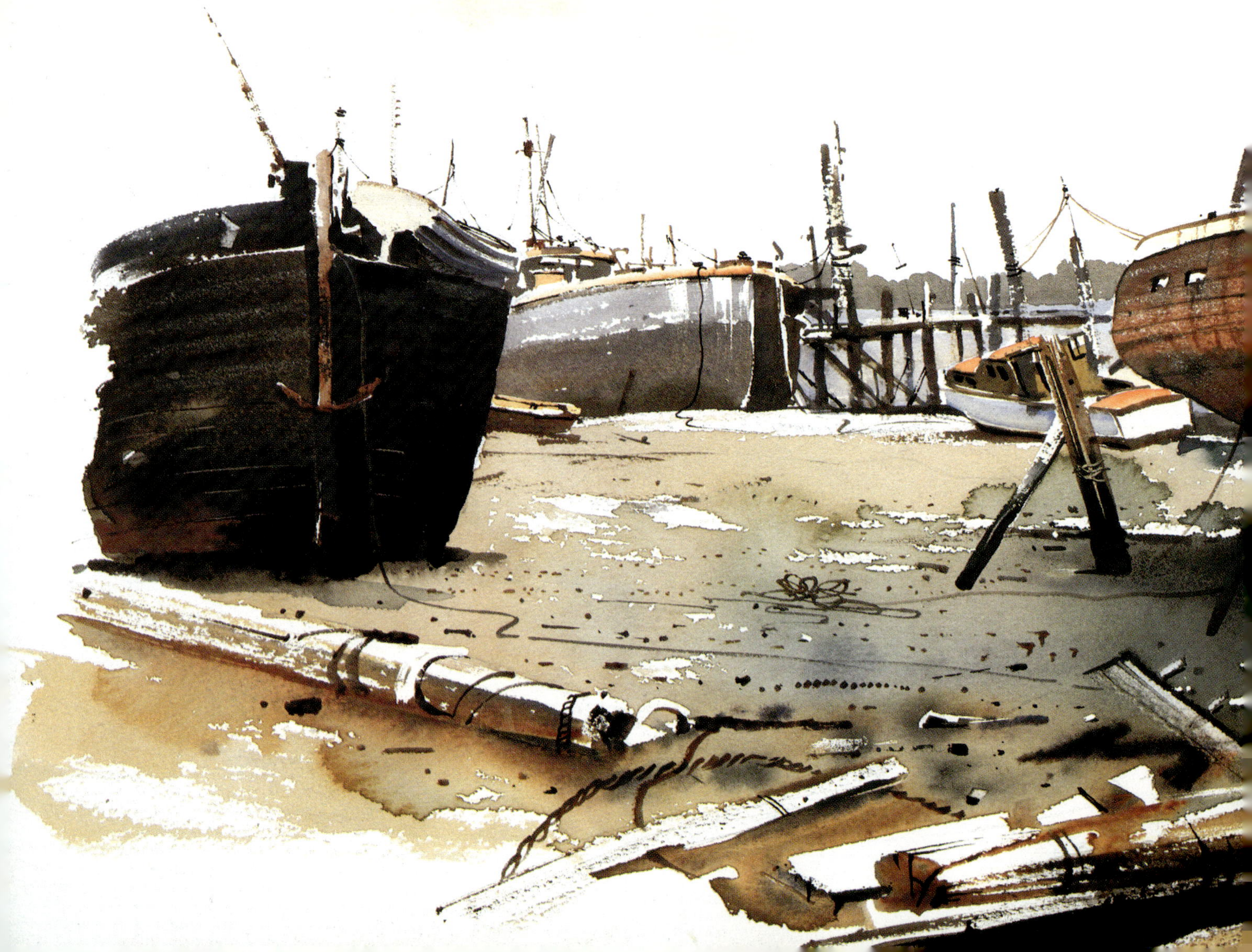

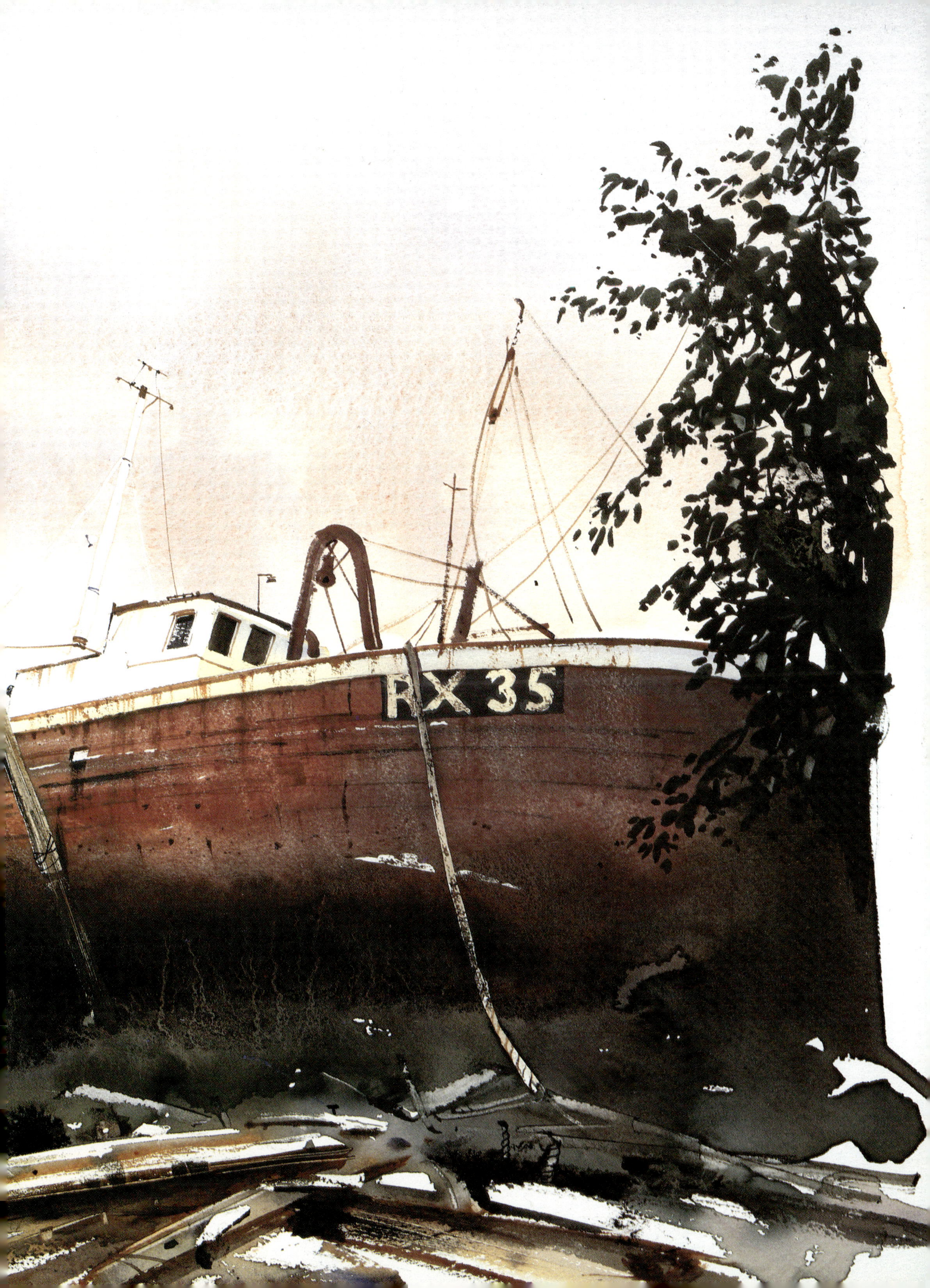
RX 35

The hull was painted with an uneven mixture of Indian Red, Bright Red, and Cobalt Blue. When that was dry, I smudged in some Burnt Sienna, using drybrush to streak the paint downward to create a vivid rust caused by exposure to salt water. The timbers leaning against the hull have little character, their purpose is to break up the shape of the hull. The dark horizontal lines running along the side of the ship are inconsistent strokes of a darker mixture of the base color. The light, broken-textured streaks that give the hull shape were put in *lightly* with a razor blade dragged along on its side.

To create the shapes of debris in the shadow, I lifted out narrow strips of the mixture of Ultramarine Blue and Indigo by gently scraping into the almost-dry color.

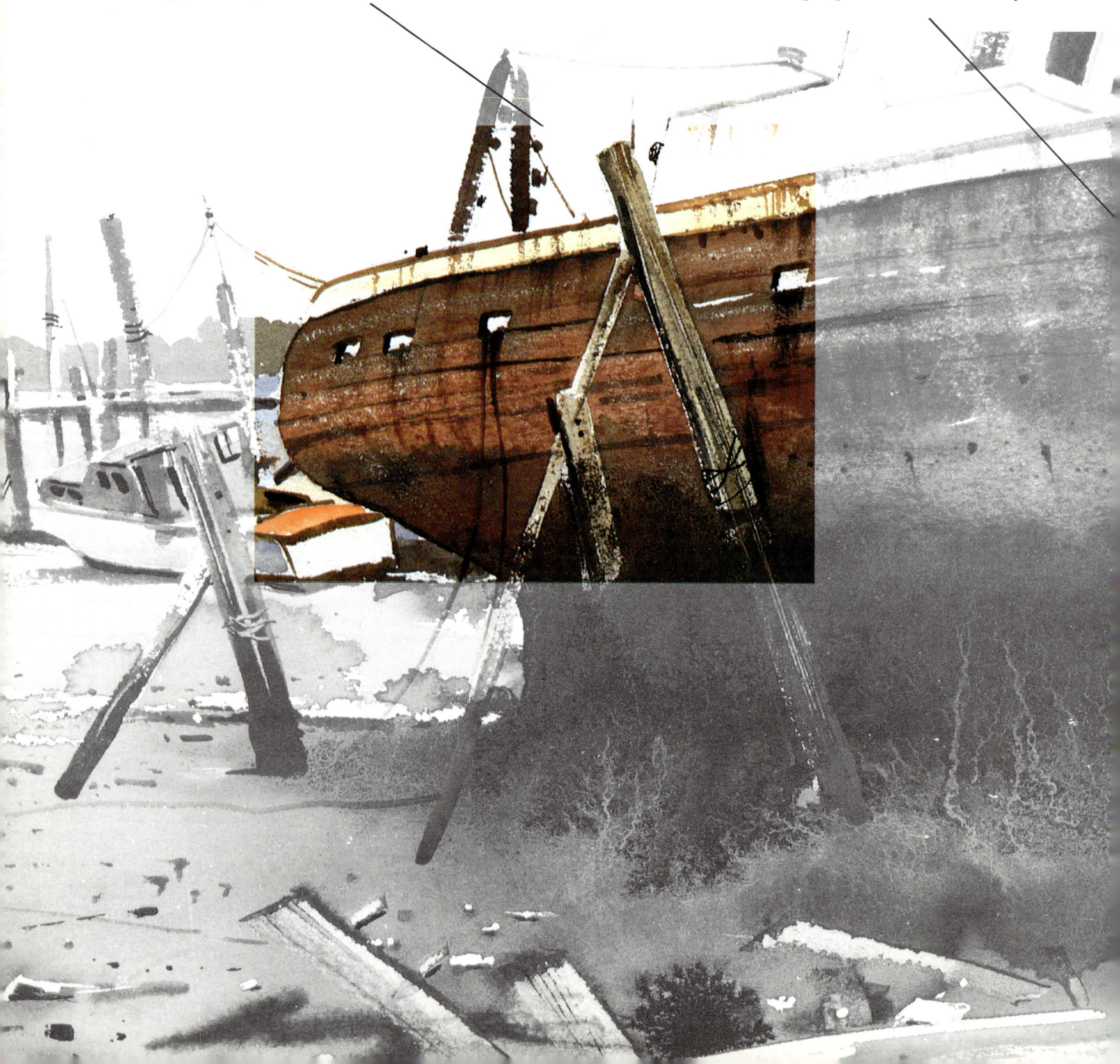

I laid a very fine wash of Naples Yellow along the top edge of the hull and the *RX 35.* Before the boat was painted red, I masked out the letters and numbers on the bow, taking care not to draw them too accurately or with great typographic precision. When the red hull was dry, I removed the masking fluid from the letters, dirtied them up a bit with some scratchy rust-colored paint, and then used Prussian Blue to paint in the dark background behind the *RX 35,* to give a weather-beaten look.

This mass of foliage is a rich combination of Ultramarine Blue, Indigo, and black ink, but the color is really quite unimportant compared to the overall texture of the leaves. I built up this tree by developing a group of dabbed-in brush marks. Try this for yourself and aim to achieve interest by varying the shape and size of each mark, and varying the density of marks in each group.

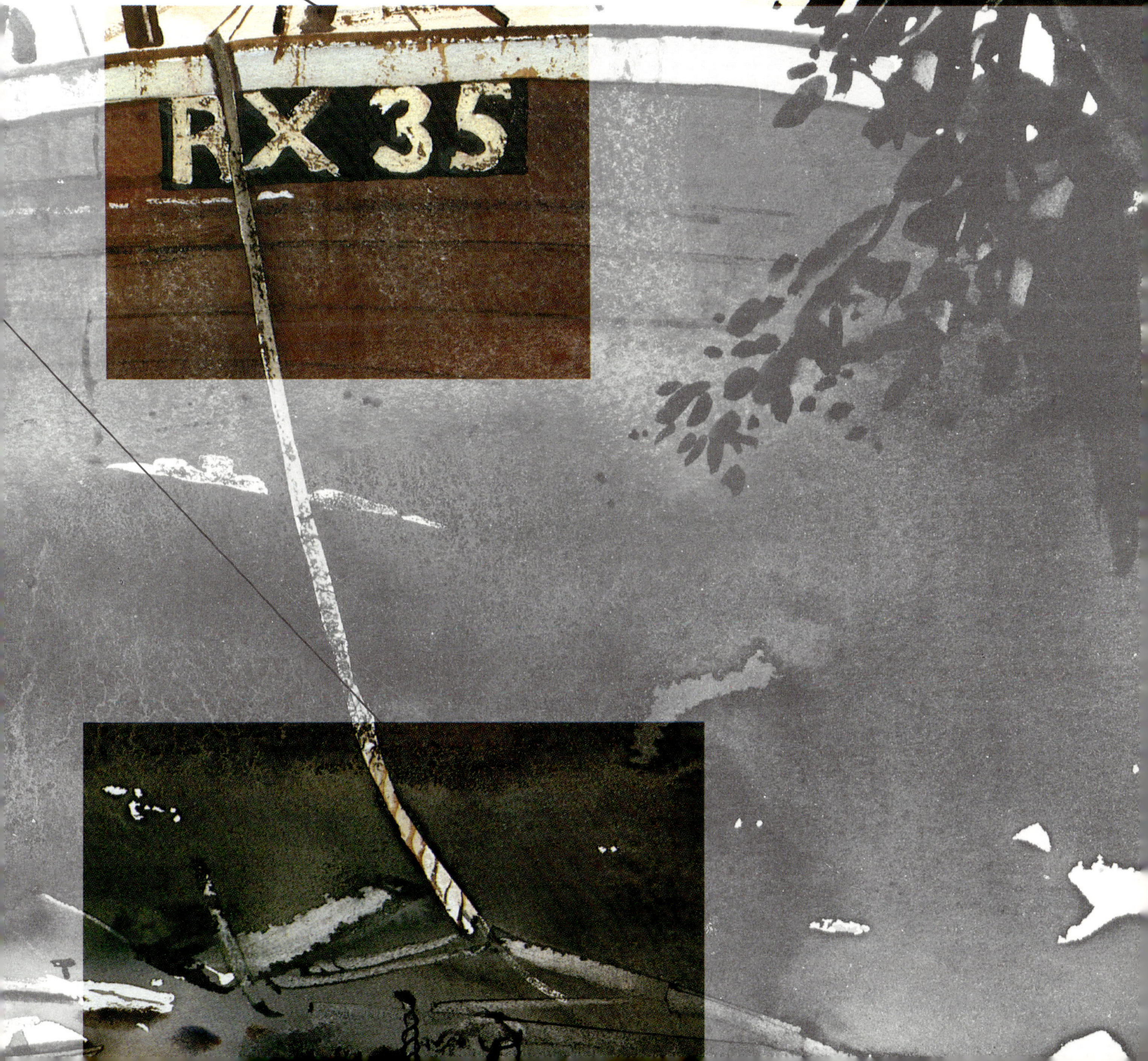

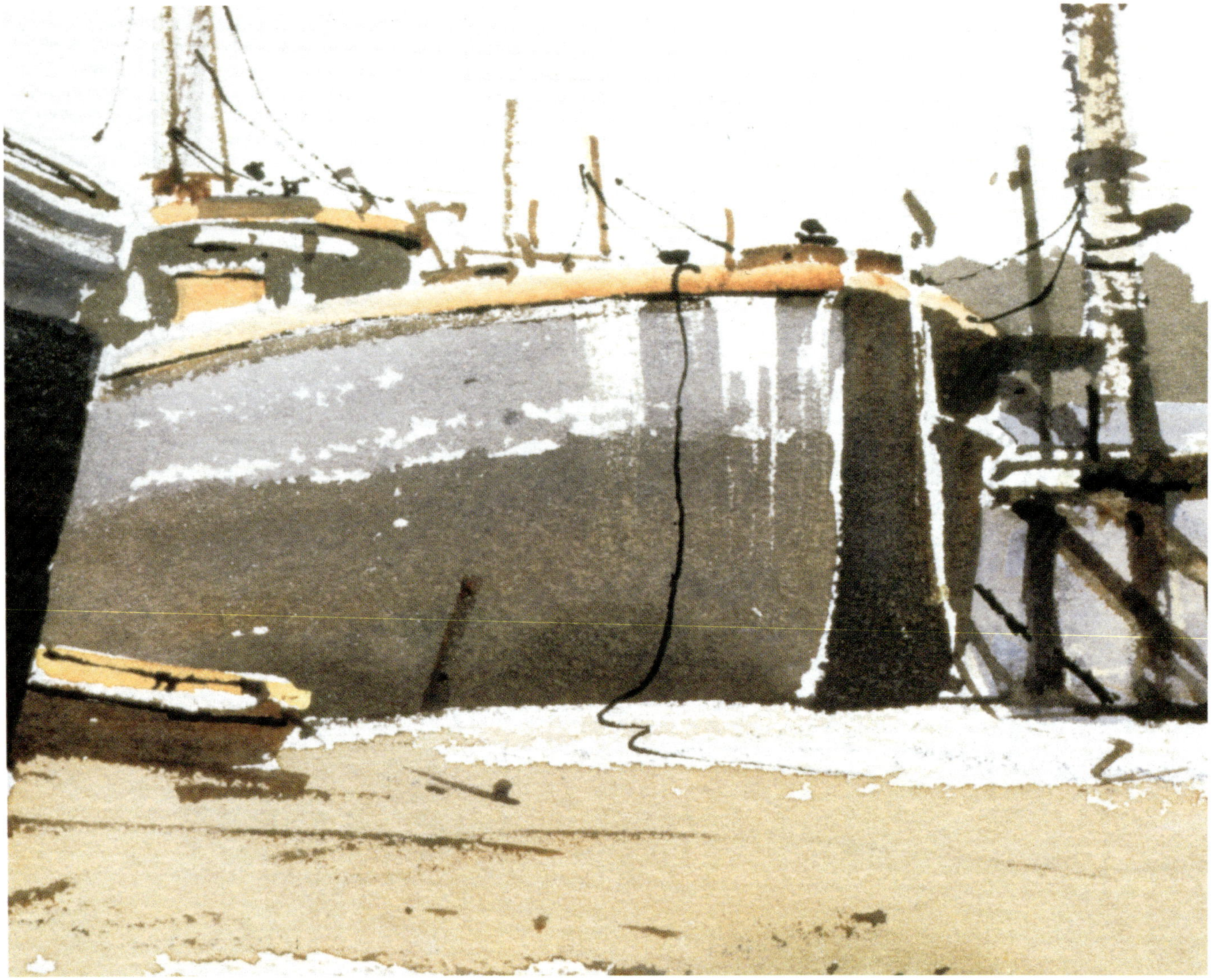

I painted the hull of this boat a light color in contrast to the other two large dark hulls. Because it was not the center of attention in the painting, it was suggested quite simply with quick confident brushwork. Notice that on either side of the bow is a dangling length of rope: one is black, the other white. In reality, the ropes were neither of these colors but it does not matter in the painting, for the ropes *feel* and look right because of their shape and character.

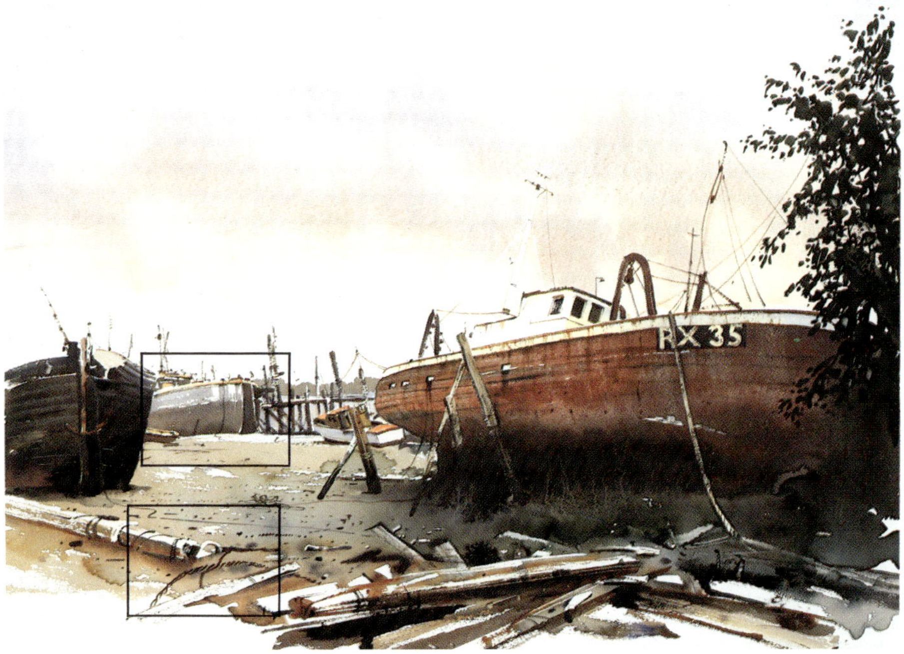

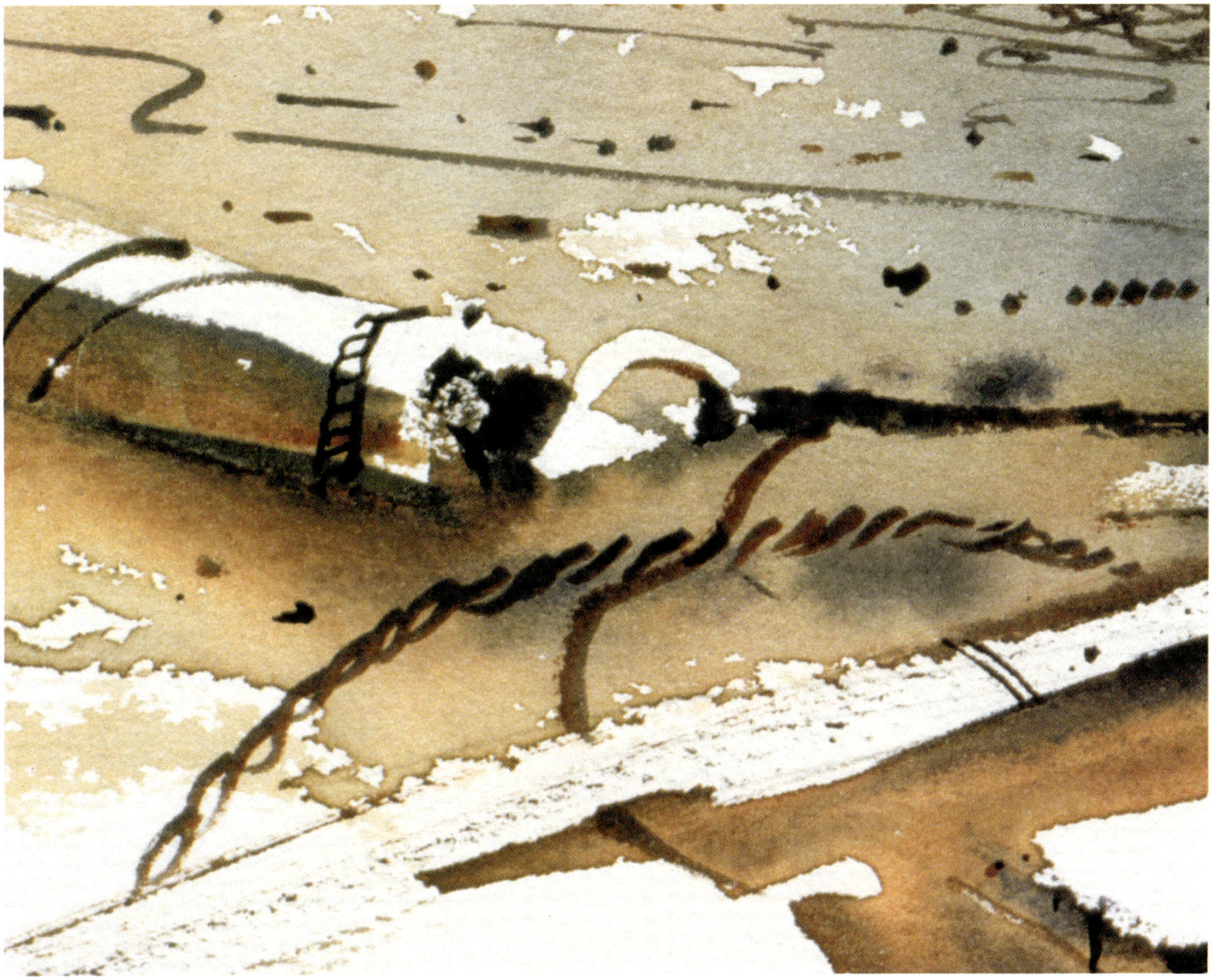

Sometimes it is wise not to rely on masking fluid to retain lighter areas in a painting. If you practice painting the negative shape around a subject, the subject itself will have a more spontaneous look and you will learn to think about a shape itself and not the object that makes it. The timber in the top left was just a white area of paper until a little drybrush work at this end suggested end-grain and the coil pattern of rope gave it form. Notice that the length of steel cable arcing across this area looks extremely coarse here, but in the context of the whole painting, it does not look overstated.

CALM WATER, SMALL BOATS

Living close to the sea, or to a lake or river, provides the painter with a constantly changing scene. Reflections in the water change with the light, and so even the space of a few minutes may lead to an entirely new palette and composition. Waterside shapes and colors lend themselves readily to the artist's brush, either singly or grouped as in this painting of Wells on Sea, where a montage of shapes and colors is created.

I wanted to capture the tranquil mood of the warm early evening at dockside. It's the time I like best for painting. The setting sun casts deep shadows and gives the sky a variety of strange light effects.

I wanted an overall blue cast and so I painted a wash of Ultramarine Blue over the foreground scene. First, however, I picked out those areas that I wanted to remain white with masking fluid. The blue wash has the effect of harmonizing the picture, holding all the elements of the painting together. To maintain the soft and tranquil feeling of the scene, the brush and colors must be used in a soft way. The colors were all gently blended together with a brush full of clear water to soften the edges.

Nearly all the colors have mellow deep tones, with just an occasional bright color jumping out or a bright white highlight appearing where the masking fluid has been removed.

To contribute to the calm effect, both the composition itself and the individual houses and boats were kept to a basic expression. Though there are many boats in the painting, the effect is made simple by the similarity of forms and the strong horizontal patterns.

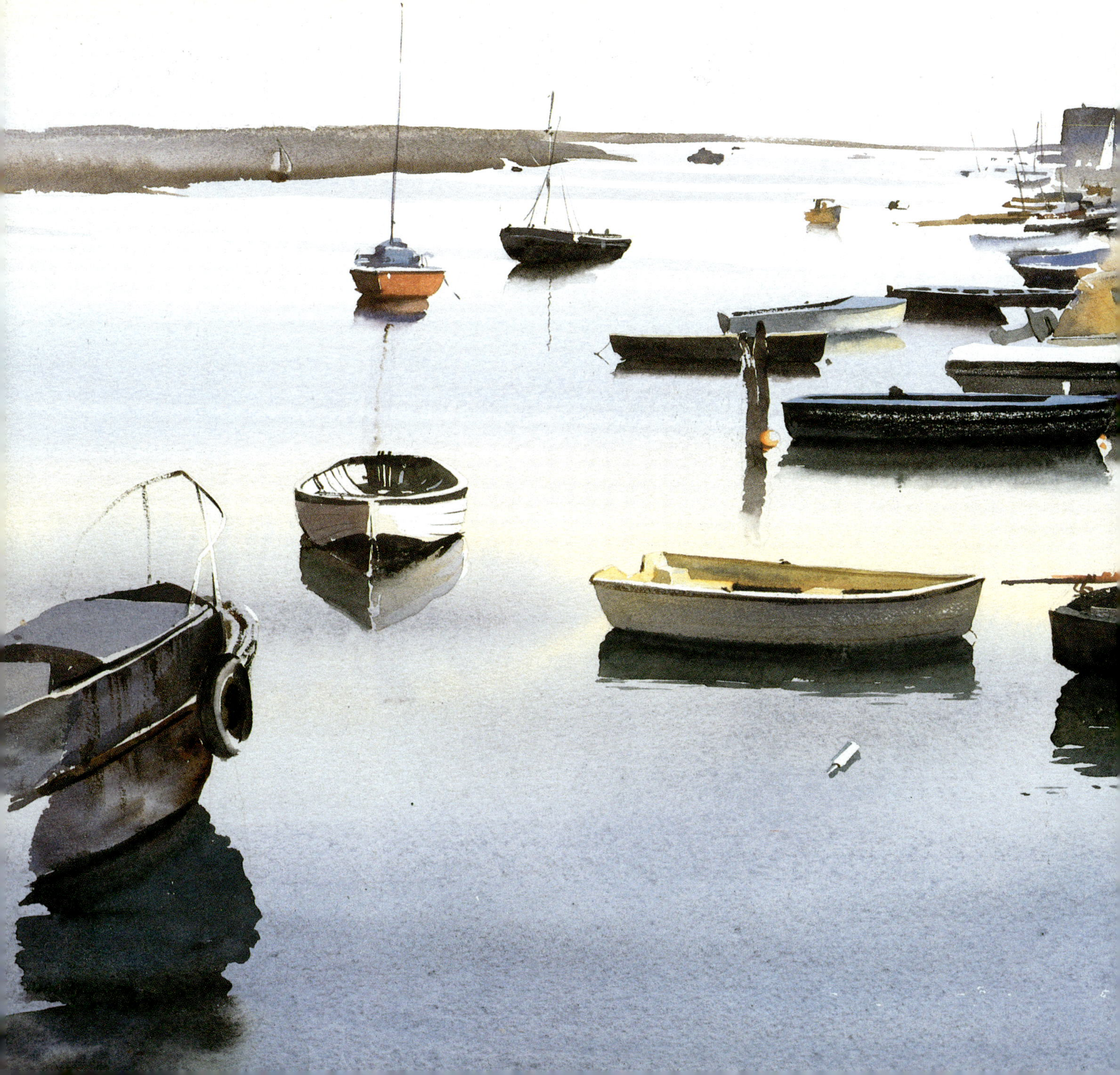

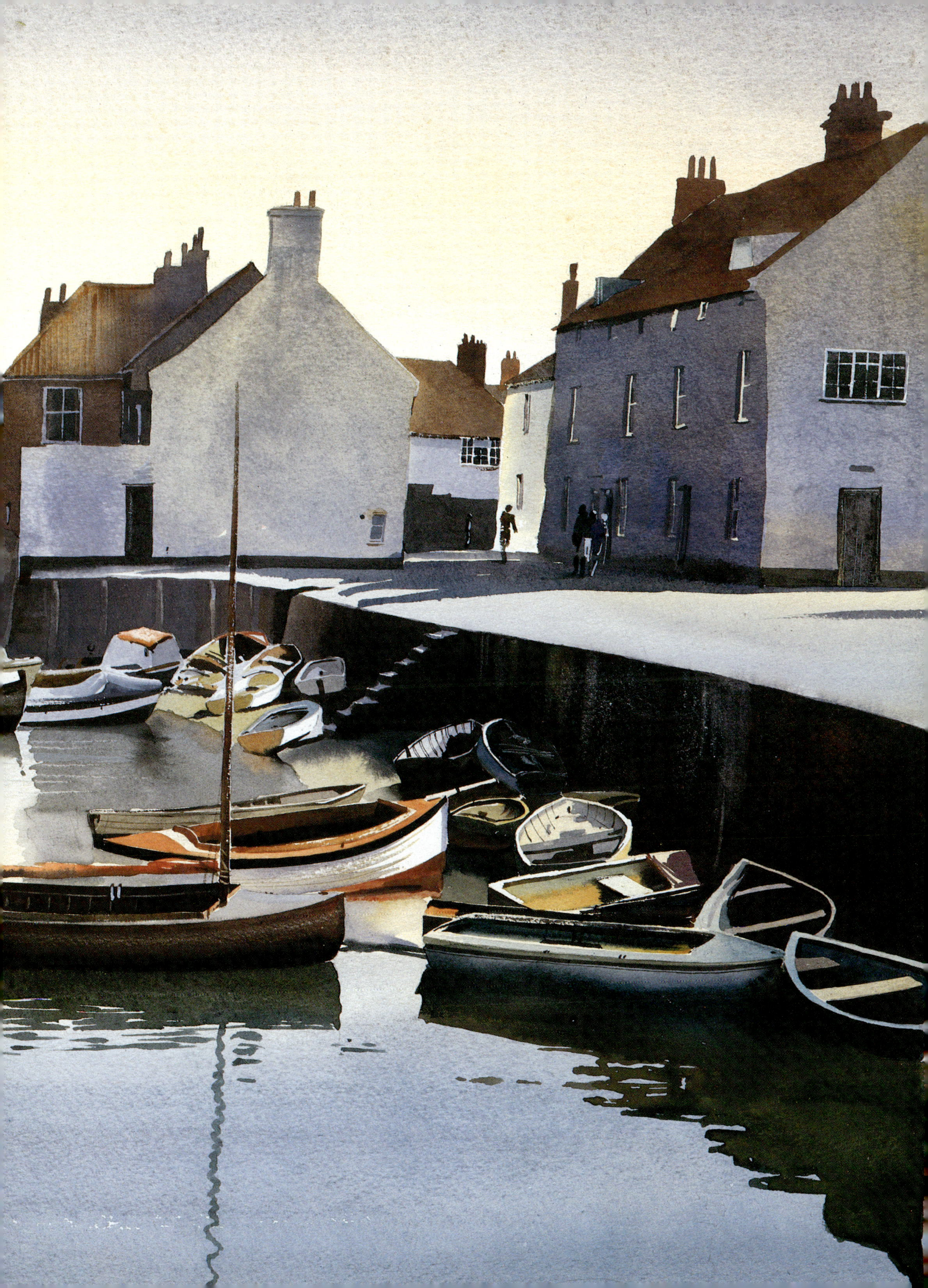

Thick paint, then razor scratches on the hull gave this weathered effect to an ordinary boat form. I carried this dark-light pattern into the reflection, where it is of course reversed.

The bright furled sail not only enlivens this dark boat but also provides a connective to the reddish tones of the adjoining boats. The reflection here lends itself naturally into ripples, which help to relieve the solid mass of the boat.

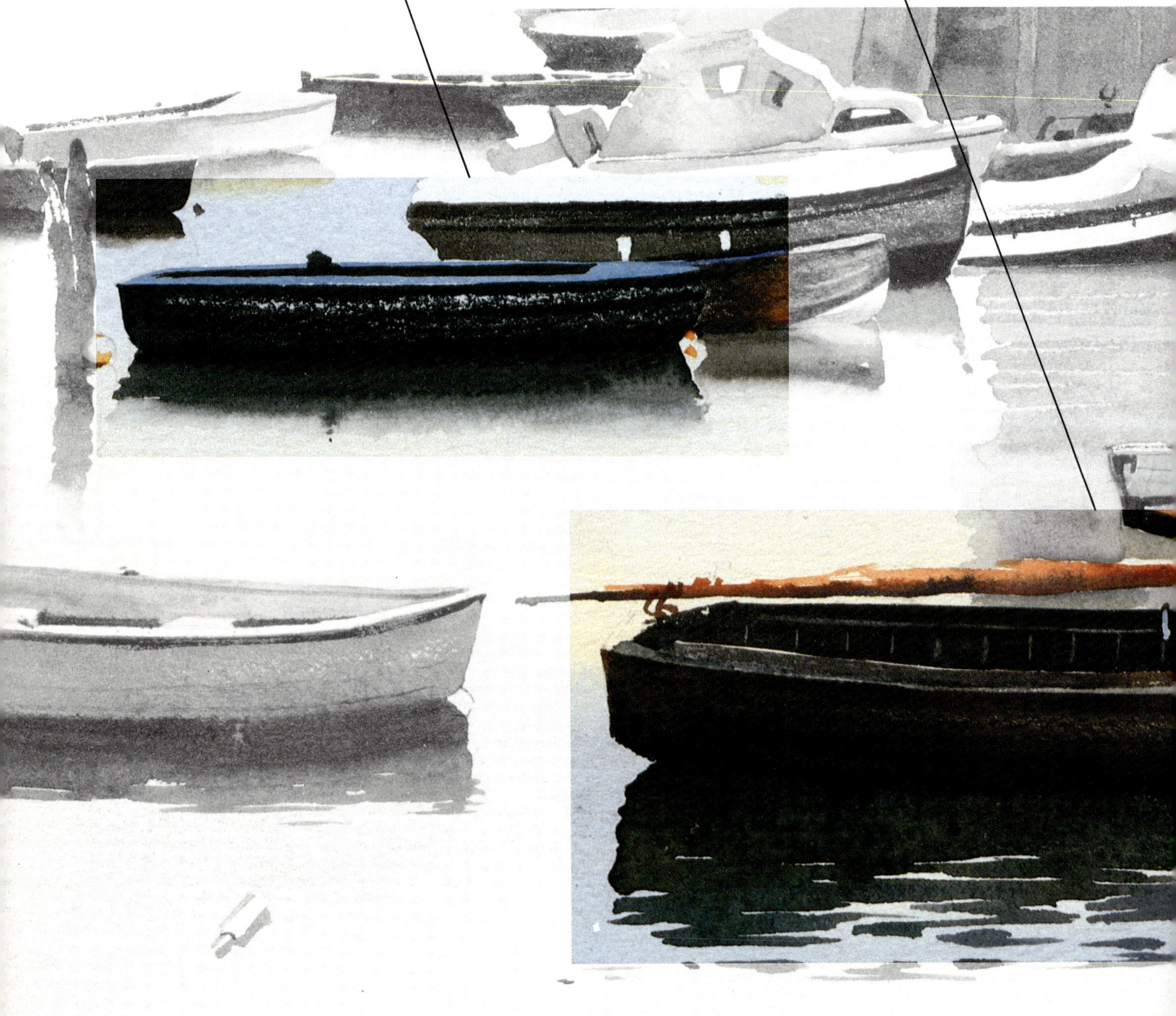

The beautiful curves of the rowboats are clearly defined here, as they are beached slightly, so that the viewer appears to be seeing them from above. Because I wanted to emphasize these curves, I painted them in first with masking fluid to make sure they would not get lost in the darks of the surrounding area.

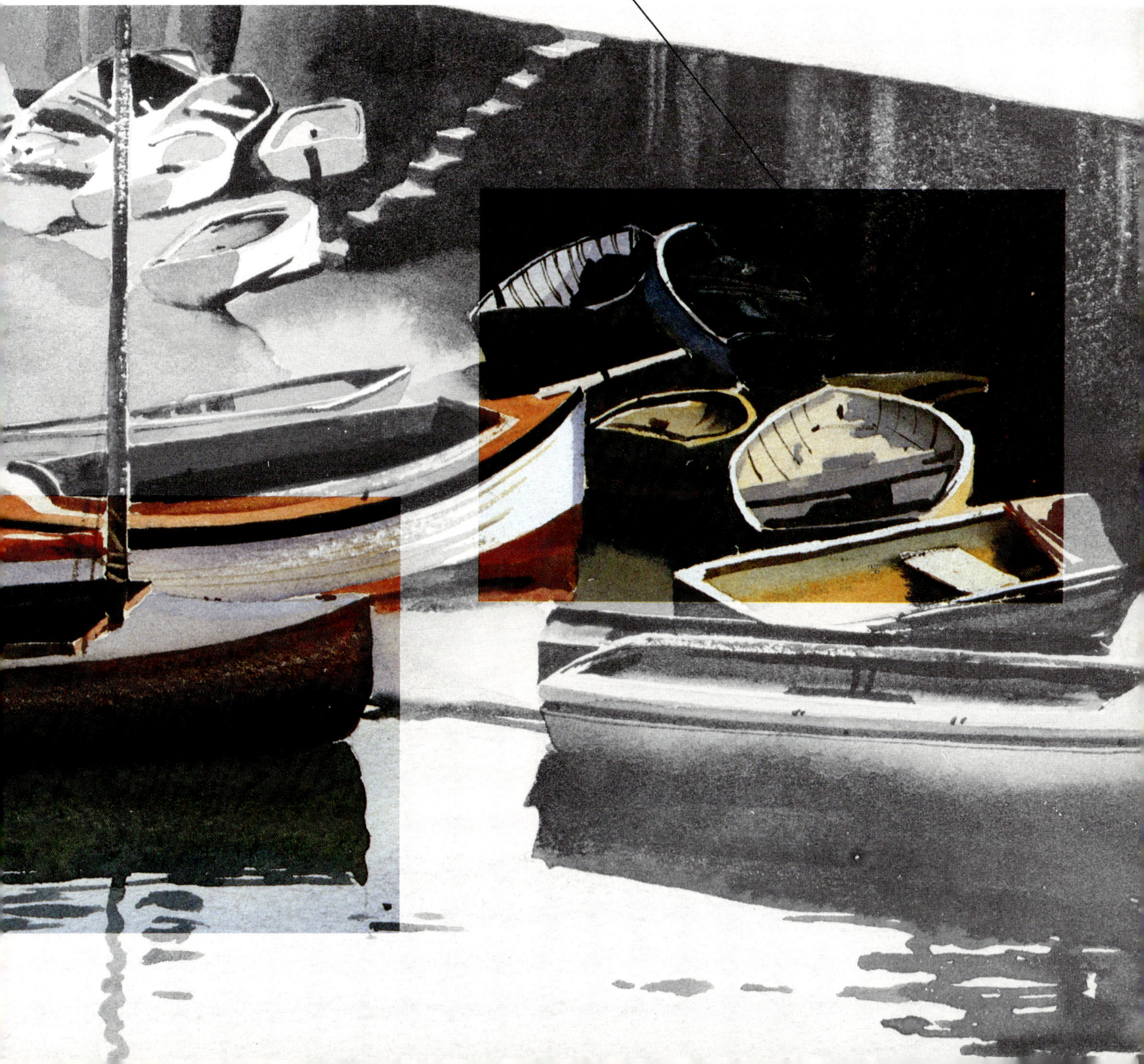

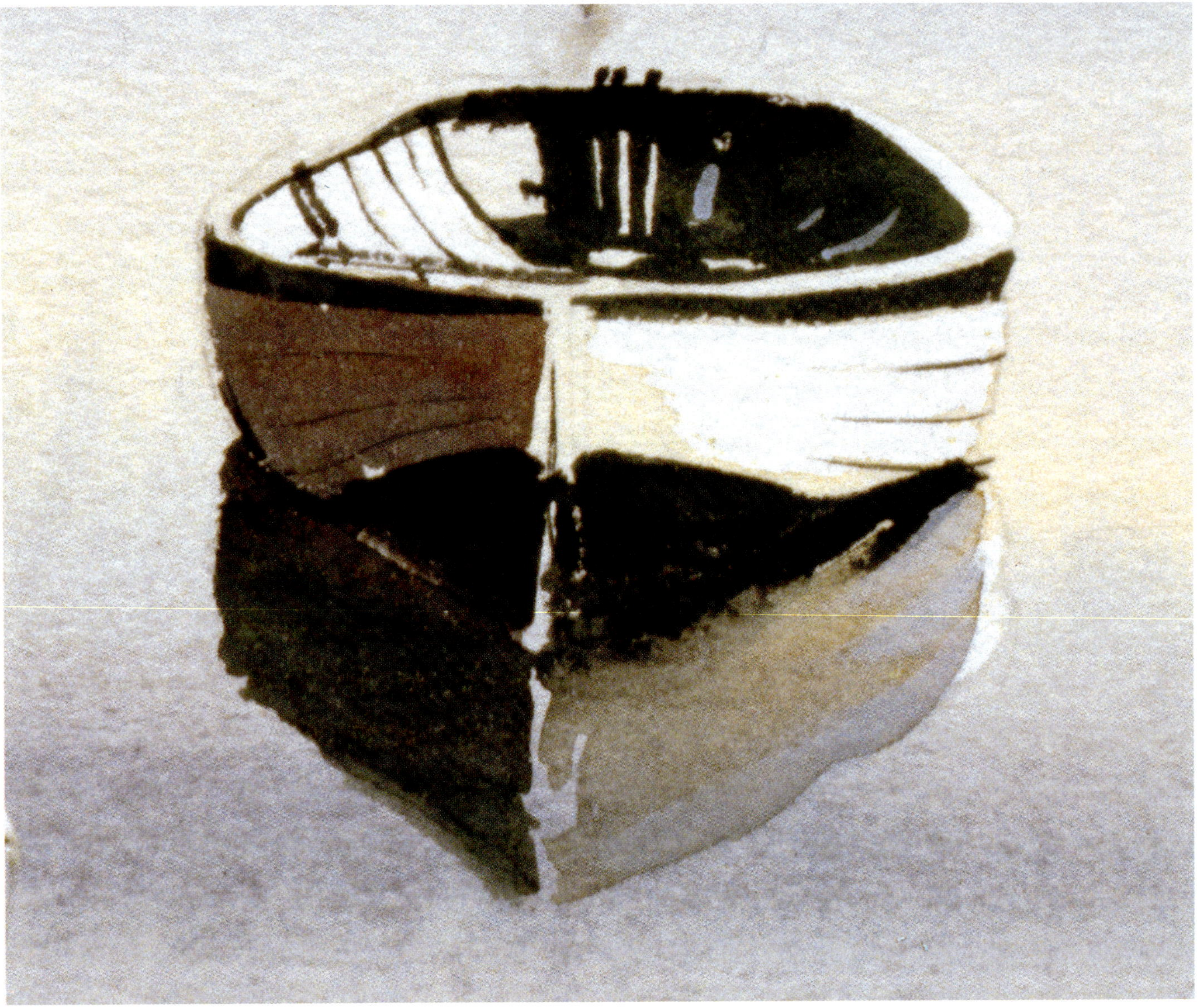

Here we have a simple pattern of black and white, the white having been blocked out with masking fluid first. The intense darks of the bow and stern were enlivened by bits of white highlights and the shape was clearly but easily presented with a few directional strokes. The reflection gives a hint of a warm color, and there is a dab of this shade on the bow to harmonize.

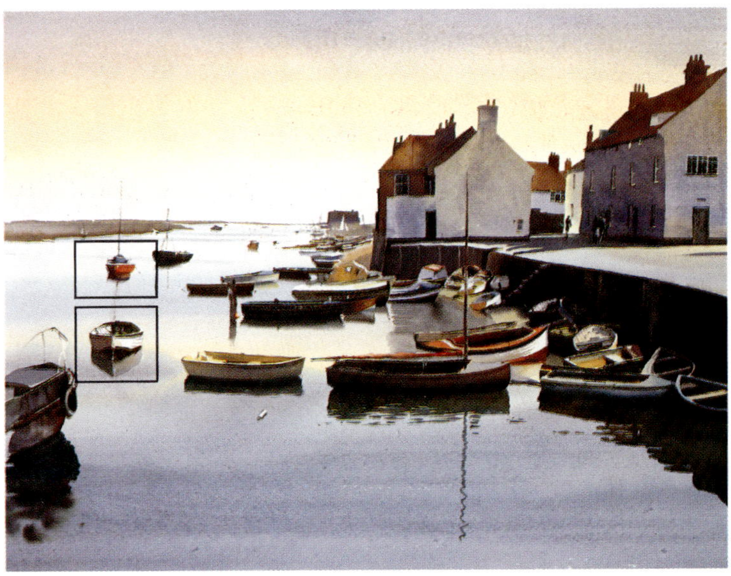

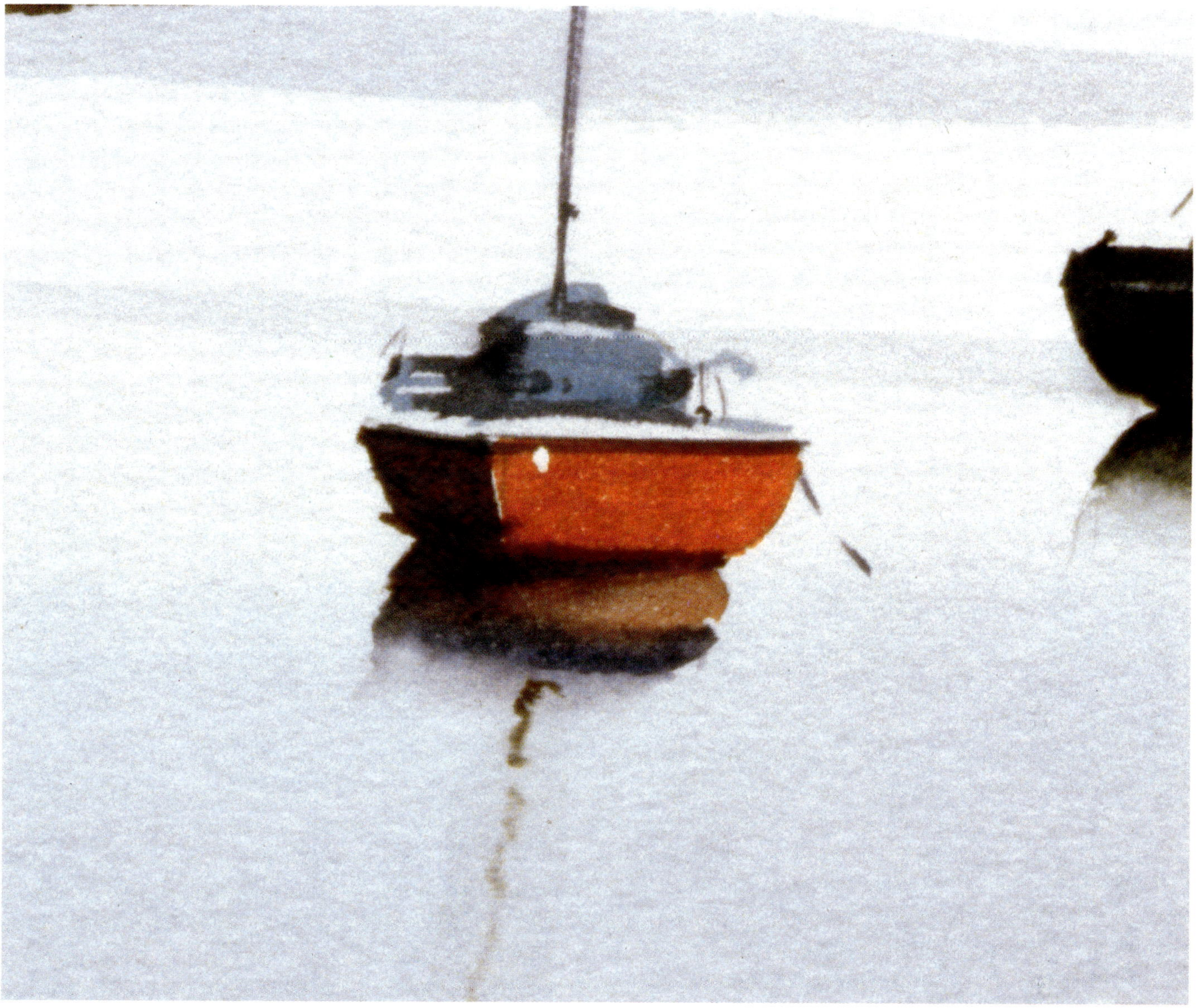

The bright red boat in the distance makes the background lively and helps to unify the highlights and warm colors, dotted as they are about the painting. The waving reflection of the mast is a useful device to connect the boat with other elements, such as the boat in the foreground, and with the water itself.

STONE AND CEMENT

CRUMBLING CEMENT WALLS
This scene provided a delightful theme of order and chaos that appealed to me immediately—tidy traditional door with a labeled letter slot and lacy window complete with a wall literally falling into the street and weeds growing wild across door and window. Here was an opportunity for broad areas of texture, much as an Abstract Expressionist might interpret them. I wanted a delicately pimpled texture to the wall and that took some doing. I dabbed masking fluid in fine dots about the wall to produce pinhead-sized highlights for the finished painting. Candle wax, rubbed in gently on the natural surface of the rough paper, helped build up the rough stucco effect. The danger here was the possibility of overworking and creating a mud of colors, and so I worked very carefully, building up the surface slowly. In watercolor, perhaps more than in any medium, knowing when to stop is critical.

The main colors used on the wall were Naples Yellow, Burnt Sienna, and Ultramarine Blue. First I brushed in washes all over the wall, leaving large white patches. When the washes were dry, I built up textures using drybrush technique, scrubbing the brush into the paper. This was the principal technique used in the area above the door. That area, though haphazard looking, was actually carefully planned, with patterns and colors that are picked up elsewhere.

Since this two-dimensional scene has no depth, I created visual activity by using two strong diagonals. One diagonal leaps from the flowers across the door to the crack in the wall; the other starts with the flat gray wash at the upper left, a new texture in itself, and continues along the exposed lathes to the window, door, and weeds at right. Amid all this movement, the window is a quiet, restful area.

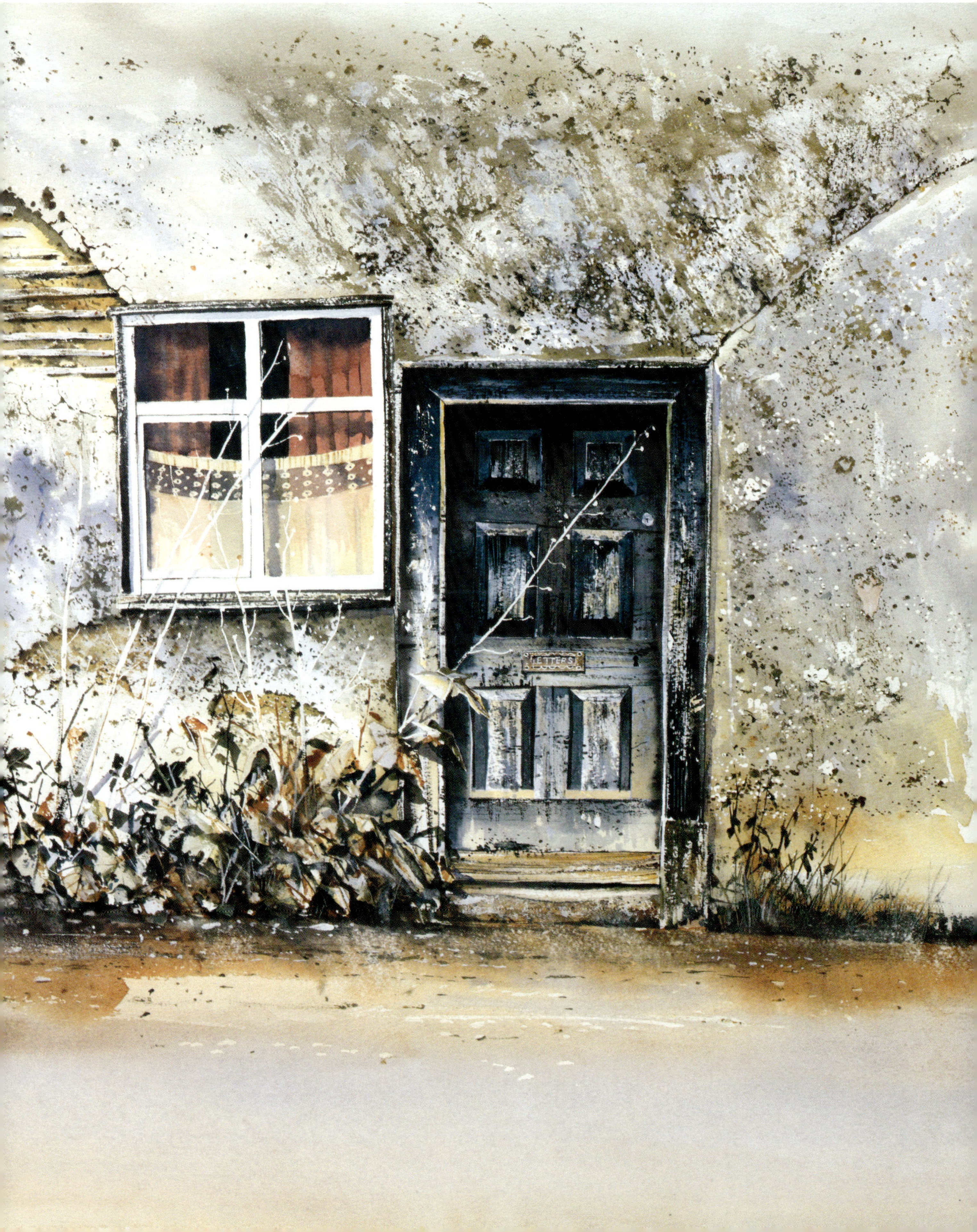
LETTERS

First I laid a ghostly pale wash of Naples Yellow and Ultramarine Blue over the wall surface that I had already primed with tiny dots of masking fluid. It was important to make this wash uneven so that the basic cement rendering had a rough finish to it.

When this wash was dry, I spent time carefully adding dots and dashes of darker wet and dry-brushed paint to build up the cracks and crevices all over the crumbling area. A few lacy, broken lines defined some irregular shapes.

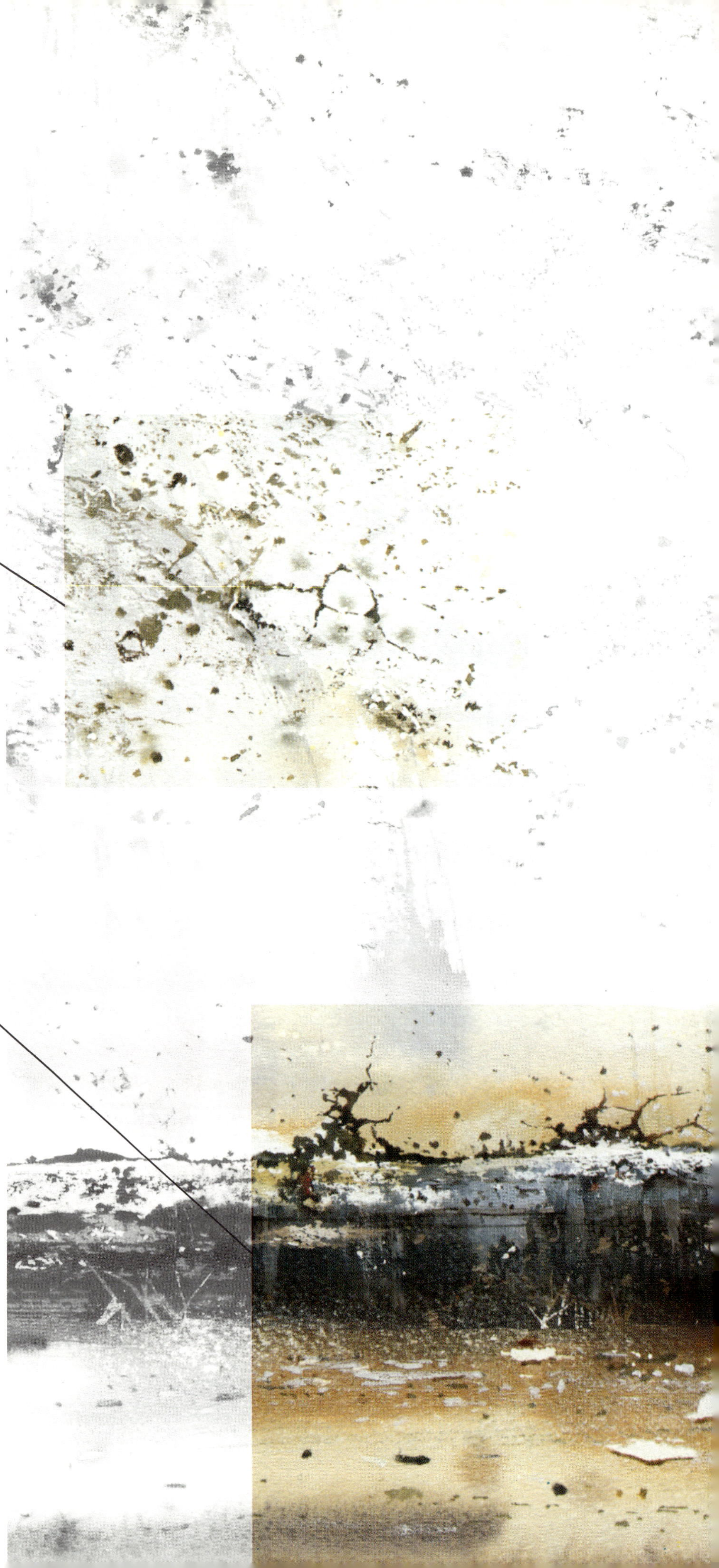

The pale wash laid all over the wall was greatly strengthened with Burnt Sienna at the foot of the rendering, giving a dirty, splattered surface by the edge of the road. The footings of the wall were created with irregular layers of Prussian Blue that was subsequently coarsened with drybrush and some rough downward brushstrokes. The broken area of white paper between the rendering and the footings was created with drybrush, and some nifty dark shadows along the lowest edge of the Burnt Sienna wash made a sharp focus of crumbling masonry.

I masked out some chunks of fallen rendering and then laid a wash of Naples Yellow over this part of the road, blending it into Burnt Sienna at the top and a mixture of Burnt Sienna and Prussian Blue along the bottom, where I left a hard broken edge. I removed the masking fluid from the chunks of cement and used a razor on its side to give extra textured light areas to the road. Just a few dark dots and shadows under the cement pieces completed this area.

I masked out the wooden slats and then painted the shape of the whole area of broken surface with a wash of Naples Yellow and Burnt Sienna. When the wash was dry, I removed the masking fluid and dirtied-up the slats with some swift drybrush strokes. Then I defined the shadows and other small, dark details with a fine brush.

To paint these busy leaves, I masked out some of their shapes along the footings before I applied the first working of Prussian Blue. This created the basic jumble of white shapes upon which to work later. I wanted these shapes to be hard-edged so I worked into dry paper. I scratched in some long stalks while the blue was still damp, but took care not to break the paper surface and create complete white lines. When the blue wash was dry, I tinkered with some pale greeny-brown washes for the leaves and defined some of the veins on the leaves with Prussian Blue. I then added the dark leaf details and upper stalks when the basic pale wall washes were dry and completely worked.

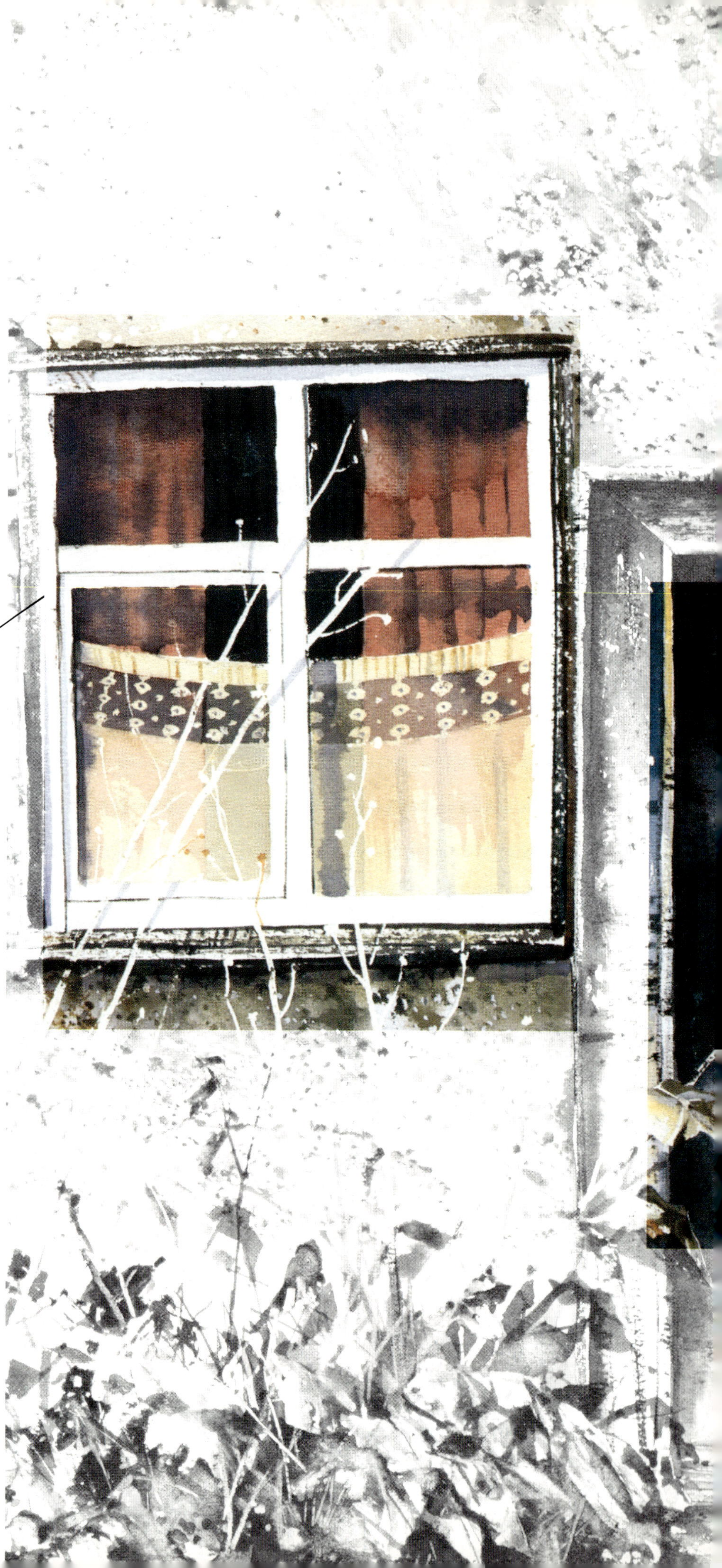

I began by masking out the tall weeds and the window woodwork and then used Alizarin Carmine and Prussian Blue to work up the drapes above the lace. Then I added a pale wash of Naples Yellow over the whole of the area to be covered by the lace curtain. I drew the lace pattern with masking fluid and then used the dark drape washes to suggest the darker drapes behind the lace. When these washes were dry, I removed the fluid and used very pale pigment over the Naples Yellow to give the slightly translucent effect over the lower part of the lace.

Finally, I removed the masking fluid from the window woodwork and put in the fine dark shadows and lines.

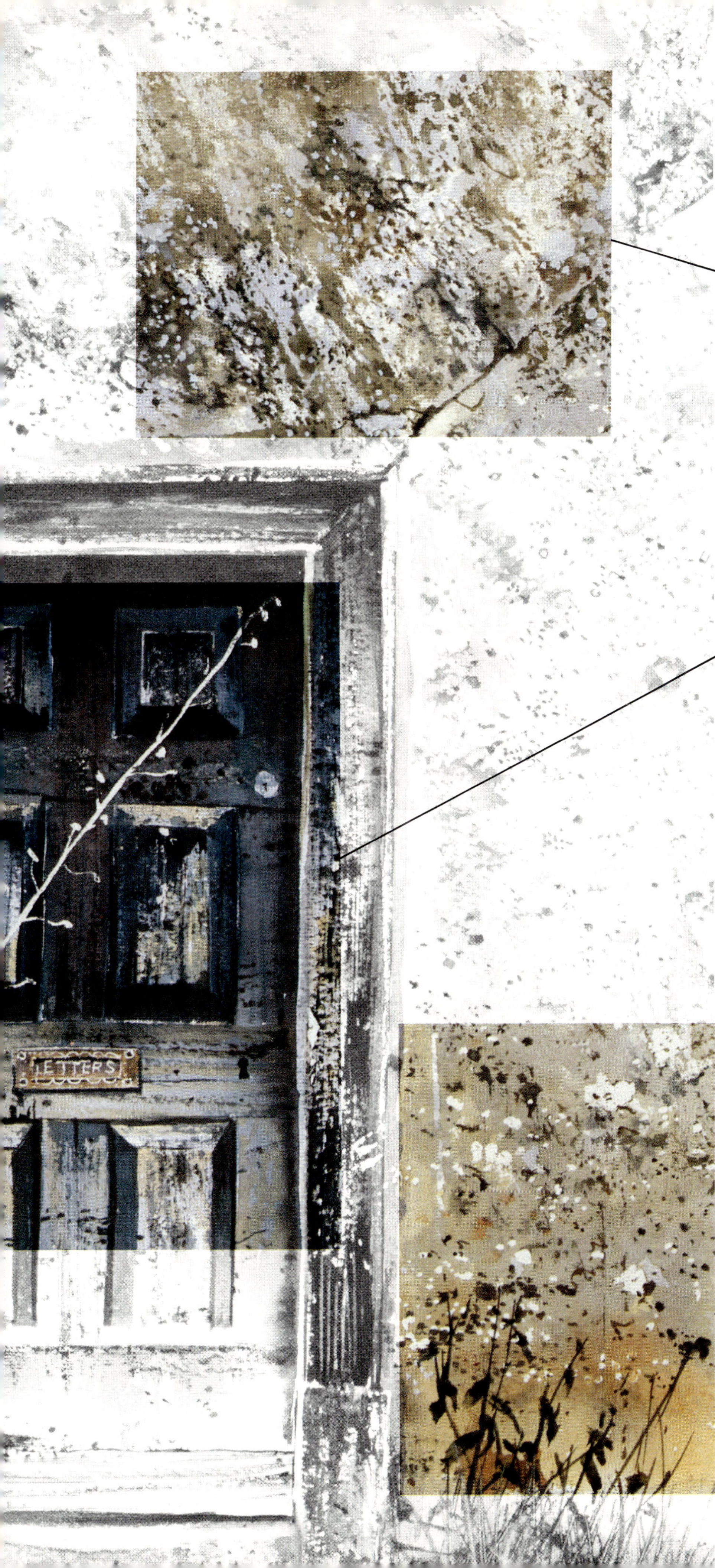

The area of wall above the door had a second wash of Cobalt Blue laid over the first to produce a deeper color. Then I took a short piece of candle wax and worked across this whole area, to make a mottled water-resistant coating for the next wash of Burnt Sienna and Cobalt Blue. This produced an extremely rough, broken texture. I added some dark crack lines, then removed all masking fluid to leave lighter dots.

Painting the door was a reasonably simple operation. Study it closely and you will see that its textures are all produced by varied brushwork and values. The color hardly changes at all. First I masked out the letterbox and the lone, tall plant stalk. Working from light to dark and from wash to drybrush, I built up a variety of surfaces and planes with Prussian Blue and just a touch of Naples Yellow.

This is the most even of all the washes on the wall, and it was laid over masked-out spots and graduated from Cobalt Blue at the top to Burnt Sienna below. As this was an area of low interest in the painting, I was careful not to make any intriguing patterns and simply used a fine brush to draw in some dark leaves and stalks after the masking fluid had been removed.

DESERTED QUARRY STONES

I made this painting before the demonstration on pages 34-37. Although the rusty shed was the main center of interest, I was pleased with the interpretation of the crumbling abyss in the foreground. In the demonstration, I worked much more detail into the whole foreground area. This first painting shows much more clearly how I worked this passage in watercolor.

It struck me that the main feature was the abrupt sharp edge where the flat land plunged dramatically downward, with the steepness of the slope and no bottom in sight emphasizing the effect. With this in mind, I began by dotting in awkward, sharp-edged rocks with masking fluid on the upper area of the face of the slope. Then I mixed some extremely thin washes of Cobalt Blue, Alizarin Carmine, and Cadmium Orange and laid them along the foreground one by one, allowing them to run into one another, creating their own secondary colors.

When these were dry, I worked a rich wash of Burnt Sienna along the top edge of the slope and then brushed it unevenly downward, on a varying wet and dry paper surface. This created an effect of steep, uneven earth; and to give greater strength to the shadow areas, I laid in the darkest values from the top edge downward, tak-

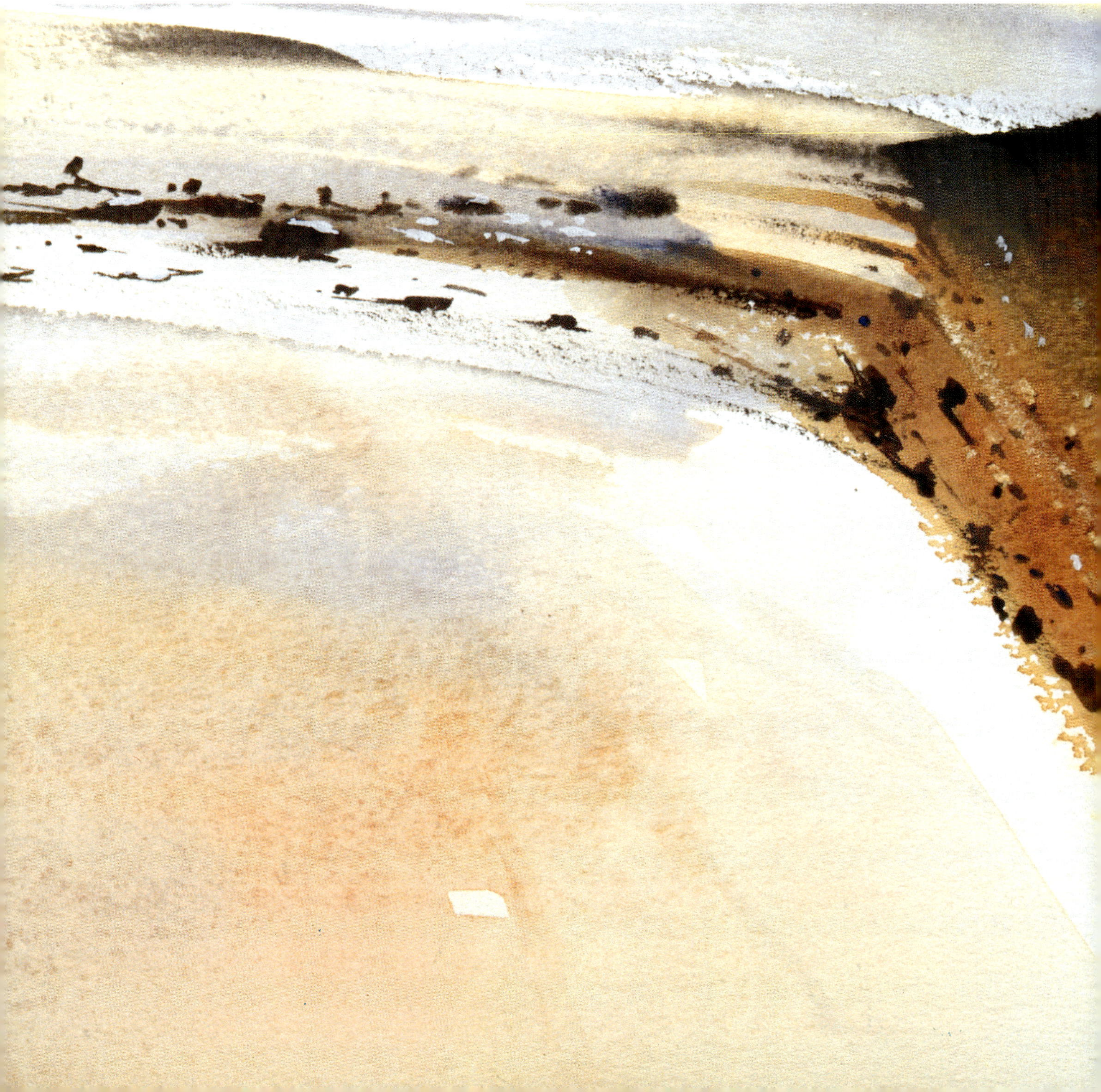

ing care to keep the color opaque along the edge to exaggerate the overhanging edge. I worked in all this paint with a wide wash brush so that where the paper was dry, a speckled texture appears at the edges of some brushstrokes.

Finally, I lifted off the masking fluid, varied the color of the rocks, put in a few dark stones, and added dashes of dark color under some of the rocks to give them prominence and greater shape.

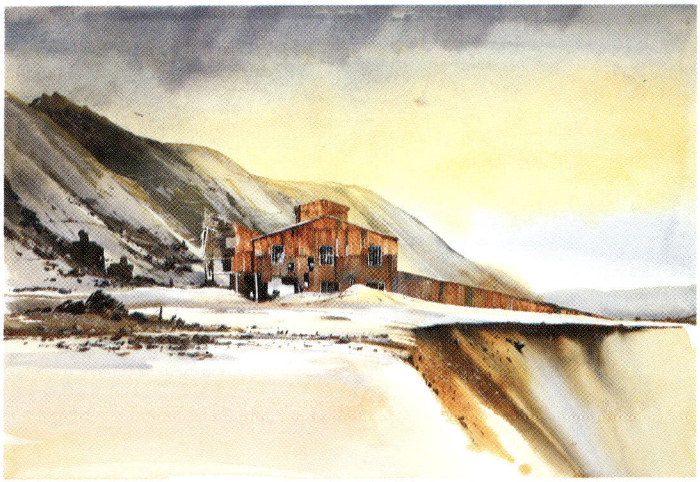

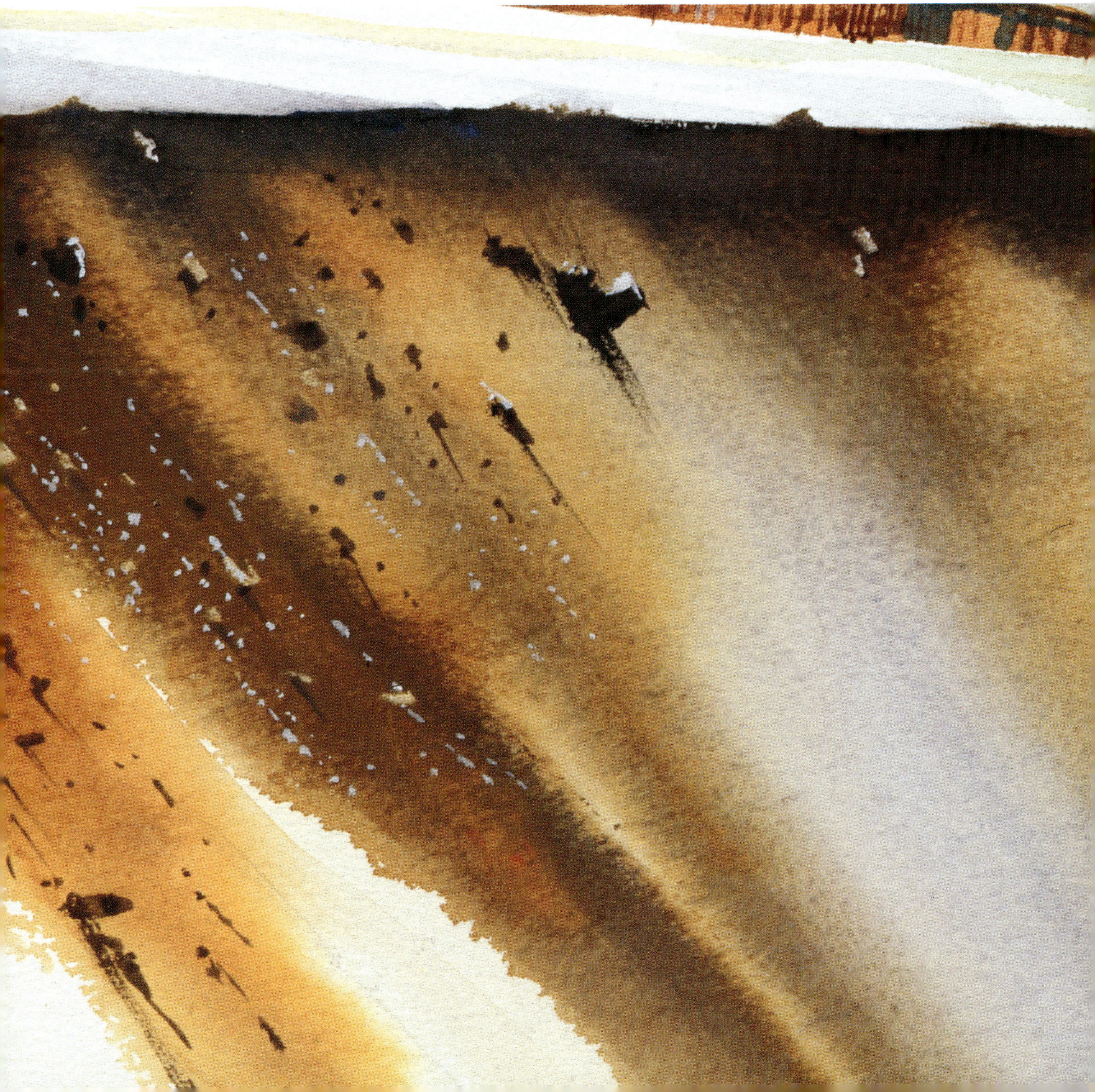

WORN STONE

If you haven't any Roman ruins handy, you may at least find some romantic decaying marble in your local churchyard. Tombstones often contain a variety of stone carvings that can be very interesting subjects to paint—provided, of course, you can maintain an esthetic distance from their morbid associations.

I always find myself looking for the oldest ones in the churchyards—some stones are several hundred years old. Some weather the passage of time well, while other, softer stones have lost all vestiges of carvings and inscriptions. This one falls somewhere in between. The carving has been lost in places; the small figure has lost its head and the form has become vague and indistinct. Also the foundations have settled, causing the stones to tilt and move apart in a disjointed manner.

I wanted to present a monumental quality to this tombstone, and that's why I placed it high up in this picture, giving the impression that I was looking up at it. The surrounding area in the painting is a blur, with detail picked out here and there either by masking out ahead of time or by adding accents with a dry brush. This vagueness accentuates the drama of the stone carving.

For the sky I used Cerulean Blue and Naples Yellow. Below, Burnt Sienna and Cobalt Blue combined in places with black ink, which was allowed to flow into the colors in places. While drying, some areas have been dabbed away with a paper tissue, which gave a worn look to the stone. There are also some technical pen lines that give the illusion of shape within the void.

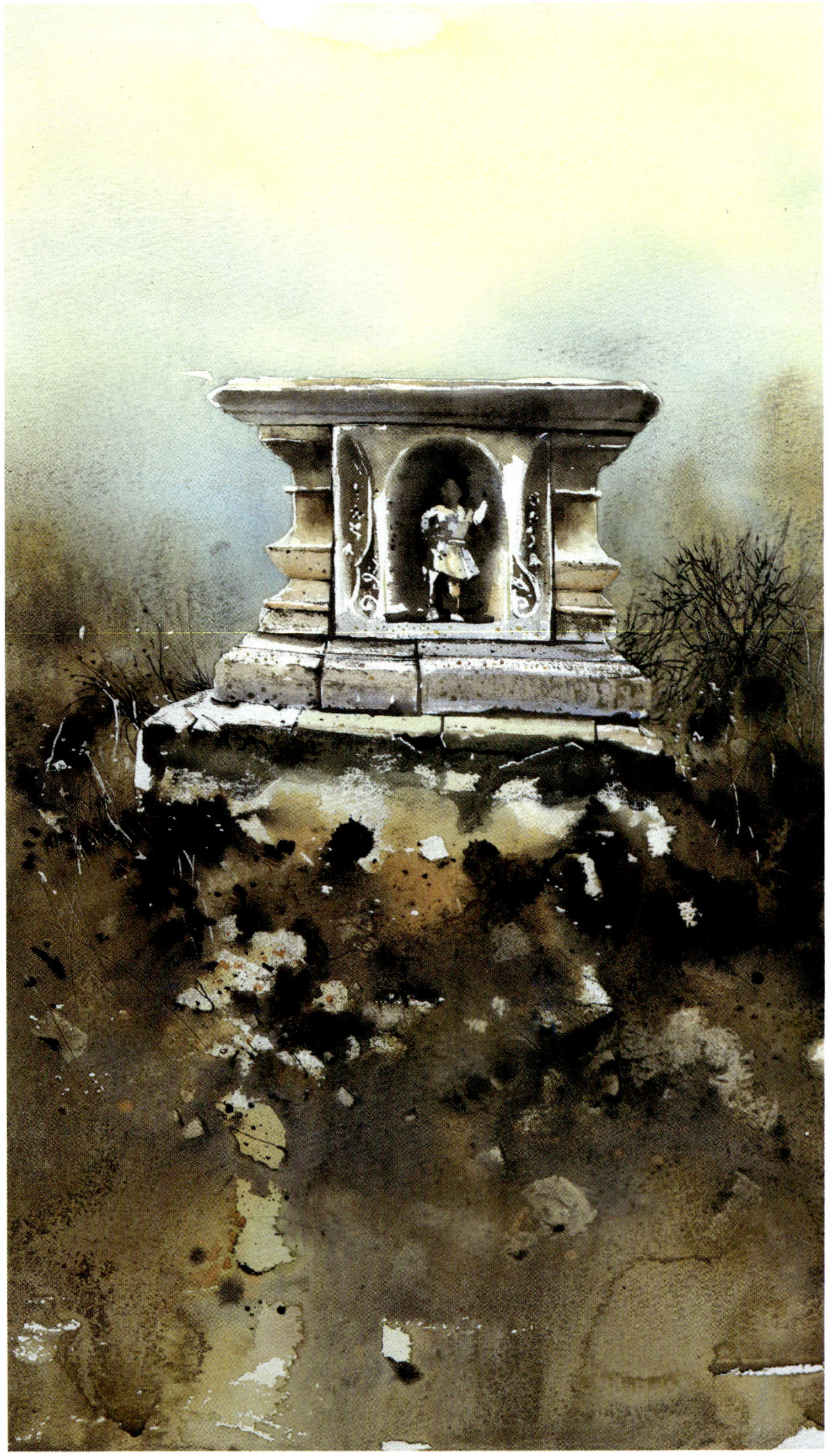

This is good practice for your next painting trip to the Classical world, on site or in a museum. After the masking fluid had been rubbed away from around the column, I penciled in the detail of the stone carving and outlined it with masking fluid. This allowed me to treat the overall painting of the stone freely. I've used Cobalt Blue, Burnt Sienna, and black ink. Detail was added with the tip of a fine brush, capturing some of the oranges of lichens and cavities in the stone. The scrollwork is essentially a matter of drawing, masking, and shading. After I removed the masking fluid from the stone carving, I added more detail there—but the figure is just suggested. I don't want a perfect figure in the niche, but one that has aged with the stone. Touches of Yellow Ochre on the figure and stone give it a feeling of weathering out-of-doors and add some warm color to a cool area. To blacken the cracks between the stones I used a technical pen.

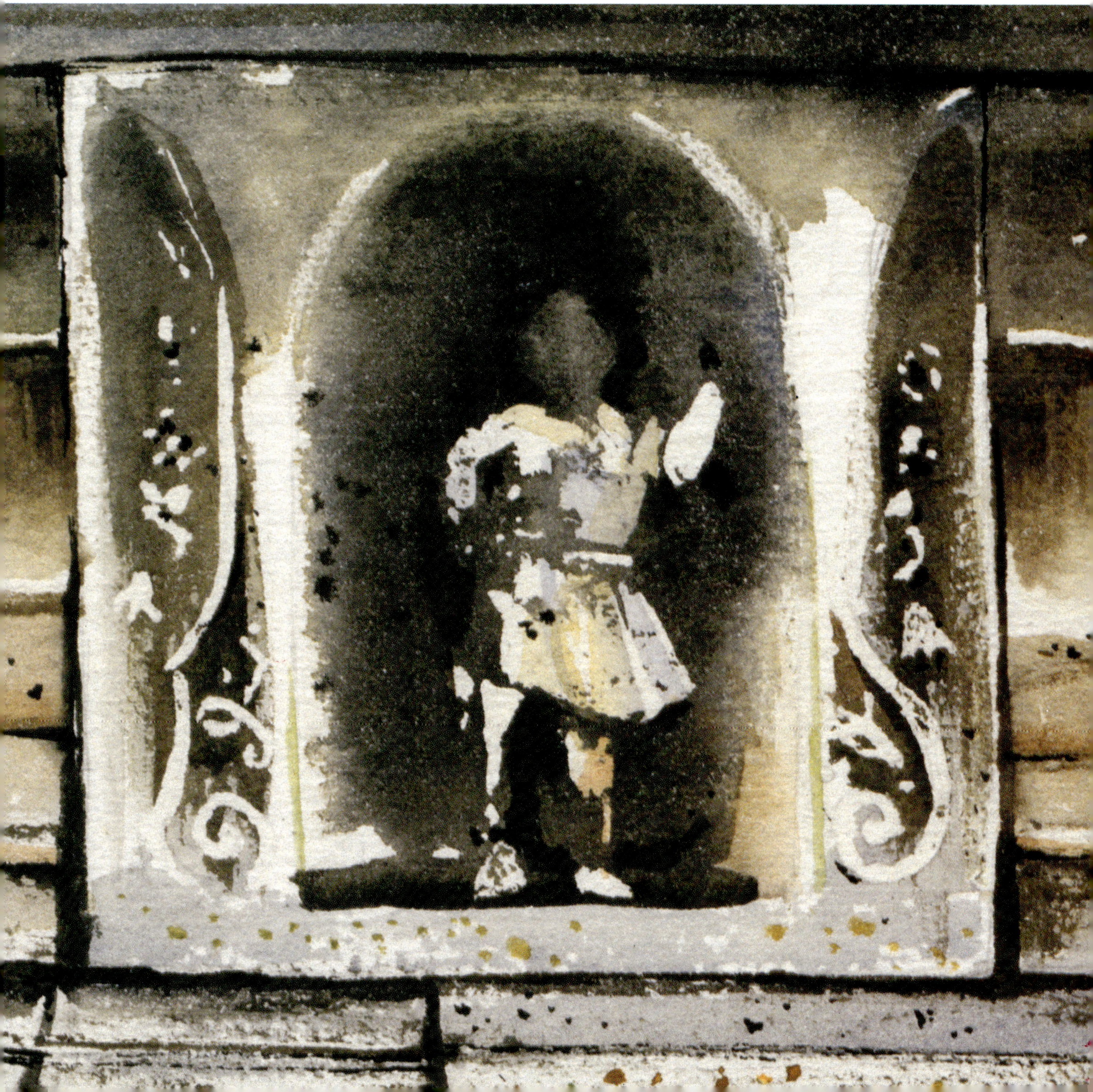

INDEX

P64
Developing ~~an~~ eye for contrasts is an essential part of painting.

70 Rust look — Cadmium Orange

75 RUST — 116

86 Photos

87 Lifting out color

82 Dabbing

89 ox-gall 89 + 90

TUBES — 97